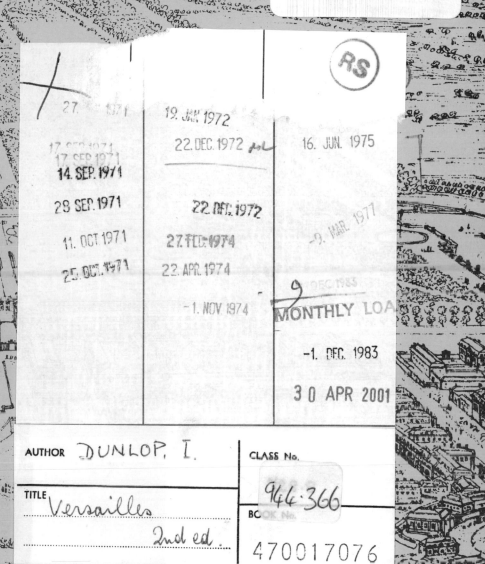

VERSAILLES

VERSAILLES BETWEEN 1664 AND 1668
DETAIL FROM PAINTING BY P. PATEL

VERSAILLES

IAN DUNLOP

WITH FOREWORDS BY

NANCY MITFORD

AND

SIR ARTHUR BRYANT

HAMISH HAMILTON

LONDON

First Edition published, 1956
Second Edition first published in Great Britain, 1970
by Hamish Hamilton Ltd
90 Great Russell Street London WC1
Copyright © 1956, 1970 by Ian Dunlop

SBN 241 01926 5

Printed in Great Britain
by Ebenezer Baylis & Son Limited
The Trinity Press, Worcester, and London

TO
DEIRDRE
WITH ALL MY LOVE

'L'évocation du passé pourrait souvent s'appuyer sur une renaissance exacte des lieux où se déroulèrent tant d'évènements importants.'

—VERLET

CONTENTS

LIST OF ILLUSTRATIONS

Between pages 72 and 73

Between pages 136 and 137

Illustrations in the Text

Endpapers

Versailles from a drawing by A. Perelle (*Bibliothèque de Versailles*)

Arch. Phot.   Archives Photographiques
B.M.   British Museum
B.N.   Bibliothèque Nationale
F.G.T.O.   French Government Tourist Office
M. de V.   Musée de Versailles

FOREWORD

By SIR ARTHUR BRYANT

IAN DUNLOP HAS based his architectural study of the most famous of all European palaces on history. To a lover of history, therefore, it is far more interesting than most architectural studies. I suspect that it will seem so to the general reader. A great building, like a tree, is an organic growth, springing not from the soil but from the social, political and economic life of its makers. In the case of Versailles, a wonderful building or rather group of buildings not only arose as a result of history; its existence, when built, affected history. By prefacing his study of the royal palace that is among the supreme glories of France with an account of that terrible, apocalyptic death-march of 1789, the author both awakens the reader's imagination and anchors his theme on the living past. Thereafter we follow the story of Versailles' genesis and growth with the same sympathy with which we follow the life of a man or woman. '*Tous les jours des plaisirs, des comédies, des musiques, des soupers sur l'eau*' in its past are, like the colonnades and galleries, perspectives and fountains that Mr. Dunlop so graphically and sympathetically describes, a part of a historical chain of cause and effect. Built after the dark clouds of the Fronde to enthrone *le Roi Soleil*, who was the hope and salvation of a France reborn, it ended only in separating the King from his people. It was a palace that sprang from the recurrent French belief that the indiscipline and political division that mar the genius and civilization of France could only be cured by the authoritarian rule of a single, strong and disinterested patriot who represented in his person the whole national genius —'*le Roi tout seul*'. It proved, as the event was to show, an illusion, yet it left behind on earth its glory, its pathos and its beauty. 'In the end, as is well known, the world beyond rose up and put an end to the pantomime, scattering the players and killing as many as it could lay hands on. By a strange oversight it left the scenery almost untouched.' It is that scenery and the story of its creation and purpose that this most valuable and illuminating book describes and unfolds.

FOREWORD

By NANCY MITFORD

M R. DUNLOP HAS lived at Versailles, he knows French and knows every inch of the château; he has written a scholarly account of it which will be useful to tourist and historian alike. He tells us all about the great palace itself, how it was built and decorated and rebuilt and redecorated; the whole complicated process is clearly described. At last we understand what happened there architecturally, when, by whose orders, and why.

Like most houses lived in by several generations it has undergone many changes. It was built by great architects for a great amateur, Louis XIV, and the chief alterations were made by equally great architects for his descendant, Louis XV, who also understood the art of patronage. The work done for these two kings spanned about 100 years. The château was saved from the tastelessness of Marie-Antoinette, as many another house has been saved, by lack of funds.

Mr. Dunlop describes the social and political life of the palace, illuminating his story with anecdotes and character studies. He has been to contemporary sources, so we are not treated to the views and moral judgments of Michelet, Carlyle and Co. The oddity of the Bourbons is clearly seen, but their vices are not exaggerated.

No house in the world so kindles the imagination as Versailles and this has nothing to do with age (by European standards it is not old) or historical associations. Madame de Sévigné, who saw it being built, was under the spell just as we are today. The Daughters of France preferred spinsterhood there to an establishment, even a throne, anywhere else; their father's courtiers

xvii

regarded exile from Versailles as a living death. No sooner was it built than every ruler in Europe, from the Mediterranean to the Baltic, wanted a copy of it. 'The inspiration of Versailles made France what Italy had been in the Renaissance, the cultural centre of Europe.' Apart from its aesthetic value, its great charm, no doubt, is the way in which it combines the centre of government with a gentleman's country seat. On one side the Marshals of France were leaving for the front, on the other the hunting horn rang out in the forest glades.

Versailles itself was the sun in a constellation of country-houses and smaller palaces, all within an easy drive of it; Mr. Dunlop gives an account of the Trianons, Clagny and Marly. 'Sire, Marly?' said the courtiers, dying for an invitation to go there. It was perhaps the most fascinating of all the palaces, though for some reason the wives and mistresses of the Kings never liked it much. Mesdames de Maintenon and Pompadour complained that it was draughty, and Marie-Antoinette preferred Trianon. Now the little palace with its painted façade, the twelve pavilions for the guests, each with two apartments connected by a tiny oval staircase, the fountains, the pergolas, the arbours conducive to conversation, all have disappeared. The house, by then considered ugly and old-fashioned, was pulled down during Napoleon's Empire.

As Mr. Dunlop points out, nineteenth-century taste was more fatal to the palaces than the Revolution, which did but little damage to secular buildings. It is a curious fact that, as soon as Louis XVI had left Versailles for ever, the Service des Bâtiments put in hand an enormous programme of cleaning and repairs. Its structure, built shoddily and too fast, has several times been in serious danger. After the First World War it was saved by Mr. Rockefeller, and after the second by an effort of the whole French nation. Now there is enough money not only to keep it in repair but also for restoration which is being carried out with scholarship and taste. In twenty years' time Versailles may look more as it did in its hey-day than the great mouldering palace we have known.

Du fond d'un vert bosquet qu'elle a pris pour tombeau
J'écoute lentement ta dernière fontaine
Pleurer sur toi, O Versailles, cité des eaux.

ACKNOWLEDGEMENTS

I would like to thank the Duc de Brissac, Président de la Société des Amis de Versailles, Madame Jean Raindre and the Hon. Mrs. Rodd for their help with the illustrations, and the Marquis de Contades for his help and hospitality: also M. Bossard, M. le Moyne, Mlle Ehrlich and M. Saltet at the Château de Versailles, and Mlle Bienvenue at the Bibliothèque de Versailles.

Figures 9a and 9b are reproduced by Gracious Permission of Her Majesty the Queen.

The frontispiece and figures 1a, 1c, 3b, 6b, 10a, 10b, 12b, 13b, 14, 15a, 16a, 17, 18a, 18c, 18d, 19a, 19c, 21a, 21b, 23b, 24, 25a, 25b, 27a, 27b, 27c, 29a, 29b, 31b and 32 by courtesy of the Musée de Versailles; 2a, 3a and 8 by courtesy of Archives Photographiques; 2b by courtesy of O. Perrin; 4a, 4b, 5a, 5b, 6a and plan 2 by courtesy of the Bibliothèque Nationale; 11a and 11b by courtesy of the French Government Tourist Office; 12a and 23a by courtesy of the Nationalmuseum, Stockholm; 15b by courtesy of Mme Jean Raindre; 18b by courtesy of the Wallace Collection; 25b and 30 by courtesy of G. Saad; 26a by courtesy of M. Marc Saltet; 26b by courtesy of Giraudon; 28 by courtesy of Princess Margaret von Hesse unde bei Rhein; 31a by courtesy of the Trustees of the British Museum.

I would like to thank B. T. Batsford Ltd. for the loan of illustrations, George Rainbird Ltd. for the loan of illustrations in *The Sun King* by Nancy Mitford, and the *Spectator* for permission to reproduce the Foreword by Nancy Mitford.

IAN DUNLOP

A NOTE ON TRANSLATIONS

THERE IS ALWAYS likely to be difficulty when it comes to translation. The problem is to enable those who appreciate French to enjoy a few quotations where perhaps the finer shades of meaning would be lost in translation, without making the book unreadable to those whose French is less fluent. While leaving a few original passages, therefore, I have tried to keep them short and to explain their meaning as far as possible by the context.

To one principle I adhere firmly: I will not translate names. I will not talk about the 'Castle of Versailles', nor even about the 'Duke of Saint Simon', for fear of being led into such absurdities as describing a meeting between *Mister* and the *Dolphin* in the *Bull's Eye Saloon*. With all due respect to those who have the Englishman's traditional difficulties with the Gallic tongue I will leave *Monsieur* (the eldest brother of the King in Court language) with the *Dauphin* in the *Salon de l'Œil de Bœuf*.

IAN DUNLOP

I

INTRODUCTION

The Approach to Versailles

*'Un des grands reproches qu'on peut faire
au Château de Versailles, c'est qu'il n'a
point une entrée digne du monument.'*
—COMTE D'HÉZECQUES

THERE IS A certain point on the ridge known as the Heights
of Satory where the trees stand back, leaving bare a little
knoll of sandy ground from which there is a magnificent
view of Versailles. Standing clear of its surrounding woodland,
and dominating the countryside from a slight eminence, the
Château displays its vast length of front, presenting three façades
of warm, honey-coloured stone finished with a neat skyline of
balustrade and trophies. High above the mass of building towers
the roof and clerestory of the Chapel—and here the historical
imagination may improve upon the scene, gilding its ornament
and crowning the whole with a slender belfry. In front, the
Orangerie, magnificently framed between the twin ramps of the
Hundred Steps, seems to carry the Palace and its parterres upon
a solid platform of masonry. Below and to the right, an ornamental water of a size proportionable to the whole layout shows
the branches of its encircling avenues, while to the left the richly
wooded slopes fall gently away from the Château to the level of
the canal—and here again the imagination can picture the same
view as it was, with the fountains playing among the trees, not
yet arrived at their full luxuriance.

If this were the first *coup d'œil* offered to those coming from

Paris, Versailles would have one of the finest approaches of any building in Europe; but it is not. To anyone arriving by one of the main routes, the Palace is always visible before it can be identified as such. The first view of Versailles can be a great disappointment, and for want of a better approach, many visitors will feel disposed to sympathize with Arthur Young's opinion: 'It is just an assemblage of buildings, not a fine edifice.' A conducted tour of the interior, with its attendant discomforts and exhaustion, may serve only to increase the initial disillusion, and that is as far as some people get.

The need for deliberate effort to appreciate is perhaps nowhere more marked than in the artistic productions of seventeenth-century France; whether it is in the writings of Racine or La Rochefoucauld, in the engravings of Nanteuil or the buildings of Mansart, 'their small bright world', as Lytton Strachey wrote, 'is apt to seem uninteresting and out of date, unless we spend some patient sympathy in the discovery of the real charm and the real beauty that it contains'.

To those who are able to make a more leisurely approach, to supplement their knowledge with a little reading and to taste its beauties *à petites bouchées*, Versailles will reveal a charm and a magnificence barely suggested by the fabric of the Palace as it is today. Nor can we long regard the building before it begins to move in us historical reflections upon the persons who have inhabited it. They bring a new life and a new interest to the place, filling the empty rooms with memories and decking the gardens with all the colourful paraphernalia of the Court of France. To those who know its history, Versailles need never present the mournful aspect of a deserted house.

The people too, whose lives thus animate the scene, stand out in sharper relief against their true historic background. Horace Walpole, a man to whom architectural context was of some importance, explained this point when sending an 'enchanting little landscape' of Strawberry Hill to his friend Sir Horace Mann with these words: 'I could rest no longer with the thought of your having no idea of the place of which you hear so much, for it is uncomfortable in so intimate an acquaintance as ours not to be exactly master of every spot where one another is writing or sauntering.' Obviously it would have been more satisfactory if Sir Horace Mann could have seen the place itself; it would have told him a lot about his friend. But to someone today, wishing to evoke the memory of Walpole, which is more useful, Strawberry Hill as it is, or the 'enchanting little landscape' as it was then, seen with all the freshness of an artist's vision? Naturally it is best when one can see both, and let the one supply the short-comings of the other, and this is, in essence, the business of the topographer; the resurrection of the past within the framework of the present.

For Versailles the topographer *par excellence* is Pierre de Nolhac. Poet, humanist, member of the Académie Française and for thirty years Conservateur at Versailles, he pieced together, from the mass of documents scarcely consulted before his time, a history of the Château which must be the foundation of every work on the subject. Certain scholars have added their elaborations and corrections to the writings of Pierre de Nolhac, offering new interpretations or fitting new pieces into the complicated mosaic formed by the incessant redecoration of the Palace; in particular the field has been extended to cover the lesser buildings which exist, or once existed, within the confines of the Grand Design. For just as the highest mountains are never seen without a complementary range of foothills, so buildings of the size of Versailles should not be considered apart from their numerous dependencies.

For the life of the Palace, contemporary writers may be allowed to speak for themselves. The letters of foreign ambassadors or of ladies of the Court, official documents and private memoirs give a picture which leaves little to be desired. The Duc de Saint-Simon, though less reliable than his friend and successor Luynes, must always remain supreme among them; 'throughout the endless succession of his pages', wrote Lytton Strachey, 'the enormous panorama unrolls itself, magnificent, palpitating, alive'.

That is the impression I would like to give of Versailles.

PROLOGUE

Autumn at Versailles

THERE IS USUALLY a stage in the autumn, precarious and ephemeral, when the whole year seems to balance between summer and winter. The trees have reached their fullest and most glorious colouring, as the broad day of summer declines towards its final sunset. Nature waits: at any moment may come that cold wind which sends the birds circling into the heavens in search of warmer lands and bluer skies, brings the leaves fluttering from the treetops and fades the royal beauty of the landscape.

If we should happen to be in France, it is at this moment of supreme beauty that we should visit the Palace of her Kings, for today autumn reigns at Versailles; in early October it places on every tree its golden coronet and spreads its leafy mantle on the ground, bringing with the pale sunshine and delicate mists a beauty not unmixed with sadness, and a sense of passing splendour which is wholly appropriate.

Sometimes, on the other hand, the autumn is cold and wet. The rains falls steadily, accentuating the loneliness of the alleys and setting the blackbirds *tack-tacking* among the bushes; from the damp stubble in the fields there rises, together with the mist, the indescribable smell of autumn, and the partridges run fearfully among the sodden furrows.

It was just such a day on the 5th of October in the year 1789; Louis XVI was out shooting in the woods of Meudon while the Assembly debated his answer to the Rights of Man and the abolition of feudal dues. Marie-Antoinette had passed the afternoon at Trianon. Despite the ominous clouds, she had ventured into the gardens; it was the last time she was ever to see them. She was alone. Her elder son had died that summer at Meudon; she had known since the spring that it was coming, and those last months had been the most harrowing of her existence. Now, her remaining children were in the Palace, her husband was out shooting, and she was alone. Artois, the Polignacs, the Abbé de Vermond—all had fled on hearing the news of the taking of the Bastille, and the little côterie of Trianon, already estranged by the troubles, had broken up. She was alone, Madame Campan informs us, 'livrée à de douloureuses réflexions'. The events of the last months had been so humiliating, so incredible: she could not forget the insult that she had received from the crowds as she walked in the procession to the opening of the States General. There were so many stories about her, so many lies. The deputies had come here to Trianon expecting to find evidence of a fantastic extravagance—rooms encrusted with diamonds, pillars wreathed with rubies and sapphires; they hardly believed the simplicity in all they saw.

She was sitting in the grotto when the fateful messenger arrived. The mob, marching from the capital, had reached the Avenue de Paris; in an hour they would be at the gates of the Palace. It was imperative that the Queen should return to Versailles.

She found the Palace upon tip-toe of expectation. The courtiers, 'sous le coup d'une inquiétude mortelle', were thronging the State Apartments, each trying to keep as closely as possible in touch with the course of events. Across the courtyards the iron grilles, some of which 'had not turned on their hinges since the days of Louis XIV', were closed and locked, and the National Guard, whose loyalty was doubtful, was drawn up in front of the main gates. Beyond was a sea of discontented humanity, calling for bread but looking as if they wanted blood. Through the windows came that most terrifying of all sounds—the sullen murmur of an angry mob.

At three o'clock the King arrived at the gallop from Meudon, omitting, in his haste, to return the loyal salute of the Regiment of Flanders, which was arrayed before the Grande Ecurie. He went straight to his apartment and remained there in an agony of indecision—now agreeing with Saint-Priest and la Tour du Pin to retreat to Rambouillet—now cancelling the order—always repeating, 'I do not want to compromise anybody.'

In the Grande Galerie, which had witnessed so many gay and sumptuous occasions of the Court, a tense and anxious silence now prevailed. 'On se promenait de long en large,' wrote Madame de la Tour du Pin, 'sans échanger une parole.' As for herself she admitted: 'I was in such a state of agitation that I could not stay one moment in the same place. Again and again I went to the Œil de Bœuf where I could observe those who came and went from the presence of the King, in the hope of seeing either my husband or my father-in-law and of hearing from them the latest news. The suspense of waiting was unendurable.'

Only the Queen's apartment, where a number of her entourage were gathered in the Grand Cabinet, afforded a scene of calm and self control. The Duchesse de Tourzel, governess to the Royal children, was perforce a witness. 'Marie-Antoinette,' she wrote, "showed on this day that great spirit and great courage which have always characterized her. Her expression was noble, her countenance serene . . . no one could have read in it the slightest sign of alarm. She reassured everyone, thought of everything.'

She was far from unconscious of the fact that she was the principal target for the malcontents, and for this very reason she gave instructions to Madame de Tourzel that, in the event of an alert, she was to take the Dauphin not to her own room but to that of the King. 'I would rather,' she said, 'expose myself to any danger that there may be, and so draw them away from the King's person and from my children.'

The Duchesse de Tourzel is one of many who have described the events of that night. It is not to be expected that, in the panic and confusion which ensued, the different accounts would be synoptic. The human mind, subjected to such violent emotion, is seldom an infallible recorder. Nevertheless it is possible to follow the general course of events through the eyes of those who were actually spectators. Madame de la Tour du Pin, whose husband was in charge of the Militia—Madame Campan, whose sister Madame Auguier was in waiting on the Queen, together with the Comte de Saint-Priest and the Comte d'Hézecques, the one a Minister and the other a Page, who were in attendance on the King—all tell what is clearly the same story. They chiefly differ as to the villain of the piece. Madame de la Tour du Pin was convinced that the Duc d'Orléans was directly responsible. Hézecques puts all the blame on La Fayette.

At ten o'clock in the evening the Comte d'Hézecques reported for duty. He reached the Château without incident, most of the women of Paris having dispersed to find some place of rest and shelter for the night. Between eleven and twelve La Fayette arrived, in the last stages of fatigue, and was at once admitted to the King's presence. In half an hour he had convinced Louis that there was no immediate danger. A detachment of the Gardes du Corps, which had been drawn up beneath the windows of the Queen's apartment, was sent to Rambouillet; most of the King's attendants were dismissed.

At two o'clock the Queen went to bed, insisting that her ladies-in-waiting, Madame Auguier and Madame Thibaut, should do the same. Fortunately for her, they decided to keep watch. The Ushers in the Grande Galerie announced that the Queen had retired and everyone departed. 'Les portes se fermèrent, les bougies s'éteignirent . . . le calme le plus absolu régnait dans Versailles.'

At the far end of the Aile des Princes, in the apartments of the Princesse d'Hénin, Madame de la Tour du Pin also retired to rest. Her husband, vigilant as ever, made his round of the sentry posts. Everything was in order. 'Not the slightest sound was to be heard, either in the precincts of the Palace or in the surrounding streets.'

Nevertheless he could not, or would not sleep. He took up his station at an open window in the Aile des Ministres—the first building on the left as one enters the first courtyard of Versailles.

It is necessary at this point to have in mind the exact topography of the forecourts as they were at that time. The Cour de Marbre, the inmost courtyard of the Palace, was divided by five steps from the Cour Royale, which was in turn separated from the Cour des Ministres by an iron grille, which today has disappeared. Except for the rebuilding, by the architect Gabriel, of

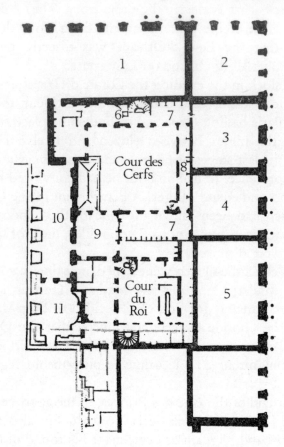

MARIE-ANTOINETTE'S APARTMENT AT VERSAILLES

1 Grande Galerie; 2 Salon de la Paix; 3 Chambre de la Reine; 4 Salon de la Reine; 5 Antichambre de la Reine; 6 Salle des Gardes de la Reine; 7 Grande Salle des Gardes; 8 Escalier de Marbre; 9 Salle du Grand Couvert du Roi; 10 Salle des Gardes du Roi; 11 Salon de l'Oeil de Boeuf; 12 Chambre du Roi

the wing next to the Chapel on the north side of the Cour Royale, the Palace remained as it had been when it was painted by J.-B. Martin in 1722. Gabriel's wing was answered on the opposite side of the courtyard by the Vieille Aile, which still retained at its easternmost extremity its tall colonnade and cupola. To the south of this wing was a narrow courtyard known as the Cour des Princes, the entrance to which was barred by an iron grille and gate, both clearly shown in J.-B. Martin's painting. At the far end of the Cour des Princes was a triple arcade which gave access to the gardens. This also was gated and barred. But there was an open passageway from the Cour des Princes, through the Vieille Aile, into the Cour Royale, which had no gate but at which a member of the Gardes du Corps was always on duty. Apart from this sentry, access to the Cour des Princes meant access to the Cour Royale; in the Cour Royale was the entrance to the Escalier de Marbre, and from the Escalier de Marbre one entered the Queen's apartment.

On this fateful night, 'by a negligence which would have been unpardonable if it were not actually culpable', the gateway to the Cour des Princes was unlocked.

At the break of day, Monsieur de la Tour du Pin, still at his open window, heard the sound of footsteps approaching in large numbers from the direction of the Orangerie. To his horror he saw that this gate, which he had presumed to be locked, was open, and an ugly looking mob was pouring into the Cour des Princes. Conspicuous among them was the figure of a farouche and hirsute savage armed with an enormous axe. His name was Nicolas Jourdan, but they called him *Coupe-Tête*.

At about the same time, Madame de la Tour du Pin was suddenly awakened to the sound of tumult in the street below. Above the hub-bub could be heard voices yelling 'A mort! A mort! Tue les Gardes du Corps!' Scarcely had she recoiled from the window when her faithful maid Marguerite, panting and pale as death, burst into her room and collapsed into the first armchair available, gasping 'O my God! We are all going to be massacred!' She had decided at daybreak to leave her quarters in the Aile des Ministres and seek her mistress, and she had walked straight into the mob just in time to see the unfortunate Des Huttes, the sentinel in the Cour des Princes, dragged before Jourdan and brutally beheaded.

More sinister, she had witnessed the arrival of a man 'in very short boots, carrying a whip', whom she recognized, or was convinced she had recognized, as the Duc d'Orléans.

In the Queen's apartment the two ladies-in-waiting were keeping their vigil with their own *femmes de chambre* in the Salon next to the Queen's bedroom. At about six o'clock they heard the sounds of the mob as it rushed the Escalier de Marbre. Only two rooms separated the Salon from the head of the staircase—the Ante-Room and the Salle des Gardes.

Madame Thibaut ran into the Ante-Room, where she found one of the guards, Miomandre de Sainte-Marie, already trying to barricade the doorway with his musket while the leaders of the mob attacked him. He turned, his face streaming with blood. 'Sauvez la Reine!' he shouted; 'on vient pour l'assassiner.' Leaving Miomandre to his fate, Madame Thibaut turned and ran back, bolting the door of the Salon behind her, and burst into the Queen's room. 'Sortez du lit, Madame!' she screamed, 'ne vous habillez pas; sauvez-vous chez le Roi!' Hurriedly throwing a skirt over her nightdress, Marie-Antoinette fled by means of a concealed door in the corner of the bedroom, through her Petits Cabinets to the Œil de Bœuf. The door to the Œil de Bœuf was bolted upon the other side.

The King at this moment, also awakened by the uproar, was hastening by means of a secret passageway contrived in an *entresol* beneath the Œil de Bœuf, which afforded a private communication between his bedroom and that of his wife. The existence of this passageway was unknown at that time even to Hézecques.

In the Œil de Bœuf, Marquant, one of the *valets de la Garde-robe*, was aroused by a frantic knocking at the door at the south end. 'He ran to open it, and was astonished to see his Queen, half dressed, flying from the blows of the assassins.' At this moment the King arrived in the Queen's room. He found it empty, except for two of the guards who had retreated into it. An instant later he rejoined his wife.

Meanwhile, in the rooms beneath, Madame de Tourzel had been alerted by Monsieur de Sainte-Aulaire. 'I leapt out of bed,' she wrote, 'and immediately carried the Dauphin to the King's room.' She found Marie-Antoinette in complete possession of herself. 'The danger to which she had just been exposed had in no way affected her courage. Her countenance was sad but calm.'

Marie-Antoinette, during that day, was called upon to display a supreme degree of courage. La Fayette insisted on her showing herself to the crowd; it was necessary, he told her, to restore order. Taking her children by the hand, she advanced on to the balcony which overlooks the Cour de Marbre from the King's bedroom. There were muskets levelled in the crowd. She was greeted by a yell of 'Pas d'enfants!' Motioning her children back into the room, she stood for an instant alone on the balcony. The muskets were lowered. For the moment the situation was saved, but the cry 'Le Roi à Paris!' could not be ignored, and the order was given for the Royal Family to return to the capital which it had virtually abandoned since the early days of Louis XIV.

Just before the departure Madame Campan found the Queen alone in her Petits Cabinets. The pent-up emotion of the last twenty-four hours had overtaken her. 'Elle pouvait à peine parler; des pleurs inondaient son visage.' In her heart she probably knew that she was about to say good-bye to Versailles for ever.

The next day, the 7th of October, began at Versailles the saddest spectacle which a building can witness: the courtyards rang to the sound of the footsteps and voices of carriers—of furniture being piled into carts, never to return; of windows and shutters being closed, never to re-open while a Bourbon sat on the throne of France; of carriages rolling out of the golden gates, never to re-enter.

It was the end. 'Une affreuse solitude régnait déjà à Versailles,' wrote Madame de la Tour du Pin. The great château stood bleak and deserted, but continuing to attract visitors, as it always had, some of whom could not understand how it managed to look so unimpressive. They had arrived too late.

The curtain has fallen. The performance is over—only the décor remains to evoke the spectacle which once was played here.

*

The story of Versailles is closely linked with the growth of power and development of character of the King who built it. The years that followed 1661, the death of Mazarin and the fall of Foucquet, mark the assumption of power by Louis XIV; they also mark the first romantic period of his amours, and the creation, around the nucleus of a remote hunting lodge of his father's, of a delightful retreat which lent itself to the pageantry of a King as well as to the quiet solitude of a lover.

In 1668 the peace of Aix la Chapelle brought France once more among the foremost powers of Europe, and her glory found its impersonation in the figure of her King. His Palace had to grow to hold his greatness, but not without passing through its awkward age. Like some enormous flower it put out shoots, developed disproportionately, and only in full maturity achieved harmonious integration. The awkward age is called the Château Neuf, where grandeur and colourful simplicity, though not unreconciled, were loosely knit together. The gardens, circumscribed by the horizon, extended in every direction their network of radiating alleys, peopled with marble statues and gilded *amorini*, and opening in accordance with some preordained symmetry into vast amphitheatres, where, amid the falling of a copious cascade, magnificent fountains rose from their groups of statuary and tossed their waste of waters into the air.

Ten years later the Peace of Nimeguen, securing for Louis the territory of Franche Comté, marked the zenith of his military career. It was the very year also of the final expansion of Versailles. Two great wings, thrown out to north and south, left the stately block of the Château Neuf a mere projection on the garden front, while on the entrance side a satisfactory solution was found to the fusion of the two styles different in scale, colour and materials. In this enormous and elegant prison the Court of France could be kept under the firm hand of the monarch.

A secondary theme to this development is provided by the smaller buildings which continually appeared, the important off-shoots of the parent growth: the Ménagerie and Trianon, both of which were to swell into little palaces; Clagny, which declined in the royal favour together with Madame de Montespan, for whom it was built; and finally Marly, 'la pièce capitale de tout le décor du Grand Siècle'. This delightful château, painted in fresco and perched, after the manner of Italian villas, on the side of a richly wooded slope teeming with cascades and fountains, was begun as a simple hermitage, but became, answering to the creative genius of the King, a miniature Versailles, 'le séjour ordinaire du Roi'. At Marly, Louis came nearest to a home life, and enjoyed the happiest moments of his maturity. Here also he tasted his deepest sorrow.

For the end of Louis' reign—it was to last for seventy-two years in all—was sombre by comparison. Death cast its shadow pitilessly across his path, as one by one his sons and grandsons died before him, and for months on end the Court was never out of mourning. Over the face of the country hung the masks of poverty and famine, the penalties of unsuccessful war. Louis countered the reverses of his old age with an ever increasing and often misguided piety, and it is in this context that the Chapel of Versailles should be considered; in it the last phase of Louis' life was faithfully reflected.

From the death of Louis the story is one of repeated and un-successful attempts to change this monument of the Grand Monarque into a residence tolerable to his successors, but try as they would to free themselves, the environment was too strong for them. The great wings shut out the precincts of the Palace from the world beyond; indeed there was no reason to suppose that any other world existed. Where the Château itself did not form the view, the gardens prolonged their endless perspectives as far as the eye could see. To the Court this was the world, and the person of the King the centre-pin of their life. Behind this decorative screen, which provided the backcloth to their fairy-land existence, events might be preparing which were to affect the very destiny of mankind, but no serious repercussion was felt. The King, virtuous and well-meaning though he might be, was lost in the labyrinth, from which, it seems, there was no escape but make-believe. The miniature refinements of the Petits Cabinets, the simplicity of the Petit Trianon and the absurdity of the Hameau belong to this world of 'let's pretend' into which the Court had degenerated.

In the hand of Louis XIV, Versailles had been an instrument for strengthening the crown against the nobility; in the hands of his successors it proved a dead weight; it helped to drag them into a financial morass from which they never managed to extricate themselves, and it separated the King from his people. At least Louis XIV had been accessible to his subjects, for Versailles was as truly 'open to the public' as it is today. His successors sought to evade this public existence, and lost the contact. The wildest and most harmful rumours circulated about the Court, and the Court was dangerously out of touch with the world beyond.

In the end, as is well known, the world beyond rose up and put an end to the pantomime, scattering the players and killing as many as it could lay its hands on. But by a strange over-sight it left the scenery almost untouched. The drama can be aeconstructed.

LA CHASSE ROYALE

The setting is a large opening in a forest, the point of con-vergence of several radiating alleys; groups of men and ladies stand about under the trees, flicking their riding whips and chatting to one another; here and there the grey coat of a *débutant* catches the eye, or the turquoise, doubled with scarlet and braided with silver and gold, which denotes a person entitled to wear the uniform of the King. Without this distinction nobody is allowed to follow the royal hunt.

For it is a *rendez-vous de chasse* at which we are now the privileged spectators. The horses, tossing their heads and pawing the ground impatiently, the continual vociferation of the hounds and the occasional note of a horn—a confused jumble of sounds, only comparable to the tuning up of an orchestra, create a note of excitement and anticipation. Occasionally the figure of the Premier Écuyer can be seen moving authoritatively among the liveried personnel of the hunt, the *valets de limiers*, holding their straining bloodhounds at the short leash, the *gardes de la forêt*, arquebus at the shoulder, the *palfreniers* and *piqueurs* in charge of the horses from the royal stables.

The alleys still continue to discharge their stream of carriages and horses into the arena. The men, descending from the coaches, present their cards to the *piqueurs* and receive their mounts, which they inspect critically: in the test of horsemanship and etiquette which is to follow, much will depend on the qualities of their steeds.

A stir in the crowd; hats fly off and ladies sweep their curtseys as the King's carriage jingles into the amphitheatre; the order is given for the repast to be served beneath the elegant canopy which has been erected by the Palace servants. During the meal the King interviews the trackers and huntsmen, who have been busy since the break of day marking down the quarry of the afternoon. They have to be able to tell from the imprints in the ground, the scent, and any other evidence vouchsafed them, the age, sex, number of points and other visible attributes of the animal to be attacked. On their observations and upon the King's interpretation of their account the success of the day's sport will depend.

His decision taken, the King gives the order for the departure, and the party moves off in carefully prescribed order to the spot where the huntsman has made his *brisée*, marking with a broken sapling the spot from which the quarry may be traced. Detachments of hounds are stationed at likely places to be released at critical moments and join with the rest of the pack. Louis XV, in his prime a hunter without equal in France, often performed the task of tracker himself, and disposed his field with faultless discrimination.

The quarry is sighted, and the musical accompaniment to the hunt begins. It was no idle sounding, but announced to the field the quality and activities of the stag; the number of points could be identified by the length of the opening call, the *gresle*. A hart royal was greeted with an appropriately imposing fanfare, and by means of the succeeding calls, *au bois*, *volcelet*, *passage de l'eau*, his movements could be traced through forest and woodland, through field and ploughland, through village and garden, until the horns sounded the 'hallali' and the beast was forced to his last stand. For la Chasse Royale knew no limits but the endurance of the animal pursued. Louis XVI was known to run a buck right to the Boulevards of Paris, and in the previous century the Duc d'Angoulême had once continued his pursuit for three consecutive days, covering a distance of nearly a hundred and fifty miles in the process. Almost equally outstanding was the feat of a Norman gentleman, M. Popipou, who started his chase near Evreux at seven in the morning and ran his quarry to ground at six in the evening in the very courtyard of Versailles. Louis XIV was delighted with his tenacity.

He was pleased to see his nobility skilled in the chase, as he himself was pleased to excel in it, for hunting was to him, as to all the Bourbon Kings, his favourite and most worthy pastime. In the minute observation and deduction which it required, the disposition of the field and hounds, the qualities of leadership and endurance which it called for, it was the best training for soldiers that times of peace afforded, and it was only as soldiers that the aristocracy of the *ancien régime* were allowed to justify its existence.

It was the Bourbons' love of hunting which led them into most of the important building ventures of the two centuries which were spanned by their dynasty. The sites of Fontainebleau, St. Germain, Versailles, Marly and Compiègne were determined by the facilities which they offered for this sport of Kings. With Versailles, however, the circumstances attendant upon the building of the Château were somewhat more complex, and a knowledge of the original site, and of certain traits in the character of Louis XIII, will assist our understanding of the palace which came to be so famous.

Louis XIII had a pronounced dislike for women; his mother had given him sufficient reason for that. Like his contemporary in England, Henry, Prince of Wales, 'his whole delight was in manly exercises', and it was with young men of athletic disposition, such as his first favourite the Duc de Luynes, that he naturally consorted. He had also favourites—for mistresses would be the wrong word—among the other sex; first a Mlle de Hautefort, whom he loved to hear reviling Cardinal Richelieu. Although nothing would make him withdraw his political support, he may well have resented the contrast afforded by the Cardinal's efficiency and his own mediocrity. It was at Richelieu's instigation that Mlle de Hautefort was replaced in the King's chaste favours by Mlle de Lafayette. The affair was complicated but not concluded by her taking the veil, and one of the strange turning-points of history is connected with this event. It was on his way to visit her at Les Filles Sainte-Marie that foul weather obliged Louis to pass a night at the Louvre with his wife, a lady for whom he bore little more affection than he did for his mother. Nine months afterwards, however, the future Louis XIV made his appearance in the world—an event of no small consequence to the future of Versailles.

A further reason for Louis' dislike of the opposite sex was that it was beginning to assume a position of prominence, and sought not only to dominate society, but to extend its influence over the Church and State as well. In the salons of Madame de Rambouillet the readers of *L'Astrée* formed themselves into a mutual admiration society and appointed themselves arbiters of taste in the world of letters, and, if they raised love from a mere lust of the flesh to a noble passion of the soul, they reduced the lover to the adoring slave of his all-powerful mistress. 'Nous surpassons

de beaucoup le sexe masculin,' they boasted, 'les femmes ont . . .
l'esprit le plus vif que les hommes parce qu'elles ont le tempéra-
ment le plus délicat.'

If Richelieu had control over affairs of State, the fair sex was
assuming control over everything else, and the young King
sought consolation in solitude and in the pursuit of the stag.
Above all other things he loved to hunt in the wild woodlands
that stretched from St. Germain to Fontainebleau, and it was on
these occasions that he not infrequently passed the obscure
hamlet of Versailles, a group of little houses and cottages
clustered round their church, their mill, and an old ruinous
castle. Here, at the Corne de Cerf, he would sometimes put up
for the night, and he acquired an affection for the place. North
of the village stretched the irregular expanse of the Etang de
Clagny; to the west and south the ground fell away somewhat
sharply, and rolled towards the distant horizon in a forlorn
landscape of forest and fenland, animated only by the incessant
mutter of bullfrogs and the plaintive cry of the waterfowl. There
was a certain melancholy charm about this wild, inhospitable
country which appealed to Louis. As he stood in the evening
looking out across the sea of treetops towards the setting sun,
his mother's apartments in the Luxembourg and the Blue Salon
of the Hôtel de Rambouillet seemed very remote, and here, in
1624, he decided to build a small house for his own use. One
thing was early decided in his mind; it was to have no accommodation for the Queen nor the Queen Mother.

A letter from Louis to Richelieu written in 1641 reveals his
attitude to the presence of the two Queens in his private haunts.
It was during an outbreak of smallpox at St. Germain, and he
somewhat reluctantly offered accommodation here for his wife
and children. 'She could certainly stay at Versailles with my
children,' he admitted, 'but I am afraid of that great number of
women who would spoil everything for me if the Queen went
there.'

The Court, when it was finally allowed to see the Château, for
Louis gave an entertainment here for the Queens and Princesses

in 1626, was duly unimpressed. Louis himself appears to have been dissatisfied, for between the years 1631 and 1634 he enlarged it to form a colourful brick and stone mansion, ranged between four pavilions round three sides of a quadrangle; the whole was surrounded by a moat and closed with a grille.

From the very beginning there were difficulties over the construction. The subsoil of this territory is composed of a fine sand, and is consequently unstable. The walls of the new pavilions, scarcely above ground, began to slip, and a new contract was hastily concluded with the architect, Le Roy, withholding payment for three years 'par sureté et assurance d'un des deux pavillons jà commencés, des quels la fondation a été trouvé douteuse'.

To this modest dwelling were added modest gardens, with water supplied by means of a horse-pump from the Etang de Clagny. A decent simplicity was all that Louis demanded for his residence, which was to remain his private property and never became a part of the Royal domain.

Perhaps Louis' feelings for his little place in the woods can best be appreciated from his words to Père Dinet, his confessor, shortly before he died. 'If God gives me back my health,' he said, 'as soon as I see my Dauphin attain his majority, I will set him in my place, and retire to Versailles with four of your Fathers, to converse with them of things divine, and have no thoughts but of the concerns of my soul and my salvation.' Versailles, however, was not destined to become the monastic retreat of Royalty.

Louis XIV and the Creation of Versailles

THE FIRST ENLARGEMENT

THE EARLIEST ASSOCIATIONS of 'le Roi très Chrétien', Louis XIV, with Versailles were not those of religious contemplation, but like his father, the young King used this pleasant sanctuary for an escape—escape primarily from Paris, forever associated with the humiliations of the Fronde; escape also from the rigours of government. For Louis had early expressed his intention to do his job conscientiously, 'faire son métier de Roi'. He was himself a formidable worker; 'il s'applique extraordinairement aux affaires', a Venetian ambassador noted, and he regulated his life with the minutest punctuality. 'With a calendar and a watch,' said Saint-Simon, 'one could say what he was doing three hundred leagues away.' In his leisure he reacted against this rigorous routine, stating in his memoirs, which he wrote for the edification of the Dauphin, that business and pleasure were two things absolutely apart. It was for his pleasure that he often made his escape to the peace and solitude of Versailles.

There was also present in Louis' mind a mistrust of the nobility, which was closely associated with his dislike of Paris. The one and the other had made an unfavourable and ineradicable impression on his early manhood. But he differed from his father in his attitude towards the Court and capital from which he sought to escape. His father had been content with retreat, but the flight of Louis was that of a queen bee, and he attracted after him a swarm of adherents, building up round his person a new court and a new government. This, in essence, is the story of the development of Versailles.

In his new creation Louis was more than commonly favoured, for it seemed that wherever he turned he was destined to be served by men of the first quality; it was this that made the century of Louis XIV the *Grand Siècle*. As Voltaire pointed out, 'it was a time worthy of the notice of the ages to come, the days when the heroes of Corneille and Racine, the characters of Molière, the symphonies of Lully, quite new to the nation, the voices of Bossuet and of Bourdaloue could be heard by Louis-Quatorze, by Madame (the Duchesse d'Orléans) famous for her good taste, by a Condé, a Turenne, a Colbert, or by this crowd of outstanding men who appeared in all fields. The times will not reappear when a Duc de La Rochefoucauld, author of the *Maximes*, at the end of a conversation with a Pascal or an Arnauld, goes to the theatre of Corneille.' 'It is with this august cortège of immortal genius,' said Cardinal Maury at his reception to the Academy in 1785, 'that Louis XIV faces the judgement of posterity, backed by all the great men who had reached and retained their positions through his discretion.'

One other factor must be considered as having largely contributed to the success of Louis' reign; this was the coincidence of a popular demand for a great king with his own conception of the office and the natural gifts which enabled him to fill it. During the Fronde he had been made to tour the provinces and had everywhere been received with acclamations. But the cry had been 'Vive le Roi tout seul!' The people's exasperation with the Government and the Court led them to look to a strong and a dignified monarch, a successor to Henri IV. Louis had a natural majesty which conformed with the demands of the times; as the Venetian ambassador reported: 'If fortune had not made him a great king, it is certain that nature gave him the appearance thereof.'

The Court of St. Germain, however, from a personal as well as an architectural point of view, did not lend itself to supplying a background suitable to this natural majesty. It had a bad record and a worse reputation. Louis' mother had been unable to control it. 'The French,' she remarked, and she might have said *the Court*, 'have never been able to govern themselves, either in greater or lesser matters.' The public reception of the Polish ambassador, who came to seek the hand of Marie de Nevers for his master, had actually had to be cancelled owing to unresolved disputes among the nobility about matters of precedence. The disgraceful incidents of the Fronde had been but the logical outcome of their natural indiscipline, freed from the rod of Richelieu. But rather than clean out this Augean stable, Louis preferred to build anew.

The earliest embellishments to Versailles, however, were not so much the result of a calculated policy towards the Court, as a carefree abandon to the pleasures of life in general and love in particular.

Within a year of his marriage, the King had embarked on his well-known series of mistresses. Although Louise de la Vallière and Madame de Montespan are almost as familiar to us as Pompadour and du Barry, Louis XIV is less often reproached for this lapse in his morals than his successor to the throne. Primi Visconti, with the ready complaisance of a courtier, put the blame on to the ladies. 'Numbers of women,' he wrote, 'have told me that it would not offend their husbands or their fathers, or even God himself. So one must have some indulgence for the King if he fails, with so many devils around him, all trying to tempt him.' The last temptress, Mlle de Fontanges, was the most brazen of them all. She is amusingly sketched by the Marquise de Sévigné: 'You must imagine her precisely the reverse of the violet which hid itself among the herbage and which blushed alike to be a mistress, a mother, and a duchess.' She is presumably contrasting the lady with Louise de la Vallière.

It is not to be supposed that Louis was faithful even to his mistresses: the Duchesse de Navailles was disgraced for having the door which connected Louis' room with that of the ladies-in-waiting walled in. To his mother he made no attempt to justify this departure from morality, admitting with tears in his eyes that

he could no longer control his passions, nor even felt any desire
to. He did, however, exercise a certain restraint, and in his
memoirs he confessed that his example was not to be followed.
Two precautions, moreover, he always claimed to have taken;
first, that the time devoted to his love-making was never to the
prejudice of his work, and secondly, that he never allowed his
mistresses to interfere with affairs of State. They did, however,
exercise a certain influence over his building schemes, for the
gardens of Versailles were the chosen site of Louis' amours.

In 1661, the year of the disgrace of Foucquet, Louis had taken
on the three artists who had been responsible for the too sumptuous ensemble of Vaux le Vicomte. At Vaux there was a noble
unity about the design, in which Château and gardens were treated
as parts of one all-embracing scheme, which announced the
distinctive character of the *Grand Siècle*. Many of the features of
the park have been recognizably adapted at Versailles, Chantilly,
Sceaux and elsewhere. But Vaux was not the only source from
which Louis was to draw inspiration; in some ways the Château
de Richelieu, with its satellite town, provided a more direct
prototype. The real legacy of Foucquet was the three artists Le
Nôtre, Le Vau and Le Brun, who were to become the creators of
Versailles. The first two of these, the garden-designer and the
architect, were to be faced with almost insuperable difficulties,
presented by the natural drawbacks of the site.

For Louis XIII had built, it would seem deliberately, on a site
which was described by Saint-Simon as 'of all places the saddest
and most barren, with no view, no water and no wood, for it is
all shifting sand and marsh'. Colbert, who anxiously watched the
royal expenditure, begged Louis not to commit the folly of
attempting anything big here. 'Oh what a pity,' he wrote, 'that
the greatest and most virtuous of Kings should be measured by
the scale of Versailles.' But Louis paid no heed; if the ground
presented difficulties, the honour would be the greater for the
king who overcame them. 'C'est dans les choses difficiles,' he
wrote in his memoirs, 'que nous faisons paraître notre vertu.'

At first he was content with enlargement and redecoration,

ceilings painted by Errard and Coypel, tapestries from the Gobelins, gold and silver filigrees from China, and countless vessels of jonquils lent their brightest colours to the scene, while out-of-doors the prospect was no less ravishing. The warm red brick, decorated with stone panels between the windows, the iron balcony which ran round the outside of the Château below the windows of the first floor, richly wrought and gilded, the blue-grey leads of the roof, the tall red chimney stacks, the iron grille, painted a royal-blue and tipped with gold, all made the pleasantest contrast with the prevailing greens of the landscape. Mlle de Scudéry, in her *Promenade de Versailles*, gives a vivid idea of the brilliance which this colourful ensemble could produce. 'Comme le soleil parut à ce moment fort à découvert, il sembla à la Belle Etrangère que ce n'était que pour faire briller d'avantage tout l'or dont le comble du Palais est orné.' It was, in fact, the external gilding which most impressed visitors. Sébastien Locatelli, the first to leave an account of Versailles under Louis XIV, wrote in 1665: 'I camini et certe cupolette sono ricoperte di rame dorato, che in lontananza fà una vista mirabile.'*

The Château itself, after the first enlargements, formed three sides of a quadrangle, with boldly projecting pavilions at each corner. Both the grouping of the buildings and the treatment of the decorations was carried out in a deep relief, so that the colour scheme was enhanced by a rich play of light and shade. The courtyard was closed by an arcade and the whole surrounded by a dry moat; the solitude of Louis XIII and the gaiety of his son were alike unassailable in this charming sanctuary.

Beyond the moat, another courtyard was formed between two symmetrically placed office buildings, reflecting the brick and stone colour scheme, but of less pretentious aspect, as befitted their inferior status. Two little pavilions, in the richer style of the main block, and connected by an iron grille, marked the entrance, and from these flowed two semicircular ramps, forming a sort of

* 'The chimneys and certain cupolas are covered with gilded copper, which, from a distance, makes a wonderful sight.'

forecourt, and gathering in the visitors in their welcoming embrace.

Not for long was this colourful jewel allowed to remain in the rough setting of forest and marshland which had so appealed to the founder. To the south, Le Vau made use of the falling away of the ground to construct an orangery, with a flight of steps on either side, and a parterre was laid out on the terrace above. This was the Parterre des Fleurs 'à balustrade dorée, bordé de cyprès et d'arbustes différents et rempli de mille espèces de fleurs'. It was particularly dear to Louis, who had a passion for flowers, and its destruction, to make room for Le Vau's enlargements in 1668, led him to the creation of the first of the Trianons. At present it is sufficient to note that it was lined with vases 'painted like porcelain'.

It is possible to make an accurate reconstruction of the gardens at the time of the fêtes from two accounts: one left by La Fontaine, who made a tour of them in the distinguished company of the 'Four Friends'; and the other by Mlle de Scudéry, with her mythical companions, Glicère, Télamon and la Belle Etrangère.

To the west of the Château a circular basin, later to take its name from the groups of Latona and her children, with its semi-circular ramps, the Allée Royale and another ornamental water known then as the Bassin des Cygnes, the beginnings of the canal and the avenue beyond, already fixed the main lines along which the gardens were to develop. 'Tout y rit, tout y plaît, tout y porte à la joie,' exclaimed Mlle de Scudéry, whose company expressed wonder and admiration in all they saw. It is rather tedious to read some of these lengthy and uncritical panegyrics, but having constructed the general scene from her more informative passages, one can agree with her comment on the great diversity of the layout—there were large spaces for the carousels and tournaments, there were retired and intimate walks 'propres à la rêverie d'un amant'. But there was still room for experiment, and many of the garden structures of this period were of a temporary nature, erected for some special entertainment and removed after they had served their purpose.

Of the permanent structures, two in particular claimed the attention of contemporaries, and rarely a visit to Versailles was completed without an expedition to the Grotte de Thétis and the Ménagerie. Of these, perhaps, the Grotte de Thétis was the most regarded, lying closer to the Château; it was something of an outing to go to the Ménagerie, but one only had to step out of the house, cross the dry moat and pass into the north gardens to come face to face with the grotto.

It presented to the Parterre du Nord a simple, one-storey façade pierced by three arches and decorated with rustic panels. Four circular medallions representing boys playing with dolphins (the Dauphin had been born in 1661) occupy the spaces between the keystones, while above the cornice the parapet bears three panels depicting the descent of Apollo's car into the sea at the end of his day, a theme which was to receive its consummation inside the grotto. The external feature which evoked most comment, however, was the ironwork of the three grilles which closed the arches. The head of Apollo, Louis' personal device, occupies the middle of the central arch, and its radiating shafts of light provide the framework to all three gates.

Within, three niches, encrusted with pebbles and shells, reflected the three arches of the front, and housed the groups of Apollo tended by nymphs after his day's work, and to either side his fiery horses groomed by tritons. Behind the central group was a water organ, which reproduced in a surprisingly realistic way the twittering of birds. 'One might well fancy oneself in the middle of a grove', wrote Mlle de Scudéry, 'where a thousand birds answer one another, and this natural music, joined with the murmur of water, produces an indescribable effect.' Just what birds were doing in this submarine retreat we can only guess, but it was best not to be too inquisitive nor to ponder too long on such interesting speculations, for the grotto, like almost all grottoes of the sixteenth and seventeenth centuries, was equipped with every facility for practical joking, in the usual form of hidden squirts of water, mostly playing upwards from the floor, from which there was no escape. 'L'eau se croise, se joint, s'écarte, se rencontre,' wrote La Fontaine, and woe betide the visitor who sought to escape by penetrating the inner sanctuary of the grotto!

The interior of the grotto was often illuminated, and was much used by Louis for the entertainment of his guests, serving now as a supper room, now as the background to some comedy. An engraving by Jean Le Pautre shows its three arches as the backdrop to a performance of *Le Malade Imaginaire* in 1674.

Twenty minutes' walk in the direction of St. Cyr led one to the Ménagerie, whose dome and cupola dominated this part of the landscape. Like a miniature château, this building had its two courts, each separated by an iron grille, which had to be crossed before the tall entrance door, with its impressive flight of steps, could be reached. Passing from this narrow court, the straight passage opened suddenly into a vast octagonal salon. Seven large windows gave each on to a balcony, which in turn overlooked a segment of the court, for the runs were disposed fanwise around the central rotunda. Each run had its name, but in practice the name did not always correspond with that of its occupant; hence the 'cour des oiseaux' housed an elephant, and later some camels, and the 'quartier des cigognes' was inhabited by a number of fat sheep. The ostriches, however, were to be found in their proper compartment, and most of the rest of the space was given up to birds; the larger ones, flamingoes, herons and pelicans, had a thick coppice for their protection, but the more exotic species, the humming birds, birds of paradise, parrots and lorikeets, toucans and cockatoos were lodged in regal splendour. The 'cour de la Volière', their predestined home, contained an aviary which was a perfect miniature of French architecture, with its central *corps de logis* and dome joined by low wings to end pavilions capped with little pyramidal roofs, it bore the appearance more of a tiny orangery, and moved Mlle de Scudéry to remark of the birds here that: 'Those of Venus were not better lodged than those of Mars.'

Louis and his friends took a great interest in the many different birds and animals that could be seen here, but should interest in zoology pall, there was the grotto below, equipped with concealed squirts in the same manner as the Grotte de Thétis. Louis was not above entering into the fun himself; Petit describes him as taking a pleasure in working the taps himself, 'sans pouvoir s'exempter d'être un petit [*sic*] mouillé'.

Every new arrival to the Ménagerie was carefully drawn by the artists of the royal workshops, and reference made to them later on for the frescoes and tapestries of the Palace. The Gobelin tapestries of this period are remarkable for the excellence of their animal portraits. Dead bodies went to the Académie des Sciences for dissection. In 1681, the elephant having died, the Academy was convoked, M. du Verney did the dissecting, M. Perrault the description, and M. la Hire the drawings; it is typical of Louis' wide interests that he assisted himself at the autopsy. In this way the arts and sciences profited from the Ménagerie as well as the guests, who came only for pleasure.

The Ménagerie and the Grotte de Thétis were the first important additions; they provided focal points of architecture in a lay out which was already too elaborate to centre solely on the Château.

There exists a charming and detailed painting by Patel of Versailles, giving a vivid idea of the place as it was between 1661 and 1668. Despite the fact that it is taken from an impossible viewpoint, it has escaped the artificiality of the typical seventeenth-century 'Perspective' drawing, and by a clever use of light and shade the artist has created an impression of a picture done from the life.

The whole layout is revealed, with the canal in the centre and the Ménagerie and the village of Trianon to left and right in the background. The Château itself is admirably depicted amid its three parterres, and the regular progression of its courts shown to their best advantage. On the left-hand edge of the canvas can be seen the ramp of the Orangerie, while immediately to the right of the north offices stands the Grotte de Thétis and the reservoirs. Beyond the confines of the Château, and forming the foreground to the picture, six pavilions, in the same style as the offices, line the Place d'Armes. The arrangement was to be repeated in more self-conscious form in the building of Marly some ten years later. Such noblemen as the Prince de Condé, the Duc de Navailles, Turenne, Villeroi and Bellefonds were lodged in these besides the musicians and players who were to provide the entertainments during the royal visit. For it was as a *maison de plaisance* that Versailles was first used, in which the King, with a number of carefully selected friends, could pass a few days of rest and diversion, away from the Court of St. Germain.

It is at the moment of arrival of just such a party that Patel has timed his picture. From the Avenue de Saint Cloud pours a stream of horsemen; behind them rolls the red coach of the King drawn by six sturdy bays. Other carriages are waiting respectfully in the oval forecourt behind two ranks of soldiers, drawn up at either side to form a guard of honour. They will follow the King's coach into the Cour Royale, where the guests will alight to enter the Château on foot, and probably they will pass straight through into the gardens; supper will be served in the Ménagerie, and at nightfall they will return by torchlight through the park, to find that the vestibule, through which they had passed hastily on their arrival, has been transformed into a theatre. For the troop of Molière, whose coaches, stuffed with costumes and scenery, had arrived from Paris earlier in the evening, is to perform a comedy. Sometimes they were obliged to perform before the play was even completely written, and in this way was created the *Impromptu de Versailles*, an improvised performance in an unfinished house.

It was Louis' good fortune to be served by men of genius not only in affairs of State, but in his architecture and his entertainments. Two men in particular assured the success of his fêtes, Molière and Lully, whose partnership lasted from 1664 until 1671. Those who seek for a reconstruction of life at Versailles at this period can sympathize with Théophile Gautier and rejoice that Molière is played again today with the original musical accessories.

The *comédie-ballet* was the child of their artistic collaboration, which left them both the richer for the experience. Writing for music led Molière to the creation of a new prose rhythm, while his comedies gradually orientated Lully in the direction of opera, in which he was to achieve his greatest success. Certain of the *comédies-ballets*, notably *La Princesse d'Elide* and *Les Amants Magnifiques*, seemed to point unmistakably in that direction; while others, such as *Le Bourgeois Gentilhomme*, were the obvious ancestors of the Opéra Comique. Literary history was being made during the entertainment of Louis' guests.

THE FETES

The first large-scale fête in which Molière played an important rôle was the *Plaisirs de l'Ile Enchantée*. Although the Queen and the Queen Mother were both present, no one was in any doubt as to the real purpose of the entertainment, for Louise de la Vallière was at that time at the height of her favour. Everywhere the gardens had been embellished to form the scenery of a pantomime, but a pantomime in which the distinction between cast and audience was not rigidly defined. Four thousand candles, besides innumerable flambeaux, lent their lustre to the setting.

An enchanted island had mysteriously appeared off the coast of France, and from its fairy shores came Roger and his knights to entertain the ladies of the Court. The first evening there was a tournament—a good pretext for the men to show off their brave demeanour and comely horsemanship in an impressive costume. The King, as Roger, took good care that no one should surpass him, his flame-coloured plumes and silver breastplate, encrusted with precious stones, and the golden fittings of his armour setting off his own majestic grace; 'jamais un air plus libre, plus guerrier, n'a mis mortel audessus des autres hommes'. When he had retired from the lists, the tournament was won appropriately enough by the Marquis de la Vallière, who received the sword of honour from the hands of the Queen.

The second day, the Enchanted Island not having left the shore, Roger and his knights offered to the Queens the pleasure of a comedy, *La Princesse d'Elide*. The perspective of the Tapis

Vert provided the background for the performance, with the palace of the Enchantress dimly visible across the waters of the Bassin des Cygnes. The greatest success of the evening was the buffoonery of the valet Lyciscas, played by Molière.

The third day the setting was the palace of the Enchantress, Alcine, who was borne across the waters on a marine monster to address her prologue to the Queen. This was succeeded by a ballet to the music of Lully, leading up to the entrance of Roger, who put an end to the spell. With a clap of thunder the whole palace burst into flames, and a magnificent display of fireworks ended the three days' entertainments.

But even the disappearance of the Ile Enchantée could not make Louis tear himself away from his darling Versailles. Further tilting in the dry moat, a luncheon served in the Ménagerie, and the ever-famous première of *Tartuffe* in the vestibule of the Château filled in the following days, until on the 14th of July the Court once more took the road for Fontainebleau.

It was not without relief that some of them saw the last of Versailles. Glorious though it had been, there were certain voices raised in complaint that there was no accommodation here for the courtiers. Ormesson noted in his memoirs of the trial of Foucquet that all the courtiers were enraged because the King took no care of them: 'MM de Guise et d'Elbœuf n'avaient pas quasi un trou pour se mettre à couvert.'

Louis, however, was well content, for he realized that there was more to be got from the fêtes than mere entertainment. Nobody could follow the King to Versailles without his order, except those on whom the greatest privilege of all, the *carte blanche*, had been bestowed. The men thus distinguished had the right to wear the blue cloak doubled with silver and gold, similar to that worn by the King himself. 'This sort of distinction,' observed Mlle de Montpensier, 'intrigued the Court.'

Louis was not slow to realize the advantages of such a system, and the Court, in time, became reduced to a position of complete dependence on himself. 'La meilleure place de sureté,' he told his brother, 'est le cœur du Roi.' Soon he began to elaborate on mere invitations to Versailles; every detail of the royal routine offered some opportunity to single out one or two for a personal favour, to reward, or to humiliate. Every evening after prayers it was announced who was to have the honour of holding the candle at the *coucher*; every word, every look, was nicely regulated according to the social rank or degree of favour enjoyed by the courtier in question. To ladies, of whatever rank, Louis always uncovered; to the *grands seigneurs* he doffed his hat perhaps only as far as the ear, and for the rest—'il se contentait de mettre la main au chapeau'. Every movement was made with an incomparable grace and majesty, even to that awkward and indefinable gesture when he made as if to rise from his seat—'sa manière de se soulever à demi'—when a lady joined his table. Such accomplishments as dancing, golf, billiards or shooting he had perfected, and he expected his followers to perform with an equal grace or not at all. In this way he kept a remarkably high standard in all things, and a visit to his Court was an experience not easily forgotten. The constant hope of an invitation to Versailles, or of some mark of favour while there, kept the nobility of France the assiduous servants of the King.

The fêtes above all else gave the courtiers something to look forward to, and something to talk about afterwards; not to have been asked would have put one at the greatest disadvantage and confusion at Court.

In 1668 Louis gave the *Grand Divertissement Royal*, the supreme moment of existence of the old Versailles, for in the same year the plans for enlargement were definitely accepted, and soon after the fête the work was put in hand. It was given in July, some two and a half months after the Peace of Aix-la-Chapelle, and the cool of a summer evening lent its charm to the ceremony.

> 'L'importune et grande chaleur
> Cédant la place à la fraîcheur,
> Ainsi que Phœbus aux étoiles,
> La nuit tendit ses sombres voiles.'

This single night, which cost 100,000 livres, not counting the costumes 'extraordinairement parées' of the guests, was planned for the enchantment of all present. At six o'clock, the *promenade des jardins*, where Louis showed off the latest embellishments and improvements. Slowly the great unwieldy cortège made its way down from the Château, past the Grotte de Thétis and the Parterre du Nord, the ladies mounted 'en calèche', a vehicle combining the ease of a bath-chair with the elegance of a Roman chariot, with colourful parasols held, like miniature canopies, above their towering coiffures; the men on foot, swarming round Louis as he stopped here and there, now explaining the latest scheme for the further elaboration of the gardens, now pausing to discuss the mythology relating to one of the statues newly erected in the alleys.

Arrived at the Cabinet de Verdure, they found the buffet loaded with delicacies, and all the trees around hung with fruits, fat oranges from Portugal, currants from Holland, and every sort of pear, peach and plum, there for the plucking. One of the buffets held a palace of marzipan and sugar, which was broken up and consumed by the crowds when the King and his party had passed on. Even under Louis XIV the Court was never really disciplined when it came to large functions. 'Certainly, if there had been less disorder and confusion at this fête at Versailles,' wrote the Marquis de St. Maurice, 'the paraphernalia of it had much pomp and beauty.'

Passing by the Fontaine des Cygnes, for which, Louis explained, the group of Apollo's chariot was already ordered, they arrived at the theatre, erected by the ingenious Vigarani in the Allée de Saturne. It was constructed entirely of foliage, hung with tapestry on the inside, and lit by thirty-two crystal chandeliers. Here was performed 'une agréable comédie de Molière'—*Georges Dandin*—with a symphony by Lully to which opera and ballet were performed in the intervals of the comedy. No one was more brilliant at these improvisations than Molière, who was actor, author and producer all at once. He never hesitated to poke fun at his audience, often having a foil among them whom he heckled from the stage. The Marquis, the Précieux, the

Savants, the Hypocrites, all came under his lash, and only the latter made any serious protest. *Tartuffe*, which was played for the first time at Versailles, has never ceased to evoke the opposition of the more respectable classes.

After the theatre, a more serious repast was offered in another octagonal Salle de Verdure contrived at the intersection of several alleys. Its walls were lined with marble fountains from which water overflowed abundantly into little rivers designed for its conduit, the silver guéridons, ablaze with candles, the festoons of flowers, and the formal setting of the buffet, this time a Mount Parnassus, provided the décor for this midnight supper. Mlle de la Vallière, still *maîtresse déclarée*, sat at the King's table, while at that of the Duchesse de Montausier were both Madame de Montespan and Madame Scarron (later Marquise de Maintenon), the two women who were to play the greatest rôle in Louis' life.

The supper was followed by a ball, held in another specially constructed salon, solidly built of marble and porphyry and lined with private boxes, underneath which were grottoes, each contributing its little stream to the basin at the entrance to the salon; again the chandeliers lent their enchantment; 'l'éclat des eaux disputait de beauté avec les lumières'.

After this surfeit of entertainment, the guests make their way back in the small hours of the morning through the dark alleys of the Petit Parc at the close of this memorable night. But even now, a further surprise awaited them. The Château itself, and the gardens, right down to the Bassin des Cygnes, were aglow with a phosphorescence which seemed their own; on the last occasion on which it was to serve as the background to Louis' magnificence, Versailles had become 'véritablement le Palais du Soleil'. The windows, the statues, the urns, were bathed in different colours, while a thousand points of light were reflected on the waters of the parterre; it was as if a new solar system had evolved around the person of Le Roi Soleil. But as the courtiers stood enraptured at the sight, the crash of gunpowder rent the air, and on every side the woods and alleys leapt into a blaze of fireworks; fountains added showers of golden rain to that of their waters, the monsters around Latona spewed fire, and the whole surface of the Bassin des Cygnes appeared to be a sea of flames; so closely were the two elements, fire and water, allied that it was almost impossible to distinguish one from another. No sooner had the fires on the earth died down than a thousand rockets streaked into the sky, breaking into great petals of light with a roar that seemed to make the very ground tremble, and the royal cypher, the inverted 'L's', traced in figures of fire, rose majestically against the sky, where already the day, as if jealous of the splendours of such a night, was beginning to show its morning lustre.

THE CHATEAU NEUF

In the autumn of 1668 the Château, which seemed to many to have been brought to its final perfection, was once more a mass of scaffolding, and the workshops thronged with masons. For the repeated and prolonged visits of the Court had shown the accommodation to be quite inadequate for Louis' requirements, and he determined on a considerable enlargement of the building.

Colbert, anxious that the King should seat himself permanently and worthily in his capital, was opposed to the squandering of further sums on a residence which, in his opinion, could never be made answerable to the grandeur of his master, and did all he could to further the completion of the Louvre. Louis, however, soon abandoned Bernini's project for his Parisian palace, and concentrated his attentions upon Versailles. Le Vau, being Premier Architecte du Roi, was given the not very easy task of designing the new enlargements.

There were two schemes between which Louis and Colbert continued to waver, even after the foundations had been laid; one was to encase the little château on three sides with new and larger constructions, and the other to abolish it and make the new building sufficient in itself. The difficulty was lack of space; 'il est impossible', noted Colbert in his memorandum on the subject, 'de faire une grande maison dans cette espace, sans renverser tout . . . et sans faire une dépense prodigieuse.' Other architects were invited to submit solutions, but the problem remained the same. The size of the inner court, determined by the restrictions of the site, would not permit of sufficiently tall façades, unless the court were to be very disagreeably proportioned. 'Le défaut universel de tous les dessins sera qu'il faut trop abaisser les bâtiments sur les cours.' The final retention of the Petit Château solved this problem by enabling a stepping up in the heights of the respective façades, but it entailed an awkward contrivance where the two buildings met, which was only done away with in the final enlargements of Mansart.

Despite the many changes in plan, the building progressed with little interruption, as is proved by the accounts. For 1669 they show 335,000 livres for masonry, a figure which rises to 586,000 and 428,500 in the following years. In 1672 it has dropped to 54,000 as the new structure reared its stately façades above the gilded roof-tops and chimney stacks of the old Versailles.

Louis frequently visited the scene of operations himself with a sharp and critical eye, and the prospect of his next visit was kept as a perpetual incentive to the workers. When he was absent, either with the Court at St. Germain or Fontainebleau, or on his campaigns, he maintained a correspondence with Colbert so voluminous that the Superintendent, fearing that his labours might be *de trop*, asked whether he wished for long or short despatches. 'De longs,' came the answer, 'le détail de tout.'

It was by his close interest in detail during the many years of construction that Louis imprinted his personality upon Versailles and made it, not a prosaic essay in classical architecute, but something personal and made to measure.

The new additions were known as the 'Enveloppe', for they encased the old upon three sides, leaving the Cour de Marbre open as an inner court, with two other enclosed courtyards on either side. From the gardens, the Enveloppe, or Château Neuf, presented an entirely new aspect. It was all of stone, three storeys high, with a balustrade to conceal the roof. Apart from the rectangular windows of the first floor, surmounted with bas-reliefs, the three main façades on the gardens were, in detail, much as they are today. The west front, however, presented a very different appearance, owing to the absence of the Galerie des Glaces. Seen from the top of the steps leading to the Parterre de Latone, the King's apartments to the left, and the Queen's to the right, projected forwards, leaving the upper storeys deeply recessed between them, with a terrace in front formed by the continuation of the ground floor between the two wings. Further to the left, to the north of the new buildings, could be seen the single-storied structure of the Grotte de Thétis.

Visitors to the Château Neuf were eloquent in praise of the garden fronts, noting in particular the statues and relief work with which they were decorated. 'Toutes les figures et les ornements qu'on y voit,' wrote Félibien in his official description, 'n'étant pas placés au hazard, ils ont relation ou avec le Soleil ou aux lieux particuliers où ils sont mis.'

It would indeed be a mistake to suppose that the symbolism behind the decoration of Versailles was disposed at random. The artists, directed by Le Brun, were expressing a view of the universe—Newton's universe—in terms of the microcosm which they were creating around the figure of Le Roi Soleil.

The three porticoes, each of four columns, with which Le Vau punctuated the western front of the Palace, suggested the opportunity of representing the twelve months of the year, and the bas-reliefs over the first-floor windows were scenes depicting the various activities proper to each month. The view that the year represents 'the perfect image of the life of man', growing through spring to the ripeness of summer, and declining through autumn to the winter of old age, provided the theme for the keystones over the ground-floor windows, whose masks show a steady progression from childhood to senility. On the south front, the proximity of the Orangerie and the flower garden fixed the symbolism of the decorative scheme; Flora, obviously, and her lover Zephyr, 'qui, par la douceur de son haleine fait sortir des fleurs hors de la terre', and Hyacinth and Clytie, who

37

were turned into flowers by the sun. To the north, where the proximity of the Grotte de Thétis and the reservoirs was of first importance, the statues conformed with the aquatic nature of their orientation. On the entrance side the symbolism is not at once apparent; it is derived from the Palace kitchens, and represented the four elements, which supplied fruit, fish and fowl to the royal table, and fire to cook them with.

The architectural arrangement on this side, however, was less happy; the sweeping curves of the forecourt were retained, although considerably advanced into the Place d'Armes. Four isolated pavilions, reminiscent of the former offices, but larger and set wider apart, flanked the outer court, while the offices themselves had been incorporated in the main block and ornamented with a balustrade and vases on the walls facing towards the courtyard, and with a colonnade and statues on their extremities towards the town. This was certainly an unsatisfactory and ungainly arrangement, and the low, flat roofs of these wings presented difficulties on the north and south façades where they met the taller buildings of the Enveloppe.

From a distance, the Palace now presented a somewhat disorderly appearance; nearer to it, it had its particular charm in the old courtyard, the Cour de Marbre, which was now formed into a delightful inner sanctuary. Two shallow flights of steps preserved the harmony of its proportions and safeguarded it from the intrusion of vehicles. The entrance to the vestibule was accentuated by a balcony supported on eight marble columns, *rouge de Languedoc* in conformity with the general colour scheme; the stone plaques between the windows were adorned with busts, and the court itself was paved with marble flags, red and white and black, from which the court was to take its name. To this friendly and colourful retreat the babble of running water and the song of birds lent their accompaniment, for in the centre of the court a large fountain had been constructed with its group, modelled by the Marsy brothers, which gave it the name of 'Fontaine des Enfants'; and in the inner corners, above little grottoes in the shape of cockle shells, were two wrought-iron aviaries, capped with domes, and of course gilded.

In the old Château the three rooms in the centre of the ground floor could be opened up to form a theatre, and it was here that most of the comedies of Molière had been performed. On special occasions, such as the fêtes, outdoor theatres had been constructed; the Cour de Marbre, already elevated by five steps, lent itself admirably for this purpose. An engraving by Le Pautre shows beautifully the scenic arrangement for the production of *Alceste* in 1674. Windows, balcony and cornice are ablaze with candles, and a double line of orange trees form the wings to either side of the stage, while great bunches of flowers have been placed to act as mutes to the waters of the fountain. In front, two boxes have been contrived for the orchestra, and chairs set in an amphitheatre for the guests.

Although *Alceste* was not considered outstanding among Lully's works—his own favourite was *Roland*—it was very well received by King and Court. 'C'est une chose qui passe tout ce qu'on a jamais ouï,' wrote Madame de Sévigné, 'le Roi disoit l'autre jour que s'il étoit à Paris quand on jouera l'opéra, il iroit tous les jours.' By birth an Italian, Lully had worked with French teachers and had managed to assimilate completely the style of his adopted country, becoming, in the words of La Laurencie, 'plus français que Charpentier, que l'on traitait d'italien'. Showing what Schweitzer calls the 'audacity of genius', he knew when to put himself above the rules which held so many of his contemporaries in shackles, and gave to France a music which was quite unknown before his time. By force of personality he held together the difficult and temperamental members of the Opéra, and made it not only a musical but a business success. He was lucky to number Corneille, Molière, La Fontaine, Quinault and Racine among his librettists, but it is typical of the century that it should have been so.

The performance of *Alceste* was part of a prolonged *divertissement* given by Louis in July and August of the year 1674 to celebrate the annexation of Franche Comté. As usual, Madame de Sévigné is ecstatic: 'Tous les jours des plaisirs, des comédies, des musiques, des soupers sur l'eau,' she wrote, 'on va sur le Canal, on y trouve la musique; on revient à dix heures, on trouve la comédie; minuit sonne, on fait medianoche.' These midnight suppers had become a regular feature of the fêtes; sometimes they were held in the Château, sometimes at the Ménagerie or in a temporary pavilion; on one occasion in the Cour de Marbre, specially adorned by Vigarani with a Trajan's column of candles. The dramatic part of the entertainments had also been worthy of note; for besides Lully and Quinault, both Racine and Molière had contributed, *Iphigénie* being played on the 18th of August, while the performance of *Le Malade Imaginaire* against the background of the Grotte de Thétis had been a month earlier. A great classical proscenium, decorated with the same rustic panels and roundels as the grotto, and bearing the royal arms wreathed in laurel leaves in its broad pediment, enclosed the stage, lit by five great candelabra, and lined on either side with orange trees. Tapestries stretched upon frames formed an auditorium for the guests, in the centre of whom, on three high-backed chairs, sat the King, the Queen, and the Duc d'Orléans.

There were firework displays of the usual sort, with elaborately architectural set-pieces, and most beautiful of all had been the illumination of the Grand Canal on the last evening. The Court had made a nocturnal progress 'en calèche et à flambeaux' passing along the dark alleys with their lines of statues, which had assumed a somewhat ghostly appearance from the upcast shadows, like so many figures before the footlights.

Le Pautre's engraving, illustrating Félibien's account of the fête, gives a good idea of the general layout and luminosity of the scene. It gives no idea of the colouring—'la savante disposition des lumières et des couleurs'. The pavilions marking the centre of the cross were of various marbles, some of a sea-green translucency, while others in coral and amber suggested the reflections of a setting sun. Loveliest of all was the palace of crystal at the far end of the perspective, built in a proportion calculated to show to advantage from so great a range, for it was thirty-six feet high. It seemed to have been made, not of marble, but of topaz,

'LE PASSAGE DE LA REINE' THROUGH WHICH
MARIE-ANTOINETTE FLED ON THE NIGHT
OF OCTOBER 5/6, 1789

ENFILADE THROUGH THE QUEEN'S APART-
MENT FROM THE CHAMBRE DE LA REINE

THE FORECOURTS OF THE PALACE SHOWING THE GATE, LEFT OF THE COLONNADE, THROUGH
WHICH THE MOB ENTERED THE COUR DE MARBRE. DETAIL OF THE PAINTING BY P. D. MARTIN

LOUIS XV AT A RENDEZ-VOUS DE CHASSE
TAPESTRY BY OUDRY

THE ROYAL HUNT AT MARLY
SKETCH BY A. VAN DER MEULEN

THE MÉNAGERIE
ENGRAVING BY A. PERELLE

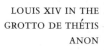

LOUIS XIV IN THE
GROTTO DE THÉTIS
ANON

FIREWORKS AT VERSAILLES, 1668

A PERFORMANCE OF *ALCESTE* IN THE COUR DE MARBRE
ENGRAVINGS BY LE PAUTRE

THE ENVELOPPE FROM THE PLACE D'ARMES
LOUIS XIV RECEIVING JAMES II IN EXILE
DUTCH ENGRAVING

THE ENVELOPPE FROM THE GARDENS.   ENGRAVING BY A. PERELLE

THE CANAL WITH ITS FLOTILLA

THE PARTERRE DU NORD.   PAINTING BY E. ALLEGRAIN

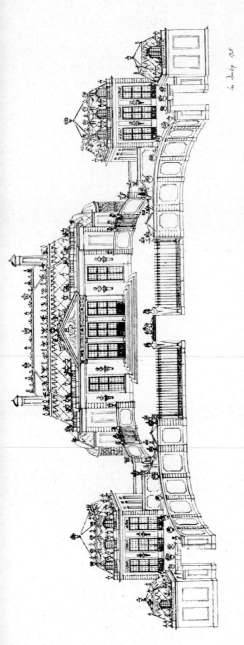

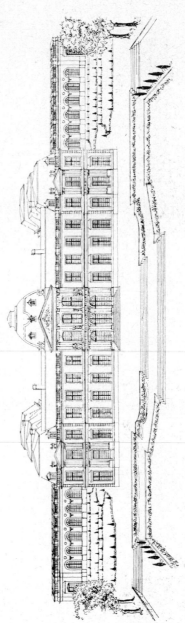

THE TRIANON DE PORCELAINE.   RECONSTRUCTION BY IAN DUNLOP

THE CHÂTEAU DE CLAGNY.   RECONSTRUCTION BY IAN DUNLOP

THE GRANDE GALERIE.   ENGRAVING BY COCHIN

emerald and ruby, casting their reflections like a tray full of precious stones on the untroubled surface of the canal. On this enchanted ocean the Court now proceeded to embark in the little flotilla which Louis provided for the purpose, and made a further inspection of the illuminations to the delightful accompaniment of Lully's music. In the profound stillness of the evening one could hear the violins following His Majesty's barque, and as the ships drifted gently out into the night, trailing their silver wakes behind them, one could see the oars rising and falling with a lazy monotony, leaving pools of light upon the dark face of the waters.

A comparison between the illustrations to the fêtes of 1674 and those of the *Ile Enchantée* reveals the astonishing progress in the development of the gardens which had accompanied the building of the Enveloppe. This had necessitated the ordering of a considerable quantity of new statues. Patel's painting shows a garden outlined largely by trim clipped hedges and neat balustrades. The iron grille that separated the Château from the Parterre des Fleurs was lined with terms, some twelve feet in height, and a similar decoration had previously been accorded to the 'demi-lune' (Latona) and the Parterre du Nord. A few statues had stood, solitary sentinels to the entrance of each allée, but there was no particular scheme into which they fitted, most of them representing lesser deities, Pans and Hamadryads, in keeping with the sylvan surroundings of the place.

In 1666, however, the year that saw the installation of the Grotte de Thétis, a new impulse was given to the statuary by the commanding of the major groups which were to punctuate the central axis of the gardens: the three destined for the grotto itself, that of Latona and her children, and one of Apollo's chariot for the Bassin des Cygnes. It is worth noting the names of the artists from whom they were ordered; Girardon and Regnaudin were to be responsible for the big group of Apollo in the grotto, Marsy for the horses, and also for Latona, while Tubi was to furnish the figures of Acis and Galatea for the grotto, and to model Apollo's chariot. All these were young men who received their commissions over the heads of the regular sculptors, and who formed a team whose work was so subordinated to the general effect that it is difficult to believe that the statuary came from so many different hands.

The central group of these three was that of Latona. Originally she was placed facing the Château, but later was turned to face out over the park. Latona, it will be remembered, was the mistress of Jupiter and the mother of Apollo. One day, while fleeing the wrath of Juno, Jupiter's espoused wife, she was prevented from quenching her thirst by the peasants of Lycia, who troubled the water with stones and clods of earth. Outraged by their inhuman conduct, she appealed to her lover to avenge the insult. He did so by turning the offending peasants into frogs. The group shows Latona with her children in the act of appealing, while around her a number of frogs continue to direct jets of water where once they had thrown stones. Some of them retain human form, save for the hideous grin and emaciated fingers which betray their present metamorphosis.

As the mother of Apollo, Latona would certainly have occupied a place of honour at Versailles, but to more shrewd observers was there not here a lesson in the fate of those who dare to sling mud at the mistress of a King?

Most of the statues in the garden were carved from white marble, but many of the figures which adorned the fountains were cast in lead. It must be remembered that all the ornaments which were made of lead at Versailles were originally gilded, and re-gilded every year, so that they never became dull or tarnished. The effect may be judged today by the golden figures of the fountains of Linderhof. To modern eyes it is inclined to seem garish.

Louis was never happier than when he was showing off his gardens to the many distinguished guests who presented themselves. 'The King arrived in a coach which he drove himself,' wrote Michieli, 'drew up the horses in front of the grotto, where I had positioned myself to greet him, descended with a radiant countenance and invited me to a turn in the gardens. . . . During two hours on end, escorted only by a few gentlemen, he insisted that I should accompany him into the most sequestered spots, into the most delicious retreats where solitude refreshes him from the fatigues occasioned by his preoccupations.'

But even Louis' relaxation from his fatigues was not wholly disinterested; their walk leading them along the banks of the canal, and the discourse turning to matters of vessels suitable for its navigation, Michieli at once submitted that the gondolas of his native city could not be improved upon for the purpose, to which Louis assented 'avec un gracieux et courtois sourire'. The Ambassador took the matter up later with Bellefonds, who archly suggested that the King would certainly like to have gondolas, but that he could not afford to buy any. (The Comptes des Bâtiments for these years do not offer any convincing evidence of economies of this sort.) As was no doubt intended, Michieli at once wrote off to Venice, where the Senate duly passed a resolution for the immediate construction of two gondolas 'du plus beau modèle, destinées à être offertes au Roi de France'.

More usually it was to ladies that Louis turned for company in these little expeditions round the grounds. Mlle de Lafayette, the celebrated authoress of *La Princesse de Clèves*, visited Versailles in the same year as Michieli. 'Elle y fut reçue très bien', wrote Madame de Sévigné. By this she meant that the lady was accorded a long ride in the royal coach and the pleasure of conversation with her sovereign. When Tallemand des Réaux asked Madame de Cornuel whether she did not think this to be an enchanted garden, she correctly answered him: 'Oui, mais il faut que l'Enchanteur y soit.'

The expansion of the gardens, as of the Palace, had been the expression of Louis' own ascendancy. 1670 had been a great year for France. England had been bought out of the Coalition by the Treaty of Dover, and the fate of the Netherlands had seemed assured; it was the year that saw the production of Racine's *Bérénice*, of Molière's *Bourgeois Gentilhomme*; Versailles, though incomplete, was beginning to appear in its full majesty, compared to which the radiance of the Vieux Château was but the roseate glow which precedes the sunrise. This was indeed the dawn of Le Roi Soleil.

It was therefore appropriate that the following years should have marked the completion of the Château Neuf and the placing of the most important group of garden statuary, that which gave its name to the Bassin d'Apollon.

It is a pity that it is impossible to view this piece from a higher vantage point, from which one could appreciate the splaying out of the figures, the horses tugging at the reins, the tritons scattered to either side, announcing with the raucous voice of their conches the coming of the dawn. The chariot of Apollo is labouring, like a swan about to take off, before it breaks forth upon another day. The whole group gives the most magnificent impression of eruption—*surgissement* was Camille Mauclair's word—as the horses rear and strain in a final effort to get the chariot clear of the water; one can almost feel the dilation of their nostrils and the quivering of their flanks, and one expects at any moment to see driver and horses rise into the air and commence their vast trajectory across the sky.

THE FIRST OFFSHOOTS

1. *The Trianon de Porcelaine*

'Sans Parangon waved three times with his wand, and instantly there rose up a Palace of Porcelain encircled by a Parterre of Jasmines filled with a great quantity of little fountains, and the whole scene presented the most charming appearance that could well be imagined.' Preschac, in his fable 'Sans Parangon et la Reine des Fées', gives, in appropriate form, the essence of one of Louis' most interesting experiments in architecture.

L'appétit vient en mangeant; the more the King indulged his taste for building, the more insatiable it became, and it seems that he delighted in overcoming the natural difficulties of place and time. The enlargement of Versailles had entailed the destruction of the Parterre des Fleurs, and Louis sought to reinstate this in a remote corner of the park; being remote, the garden would require its own architectural focus. In the autumn of 1669 Le Nôtre and Le Vau, and a host of workmen, were set to the task; by the following spring it was finished. The Trianon de Porcelaine had made its appearance upon the changing panorama of Versailles. Preschac was not being over-fanciful; there seemed almost an element of magic about the speed with which this exotic little château had come into being, as if, suggested Félibien, it had sprung up with the flowers of the garden.

The underlying reason for this sudden creation of a garden and pavilion in a secluded part of the grounds was doubtless the ever increasing favour of Madame de Montespan, a sufficient inducement for Louis to seek refuge from the ever growing throng at Versailles. It is possible to picture the circumstances in which he made his choice of this site, for the enlargement of the canal, started in 1668, had considerably extended the use that could be made of it. One arm now extended as far as the Ménagerie, and the other to the little hamlet of Trianon, which Louis bought in the same year. On the canal was kept a flotilla of ships, for ornament and for use. In particular there were the two gondolas already referred to.

It was one of Louis' favourite pastimes to embark in one of them 'pour goûter la fraîcheur du soir', and Madame de Montespan was his chosen companion; apart from the need for balancing the Ménagerie in the general layout, it was as a destination for their expeditions that the first Trianon was planned. It was essentially to be a garden—a garden of jasmines and jonquils and wallflowers, whose scent had a peculiar fascination for Louis, to which a pavilion, something a little fanciful, in the new Chinese taste, perhaps, would form an important accessory. Le Vau was the architect, but he died in 1670 before the building was complete, and was succeeded by François Dorbay. In the summer, when the Court visited Versailles, the new gardens were open to an admiring public.

A graceful double staircase, the *Fer-à-Cheval*, led from the canal to the level of the lower parterre, which was surrounded by a trellis screen designed to shelter the gardens from the wind, and its occupants from any inclemency of the weather. The parterre was lined with orange trees, not standing in clumsy tubs waiting to be wheeled laboriously back into an orangery, but growing in the soil. To achieve this, Le Bouteux, the head gardener of the first Trianon, had contrived a collapsible greenhouse whose partitions could be erected round the trees or taken down as the season of the year demanded. It was the only concession made to the elements. The garden was kept supplied with flowers all through the year by the expedient of lowering them fresh from the hot-house into the beds they were to occupy. Thus, even in midwinter, Louis could take his guests for a stroll among the flower-beds before entering the pavilion where luncheon was served.

At the end of the repast they would be again ushered into the gardens; imagine their surprise on finding that the beds had assumed, during the meal, an entirely new aspect, and a fresh border of the brightest colours now lined each of the walks. For it was not infrequently that the flowers had to be changed twice in a day, and Colbert was hard put to it to keep Le Bouteux supplied. 'Je vous prie,' he wrote to the Intendant des Galères at Marseilles, 'd'acheter toutes les jonquilles et tubéreuses que vous pourrez trouver.' In answer to his request came three thousand jonquils, thirteen hundred hyacinths and a promise of further supplies from Sieur Arnoul. Meanwhile Le Bouteaux kept the almost unbelievable number of one million, nine hundred thousand flower-pots in use to achieve these transformation scenes in which Louis so delighted. At Versailles he had determined to overcome nature; at Trianon it was the seasons over which he had obtained the victory:

> 'Pour le plaisir des yeux changé l'ordre du temps,
> Fait des plus grands hivers un éternel Printemps.'

The Duc de Saint-Aignan, author of the lines just quoted, was not the only one to leave verses on the subject of this new building venture of Louis'. It has also been described in couplets of exceptional mediocrity by the fountain designer, Denis. Despite the platitudes of his style, this observant gardener has managed to leave some interesting details of the first Trianon, and this account owes much to his description.

There were many seats, covered with a fine moss, from which the gardens could be appreciated, and a little bower, the Cabinet des Parfums, erected in one corner, from which their fragrance could best be enjoyed. The general colour effect was a blaze of gold, achieved mostly by the wallflowers, and to set this off the pavilion and the architectural features of the garden were made in the semblance of blue and white porcelain. It will be remembered of the original Parterre des Fleurs that the vases had been painted in the same way.

Some five years earlier, the west of Europe had become acquainted with the famous Tour de Porcelaine at the Imperial Palace of Nankin, built 'avec une telle bienséance, proportion et symétrie que les premiers architectes de l'univers ne pouvaient rien trouver à redire'. The taste for chinoiserie (the word is comparatively modern; *lachinage* would have been the one familiar to Louis) had already come to France under the influence of Mazarin, and in Delft the factories were producing exquisite tiles of blue and white porcelain for decoration. It was in this style that Louis decided to build his Palais de Flore; the classical influence, however, was too strong for Le Vau. Having planned his building with a disposition reminiscent of the Villa Pia at the Vatican, fixed its proportions with a Doric order and loaded it with a heavy mansart roof, he relied on a profusion of bizarre and colourful decoration for an effect which he hoped would pass for a tolerable imitation of the architecture of the Far East.

The roof was entirely covered with porcelain tiles, blue, with a little green and yellow, on a white base, and the balustrade and both levels of the roof carried a great quantity of china urns; between the urns on the balustrade a number of gilded *amorini* were grouped in the lines of a festoon, while on the tier above them a similar line of birds, painted in natural colouring, presented to those standing in the forecourt a jagged skyline, suggestive, perhaps, of the temples of Nankin.

The blue and white pattern of the roof was carried down on to the façade by the painting 'en façon de porcelaine' of the broad wooden casements of the windows, repeated in the iron grilles, similarly painted, and finally reappeared in the fountains and statuary of the gardens. Thus was a noble harmony and unity established between art and nature, perhaps the most typical feature of the Grand Style.

Within doors the taste for *lachinage* was more lavishly indulged. A spacious vestibule occupied the centre of the building, leading on either side into two little suites, each composed of a bedroom, cabinet and garderobe, and opening on to the gardens and forecourt respectively. Some of the rooms, notably the Chambre de Diane, were panelled with tiles of Delft porcelain, and must have been deliciously cool in summer. One of these panels has been identified by M. Robert Danis in the Salle des Bains de Marie-Antoinette at Rambouillet, and three panels remarkably similar to this are to be seen today in the kitchen at Amalienburg, a pavilion which occupies in the grounds of Nymphenburg a position which in some ways corresponds with that of the first Trianon at Versailles.

The cabinets were hung with Chinese brocade, and each opened into a little aviary, whose inmates provided music for the room, just as the garden provided the perfume. The Chambre des Amours was fitted with an 'extraordinary' bed, and a suite of furniture in blue and white taffeta.

The large side pavilions served for the accommodation of the Princes of the Blood and kitchens, and afforded a permanent lodging to the concierge of the Château. It was through the gate on his side of the Cour d'Honneur that the Trianon was generally approached, the main entrance, flanked by a tiny chapel and Salle des Gardes, being reserved for State visits. Such an occasion was the Embassy from the Court of Siam in 1684.

Whatever their real opinions on this so-called imitation of the

Chinese style, the ambassadors expressed themselves, diplomati-
cally enough, enchanted with the spot, and seemed particularly
impressed with the Cabinet des Parfums. 'C'est en cet endroit',
wrote the Sieur des Combes, 'où les Zephyrs se parfument, pour
ensuite couler le long des allées du jardin de Versailles et réjouir
par ses suaves odeurs ceux qui s'y promènent.' On one occasion,
related by Saint-Simon, Louis and his followers found the scent
of the flowers so intense and oppressive that they were obliged to
quit the gardens.

Despite its many attractions there were two circumstances
which contributed to the early destruction of this charming
pavilion. One was its small size. When Madame de Montespan
fell from favour, and the Trianon was no longer required for
Louis' amours, the smallness of its accommodation rendered it
unsuitable for further use; like most of Louis' houses, it had to
grow with him. The other drawback was in the nature of its
construction. The porcelain tiles were not meant for outdoor
use, and each year the frost brought a fresh batch of them
clattering from the roof. It was a constant and troublesome
expense to keep the place up.

2. *The Chateau de Clagny*

To anyone approaching Versailles from St. Cloud after the
year 1680 a beautiful prospect was offered from the avenue, just
at the point where, today, it crosses the railway. At the end of a
broad alley an imposing-looking residence presented its full face
to the road; as the traveller crossed the alley he got a sudden
vista of stone walls rising majestically from neat gravel paths, of
lofty Mansart roofs broken by a series of taller pavilions, of
wide-flung wings and formal gardens displayed in ordered
symmetry around the central block, which reared its gilded
dome above the whole mass of the building. Then the Château
disappeared behind the trees and plantations of the park. A little
later, at about the point where the Palace of Versailles first comes
into sight, a drive struck off to the right and, skirting part of an

extensive garden, brought the visitor before an iron grille; this was the entrance to the Château de Clagny.

It was in 1674 that Louis had determined on the building of this house for the accommodation of his natural children, that is to say, for Madame de Montespan and her offspring.

Four years previously, during the building of the Trianon de Porcelaine, Le Vau, the royal architect, had died, leaving his assistant, Dorbay, to carry on with the work. It was not Dorbay, however, who was chosen to be the architect of Clagny. Through the influence of Le Nôtre the commission was given to Jules Hardouin Mansart, a young man who had never yet had occasion to show the measure of his genius. Such an opening must have been the fondest dream of all young artists of his age, the 'tide in his affairs which, taken at the flood, leads on to fortune'. Before the century was out he was to enjoy a position of confidence of the King which gave him almost unlimited scope for his creative powers, and made him the envy of Dukes and Peers.

Now, at the age of twenty-eight, he put all the care and skill he could command into the designing of Clagny. Keeping within the bounds prescribed by the classic tradition, he showed an appreciation of the possibilities of the style which earned for Clagny the description of 'perhaps the most regularly beautiful house in France'.

Like the old Versailles, the building was to form three sides of a quadrangle, open towards the east. Each of the blocks thus formed was punctuated by three slightly projecting pavilions, a way of breaking a façade described by Evelyn as 'the French pavilion way'. The central block contained the State Apartments, each room opening into the next without other means of communication, for there was no corridor. An impressive feature would have been the vista through the suite, the natural result of the alignment of doors which was one of the great successes of the seventeenth-century layout.

The block which lay on the north side of the Cour d'Honneur was devoted to living-rooms, which overlooked the gardens, and a suite of smaller cabinets overlooking the courtyard which also provided an alternative means of access to the larger rooms. The block which lay on the south side contained the Grande Galerie, lit by thirteen windows on the garden front, and backed by a similar range of cabinets overlooking the court. With its lofty barrel-vault ceiling, divided into compartments and enriched with painted panels and gilded coffers, the Grande Galerie presented the most sumptuous appearance. It would have been a lovely room for receptions, which usually started at six o'clock when the evening sun fell obliquely on to the south windows, picking out the crimson fold of a curtain or the gilt scroll of an armchair and projecting a bold pattern of light and shade across the carpet. From the tall, round-arched windows in the centre one could pass into the gardens, while the three doors at the western extremity gave direct access to the Orangerie.

This, instead of being detached, as was the custom, formed part of the main building, running southwards from the end of one wing, while it was answered upon the other side by a similar range of buildings containing more rooms and offices. The two low wings thus formed, exactly half the length of the main façade, flanked the entrance to the Cour d'Honneur. Seen from the garden side, they formed the architectural background against which the west front, with its imposing frontispiece and dome, stood out superbly.

This was the plan later adopted on a gigantic scale at Versailles. It is interesting to notice that Mansart wanted to screen off the Cour de Marbre with a building centring on a dome very similar to that at Clagny. There was a certain lack of originality about his Grand Design for Versailles. It seems that architecture was reduced to a mere judicious juggling with a small repertory of accepted forms. At Clagny it was generally admitted that a happier arrangement of these forms could not have been hit upon. The design was successful, and was to gain for Mansart the position of First Architect to the King and the job of making the final enlargements to Versailles.

In 1674 the work was started at Clagny. The gardens received first attention, and soon formed a favourite promenade for courtiers. There were twelve hundred men engaged on the construction, Madame de Sévigné wrote, and the building was rising before their eyes. By the following year the gardens were beginning to take shape, and she was able to describe their more remarkable features. Le Nôtre had preserved a shady coppice whose tall shafts were revealed in all their natural beauty, and by way of contrast he had laid out an artificial wood of orange trees, whose massive tubs were concealed behind a palisade of dianthus and tuberoses. To Madame de Sévigné it was 'the most beautiful, the most astonishing, the most enchanting novelty that could possibly be imagined'. She was always superlative in her enthusiasm.

At the end of the gardens lay the Etang de Clagny, spreading out like a vast wedge of water towards the Park of Versailles. It is just possible that in winter, when the leaves had fallen, Madame de Montespan could see on the horizon the little Trianon de Porcelaine shining through the trees and reminding her of her greatest triumphs.

Now she was enjoying their fruits. She had only to ask in order to receive. When Louis was absent on his campaigns he wrote repeatedly to Colbert instructing him to grant the Marchioness her every wish. 'Continuez à faire ce que Madame de Montespan voudra.' This often had special reference to the building of Clagny. 'Madame de Montespan is very keen that the garden should be ready to be planted this autumn,' he wrote from his camp in Franche Comté; 'do everything necessary that she may have this satisfaction.' He followed each stage in the construction of Clagny with his usual attention, while his mistress presided in person, directing operations, visiting the workmen and giving audiences in the unfinished building. So frequently was she on the site that Madame de Sévigné compared her with Dido at the walls of Carthage.

She was not, however, destined long to enjoy this splendid mansion, for a year after its completion she was ousted from the King's affections by Madame Scarron, later Marquise de Maintenon. She thereupon retired to a life of ascetic piety. She devoted

most of her time to the making of clothes for the poor, to whom
also she devoted the greater part of her revenues. In 1707 she died
rather suddenly, having called her servants into her presence and
made a public confession 'with a humility so decent, so profound
and so penitent that nothing could be more edifying'. The fear of
death, which had dogged her later years, left her completely now
that the hour had come, and having received the last Sacrament,
she quietly yielded up her spirit.

Louis was not in the least moved by the death of his discarded
favourite, explaining to the Duchesse de Bourgogne that she had
been as good as dead for him ever since he dismissed her.

Clagny also declined steadily in the Royal favour.

It served as a residence for the Duc du Maine and later the
Prince de Dombes; but remaining a crown property, it became
increasingly redundant to Louis XV, who grudged it the considerable sums necessary for its upkeep. By 1775 it was in so bad
a condition that only a costly reconstruction could have saved it.
It was therefore decided to demolish the old Château. A painting
by Rigaud shows it in the last stages of dismantling; the noble
west frontispiece stripped of all its finery, the windows appearing
as gaping voids and the proud columns prostrate in the dust. In
the foreground, on a heap of masonry, a few peasants seem to
survey the passing of this great house which had made the name
of one of their country's greatest architects and had been found
worthy to serve as a model for the completion of Versailles.

THE COMPLETION OF VERSAILLES

It was not only as a plan that Clagny resembled Versailles; it
was not only in form that it represented the typical French
château of the period. It is symbolic in its complete detachment.
It was a building designed in a studio and superimposed upon
a landscape. It had scant means of contributing to its own upkeep, and became a perpetual expense to its owner; ultimately
this was to be the cause of its destruction.

It is in this respect that the French château differs mainly from the English country house. The broad acres of monastic land distributed by Henry VIII to the new Tudor aristocracy produced a large proportion of the great houses of England out of their own resources. If there was not a ready-made quarry to hand in the form of the actual fabric of an abbey, stone was often available on the land, or brick could be made on the estate. Lesser houses, such as Losely and Gorhambury, were put up for something between two and three thousand pounds—less than the cost of a single entertainment of Queen Elizabeth by Cecil. With timber felled in his own woods, workmen supplied from his own rent roll, and often an older house to serve as the nucleus to his construction, the English landlord could produce a house which, if sometimes inferior to its French equivalent from a merely aesthetic point of view, is often more interesting as a genuine product of its time and its locality, and it could be maintained at a moderate expense. It became the natural focus for the activities of the neighbourhood, and the settled residence of its lord, who thus maintained a close contact with his tenantry. It would be difficult to picture a French nobleman standing up in church, like Lord George Sackville of Drayton, to comment on the singing of the choir: 'Out of tune, Tom Baker!'

The French noble was expected to keep up an extravagant equipage at Versailles, and only too often regarded his seigneurial lands simply as a source of revenue. In this he was frequently disappointed; money was still short, even if his real wealth might happen to be considerable. The letters of Madame de Sévigné give evidence of this state of affairs. Although technically a very wealthy woman, she could rarely lay her hands on any large sum of money; 'c'est une chose étrange que la quantité d'argent qu'on me doit'. In the end she became resigned; 'it is no use counting on more than a quarter of one's revenue'. At last the whole truth dawned on her, and she summed up with her usual straightforwardness: 'When one does not live on one's estates and eat their produce, I do not really know how one can manage.'

But to live on one's estates was regarded as a form of exile, and the nobleman who did so was cut off from any hope of improving his position. Surprisingly few of the nobility at that time could have been called rich, and all were obliged by etiquette and by the competition of wealthy financiers to keep up appearances well beyond their means. The Court offered them their only chance of a livelihood—a position in the Household, if they were of sufficiently illustrious family, a command in the Army or a benefice in the Church; all these were at the disposition of the King. Louis liked to keep his nobility dependent on him for favours, and it soon became an absolute necessity for anyone who hoped for any place or preferment to be constantly seen at Court; and Louis kept a sharp eye out for absentees. 'He looked to right and to left at the *lever*, at the *coucher*, at his meals, when passing through the apartments and in the gardens of Versailles,' noted Saint-Simon. It went ill with the nobleman whose absence was noticed, a certain disgrace for those who never came at all. Should such a man seek a favour from the King, his application would be cut short with a curt 'c'est un homme que je ne vois jamais'—and there was an end of the matter.

Those who were unsuccessful resorted to gambling, and enormous sums were won and lost by the throw of a dice or the fall of a card. To seek these various forms of enrichment, considered to be the only ones that did not bring dishonour upon the family, an ever increasing throng began to crowd the galleries and gardens of the royal palaces.

To house these the accommodation at St. Germain, which remained the official residence of the Court, was quite inadequate. Saint-Simon, who never approved of the move to Versailles, describes the housing conditions of the courtiers. Nearly everyone had the discommodity of being in the town, while the few who had rooms in the Palace found themselves lodged 'étrangement à l'étroit'. Of the two châteaux at St. Germain, the newer, built by Henri IV, was already in hopeless disrepair, and had been abandoned in favour of the more massive solidity of the older building. The only advantage was that of the site, commanding from its terraces a magnificent prospect over the River Seine to Paris, and adjoining one of the many royal forests.

The year 1678 marked, with the annexation of Franche Comté, the flood tide of Louis' military glory; it was no longer endurable that his magnificence should be inadequately housed. Versailles, however, was still in the unsatisfactory condition in which Le Vau had left it. It was neither one thing nor the other: it was too large for a *maison de plaisance* where the King and his privileged guests could spend a few days of carefree entertainment: it was too small to provide permanent accommodation for the Court and the Government. Nor was it satisfying architecturally. Although the west front of Le Vau's Enveloppe was very fine, the fusion between his stately classical façades and the more homely architecture of the Cour de Marbre was awkward and ungainly.

The solution to these defects was found in a further enlargement. By providing accommodation for his whole Court and offices for all his Ministers, Louis had to make the Palace so extensive that the architecture of the garden fronts can never be seen at the same time as that of the courtyards.

The original plan for a long gallery, demanded but for some reason abandoned for the Château Neuf, was taken up again, and it was to be a gallery the like of which the world had never seen, reflecting in its decoration the unique greatness of Louis' reign. At the same time new wings were to be added, and the entrance courts made to present a more harmonious appearance. Mansart, who had so distinguished himself in the creation of Clagny, and in particular of its gallery, was chosen to carry out the new enlargements.

The filling in of Le Vau's terrace with the new gallery necessitated certain re-formations of the west, and ultimately of the north and south fronts. After various projects had been considered and rejected, Mansart decided upon the elevation of the first-storey windows, replacing the bas-reliefs with round arches, and raising the apparent base of all the windows by means of a balustrade. Their increased height added greatly to the dignity of the façade, but the powerful relief of Le Vau's composition was perforce sacrificed.

Mansart, however, was only the architect of the gallery in the strictest sense of the word; from the point of view of decoration it was the work of the painter Le Brun. A large team of sculptors, plasterers and metal workers, among whom figured the august names of Tubi and Coysevox, besides painters innumerable, co-operated under Le Brun's direction, and worked so exactly to schedule that the gallery was opened on the very day for which it had been promised. The 15th of November 1684 was the date fixed for the inauguration of the gallery. Two days before, while the Court was still at Fontainebleau, Louvois had written to Louis that the parquet was finished and only one bay of mirrors remained to be set up. 'Je serai très aise,' noted Louis in the margin of the despatch, 'de trouver la Galerie achevée.'

Even today, standing in this noble apartment, unfurnished and desolate, it is possible to imagine the astonishment and admiration with which it was seen for the first time in all its freshness and brilliance.

Against the stately background of the marble pilasters the tall windows, each reflected in its corresponding mirror, and the ceiling with its riotous profusion of allegorical figures, imagine tall white and gold brocade curtains, two enormous Savonnerie carpets, and the walls lined with tables, guéridons and flower-tubs made of solid silver, but of a workmanship so exquisite that the value of the metal formed but a tenth part of their worth. Seventeen great crystal chandeliers and countless smaller candelabra lent an indescribable lustre to the scene. Seldom has *folie de grandeur* been carried to such extremes. 'This sort of royal beauty,' exclaimed Madame de Sévigné, 'is unique in the world.' It would have been more accurate to have said 'the western world'; if Versailles has had any rival it is probably to be sought in the East.

There is some fine silver furniture in the Van Dyck Room at Windsor Castle today, of English workmanship, and dating from Charles II and William III, which will give the visitor some idea of the effect which it would have produced on a large scale. Fanny Burney, writing of the King's bedroom at Knole, was much struck with the furniture there of 'solid massive silver curiously embossed. Nothing could be more impressive'.

At Versailles, however, this state of magnificence was extremely short-lived. In 1689 Louis gave the order for a considerable part of the silver to be melted down to help pay for the war. In the inventories of the Mobilier de la Couronne some twelve hundred items are crossed off with the marginal comment 'déchargé, ayant été porté à la Monnoie'; just over two and a half million livres was realized by this expedient. All the 'filigrane work', which may have dated back to the first Versailles, was destroyed at this time. Another feature of the Galerie, which can only be pictured from the prints of the time, was the dais and throne which were set up at the extreme end for certain ceremonial receptions. On these occasions the Court, in their most elaborate bejewelled costumes, lined the Galerie, the ladies standing in tiers in the window recesses. The members of the Royal Family were grouped on the dais behind the silver balustrade, and the King, in periwig and *cordon bleu*, awaited his visitor on the ample silver throne. It must have been an impressive testimony to an ambassador's bearing to be able to run such a gauntlet of magnificence.

The building of the Galerie was part of a comprehensive plan to provide accommodation for the whole Court and offices for the Government. On the entrance front the entire Palace was provided with a Mansart roof, thus softening the clash of styles which had somewhat marred the appearance of the Château Neuf, and the four isolated pavilions which composed the offices were joined into two long buildings flanking the outer court. These were destined for the reception of the Government.

Beyond, on the Place d'Armes, in the angles formed by the convergence of the three great avenues, were built the stables, the Grande Ecurie and Petite Ecurie, which contained the riding horses and the coach horses respectively. These beautiful buildings have a corresponding symmetry which helps to unite them to the Palace and perfect the whole. Within the concave sweeps of each façade stretches a network of great vaulted galleries and spacious courtyards which drew from the Elector of Hanover the confession that he was not so well housed as the horses of the King of France.

Besides horses, the Grande Ecurie housed the royal pages. To become a page of the Bedchamber one had to show proof of nobility dating back for two hundred years and have an allowance of six hundred livres. In return one received a good, but Spartan education comparable to that offered by Eton during the eighteenth century.

On the garden fronts Mansart continued the scheme of architectural decoration prescribed by Le Vau, while substituting throughout his own round arches for the bas-reliefs of his predecessor. To the south, the Aile des Princes extended its vast length as far as the extremity of the Orangerie, while to the north another wing made an answerable projection towards the reservoirs. To break the monotony of this seemingly endless façade the fronts were divided up by lightly advancing colonnades which carried their statues level with the attic storey. The skyline was an impressive alternation of urns and trophies.

Louis left his own instructions as to how one ought to look at Versailles. The visitor was to enter by the Vestibule from the Court de Marbre, pass through and down the steps on to the parterre. Without turning his head to regard the building through which he had just passed, he was to advance to the terrace overlooking Latona and pause to consider the disposition of the gardens before facing about to look at the Château. In this way can best be appreciated the value which the two long wings give to the central block, enabling it to stand out superbly against them.

The three parterres surrounding the Château, the 'arid zone' of which Saint-Simon complained, are so planned that the whole of the building may be seen with nothing to break the lines. There is something essentially secular about the long horizontal rows of windows which lead the eye rapidly over the whole surface; for it is noticeable that, whereas the creators of the cathedrals sought to obtain the greatest possible impression of vertical movement, the architects of the Renaissance seemed at pains to cover as large an area of ground as they could, as if to emphasize the extensive earthly properties of their patrons. This confinement to the horizontal plane makes it difficult for an architect to achieve a completely satisfying result. Mansart has probably been more successful than most. Although, inevitably, his façades may be criticized on the grounds of monotony, there is no vulgarity, no over-ornamentation. Versailles has an ordered majesty, a dignity and simplicity which make it the perfect setting for the pageantry of a Court.

The appearance in 1681 of the names of sculptors in the book of accounts denoted, as always, the approaching completion of the Aile des Princes, destined for the accommodation of the Duc d'Orléans and others of the Royal Blood. By the following year the arrangements were so far advanced as to permit the Court to move in, though it was not until 1684 that the Galerie was completed, and the Aile du Nord not until two years after that.

That work progressed smoothly according to schedule pre-supposes an efficient administration in the background; the efficient administrator was Colbert. Already loaded with half the government of France, he tried to delegate some of his super-vision to his son, aged twenty, the Marquis d'Ormoy. The letters which passed between them form an interesting record of the sort of administration required by Louis of his servants. Colbert had acquired for his son his own post of Surintendant des Bâtiments, apparently on probation, but the task was too heavy for the young man, who had not been showing the necessary diligence. 'If you want to do well,' wrote the despairing father to the unfortunate youth, 'you will have to get up every morning between five and six, go straight and visit all the workshops, see that the masters of the works are there, count the number of workers and check that they are right; put aside two hours for this visit, listen to all the workers, find out what they need, see that they get it straight away; then go to your office and do two or three hours' work revising all the memoirs of what is to be done, give the orders for everything, inspect, verify, arrange the prices. After lunch you must make a second visit, see the works and again count the workmen.' If things did not make a very immediate improvement, he added ominously, the boy's allowance would be reduced from eleven thousand to one thousand, his carriage and horses taken away, his valets dismissed 'et tu t'appercevras de la différence qu'il y a entre un homme qui fait son devoir et celui qui ne le fait point'.

It is not surprising that the young man did not retain his post after his father's death, in the following year, but found his own *métier* in the Army and died, as his brothers died, in the face of the enemy.

Louis ended by showing a most unworthy ingratitude to Colbert, in particular with regard to his works at Versailles. Perrault recounts how he reproached his faithful minister with the expenses incurred by these undertakings—one cannot help recalling Colbert's own prediction to this effect in 1668—and contrasted somewhat meanly the economical proceedings whereby Louvois was erecting his fortifications. As a result, Colbert took to the false economy of employing second-rate workmen. 'There were some engaged on panelling,' remarked Perrault, 'who did such poor work at Versailles that, when the rooms for which they had made the shutters were closed, you could see almost as clearly as when they were open.' This, not unnaturally, brought further complaints from Louis. In despair at the ingratitude of his King, Colbert succumbed to a fever, and not having even enough will to live to take nourishment, died a disappointed and disillusioned man. It would not have been much comfort to him to know that he would be recognized by posterity as having, by his painstaking administration, contributed as much to the creation of Versailles as Louis or any of his artists; for the dream he cherished was to see the Monarchy seated in Paris.

THE GRAND APPARTEMENT

The disposition of rooms in the completed Palace was simple and logical. The King's suite occupied the oldest part, being ranged round the south and west sides of the Cour de Marbre; in extension with this suite ran the Cabinets du Roi, a series of smaller rooms designed for the exhibition of Louis' art treasures and the crown jewels, extending along the north side of the Cour de Marbre and Cour Royale. Of the new outer shell, the suite on the south side remained the Appartement de la Reine, and was answered by the Grand Appartement, whose windows overlooked the Parterre du Nord. These three suites were linked together by the Grande Galerie. All these were, of course, on the first floor, and were generally reached by means of the Escalier de Marbre, which gave access to the King's and Queen's apartments; but on state occasions the magnificent Escalier des Ambassadeurs was used, which led to the King's rooms or to the Grand Appartement.

Three times a week, on what was called a 'jour d'Appartement', there was a big reception in these rooms when the whole of the Court assembled for four hours of gaming, dancing, music and refreshment. The first two rooms, the appropriately-named Salle d'Abondance and the Salle de Vénus, were set aside for the refreshments, the tables being constantly replenished during the course of the evening. Service was prompt, and every taste was catered for. There were suppers for those who wished to eat seriously, chocolate and sweetmeats for those of less hearty appetite; there were liqueurs for those who were not really thirsty, 'on donne de très excellent vin à ceux qui le souhaitent'. The company was free to wander at will from one room to another throughout the evening.

A fascinating account of a Jour d'Appartement is given by the Abbé Bourdelot, who was attached to the household of the Duc d'Enghien in the capacity of a doctor, and who came to Versailles for the carnival of 1683. The Duc d'Orléans had secured his invitation, and he waited in the crowded vestibule to be summoned into the royal presence. After a minute or two Joyeux entered and called him by name, the Abbé dived after him towards the Cabinets du Roi, 'the door closed, and I found myself in the middle of the Royal Household; the Queen was there, with

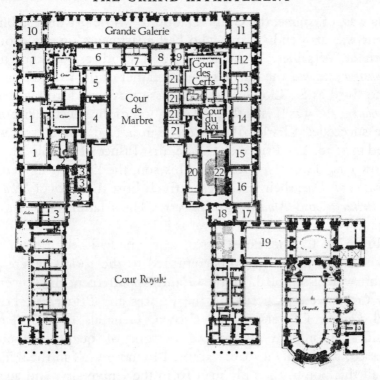

THE MAIN BLOCK, FIRST FLOOR, AS IT WAS LEFT BY LOUIS XIV
1 The Queen's Apartment; 2 Escalier de Marbre; 3 Madame de
Maintenon's Apartment; 4 Salle des Gardes du Roi; 5 Salle du Grand
Couvert du Roi; 6 Salon de l'Oeil de Boeuf; 7 Chambre du Roi;
8 Cabinet du Conseil; 9 Cabinet des Perruques; 10 Salon de la Paix;
11 Salon de la Guerre; 12 Chambre du Trône, or d'Apollon;
13 Chambre du Lit, or de Mercure; 14 Salle du Bal, or de Mars;
15 Chambre du Billard, or de Diane; 16 Salle de Vénus; 17 Salle de
l'Abondance; 18 Cabinet des Raretés; 19 Salon d'Hercule; 20 Petite
Galerie; 21 Petit Appartement du Roi; 22 Escalier des Ambassadeurs

Madame la Dauphine, Madame, and Madame la Duchesse, who
had at her side Mlle de Bourbon and Madame la Princesse de
Conti'.

It will perhaps be helpful at this juncture to notice the style
which certain members of the Royal Family were almost invariably given, not only at the Court of France, but at most of the
little European Courts which tried to model themselves on
Versailles. The eldest son of the King was known as *Monseigneur*;

63

this was, of course, the Grand Dauphin, whose private establishment was at Meudon, and who had apartments on the ground floor at Versailles. The King's eldest brother was known as *Monsieur*; he was the Duc d'Orléans, father of the future Regent, who lived at St. Cloud. The Duchesse was therefore known as *Madame*; she was 'Liselotte', the daughter of the Elector Palatine; she succeeded Charles II's sister, Henriette d'Angleterre, who died in 1670. The Prince de Condé, first Prince of the Blood, was known as *Monsieur le Prince*, and his son, the Duc d'Enghien, as *Monsieur le Duc*; their wives respectively bore the titles of *Madame la Princesse* and *Madame la Duchesse*. Their family seat was at Chantilly.

From the Cabinet des Raretés, where he had been thus introduced to Royalty, the Abbé returned to the rooms where the Court were assembled. 'In the Grand Appartement the flower of the Court were gathered, all the Princes and Princesses, Lords and Ladies, Officers of the Crown, Generals of the Army, besides an infinite number of persons of quality, superbly dressed, left hardly a space vacant. I found myself in the middle of all this pomp, the only man from the University, and accustomed to a life of retirement. What surprised me most was the room full of tables covered with cards and dice.' This room, the Salon de Mars, was situated in the centre of the suite; six portraits by Titian adorned the walls, which were hung with crimson velvet braided with gold.

It was in winter that Bourdelot made his visit, and his account affords interesting comparison with that of Nicodemus Tessin, a Swedish architect who visited Versailles in the summer of 1687. His description of the same room is very different, for in every important apartment there were two sets of hangings, one for winter, usually in velvet or damask of a plain, sombre colour to provide a rich background to the pictures by candlelight, and one for summer, of a lighter, more colourful invention. In the Salon de Mars the *Meuble d'Été* was of gold and silver brocade. There were seventeen pieces of silver furniture 'd'une pesanteur et grandeur prodigieuse(s)', two chandeliers of silver and twelve of crystal, and at either end of the room two marquetry cabinets 'd'une délicatesse merveilleuse' each bearing a number of silver statues. Tessin saw the room used as a ballroom, with the musicians accommodated in recesses to either side of the fireplace.

Normally, however, the Salon de Mars was used for gaming, on which occasions it was provided with a large table for *Trou Madame* and ten card tables, triangular or polygonal, with green velvet covers fringed with gold and silver lace, and bearing silver flambeaux at each corner. Only games of chance were played, it being considered bad form to possess any skill at cards. Among the tables the King moved easily and without restraint, the players being allowed to remain seated when he came and joined them. In the background stood a few well-trained footmen in neat livery coats and blue breeches, ready with clean packs of cards, dice boxes, or anything else that might be required; they even relieved the players of the necessity of scoring.

'The throng was dense,' noted Bourdelot, 'but without any noise and confusion,' and in this he was confirmed by the *Mercure Galant*. Madame, however, writing at a later date, painted a very different picture of the gaming tables at Versailles: 'Ils font autant de bruit que les chiens de chasse qui forcent une bête . . . l'un pleure, l'autre frappe sur la table . . . un troisième blasphème.' There is no doubt that gambling became one of the vices of the Court, but in the early days it seems to have been indulged in with a certain amount of decorum. It was the presence of the King which laid the greatest restraint upon the courtiers; later, when he took to absenting himself more often, there was a noticeable falling away in the standards.

It was traditional for a State Apartment to contain a bedroom, and the next room in the suite, the Salle de Mercure, although never slept in, was magnificently equipped as such. This also had a *Meuble Brodé* of flame-coloured hangings heavily stitched with gold and silver thread and incorporating needlework pictures of Silence, Night and Sleep. The State Bed, whose domed canopy was suspended from the ceiling, was hung with curtains of

Spanish needlework forming an openwork pattern 'faisant prendre pour ciselure ce qui est pure broderie', and trimmed with fringes 'de la dernière finesse'. It stood behind a silver balustrade, and the room was furnished to match. In the Salle de Mercure tables were usually set for the Royal Family, but it seems that Bourdelot saw it used as a billiard room, for after commenting on the excellence of Louis' play, he continues: 'From there I passed into a room [the Salon d'Apollon] which enchants with every object on which the eye falls. Here is raised the throne of the King; the hangings of crimson velvet with pilasters of gold thread, stitched and double stitched, impose respect. These pilasters are raised in relief; their bases and capitals seem to be the work rather of goldsmiths; nothing could be more august or majestic.'

It seems, however, that the *Meuble d'Eté* was considerably more majestic, and of a sumptuosity which contemporaries were at a loss to describe. It was made under the direction of Madame de Montespan at the Filles Saint Joseph, a charitable institution which she patronized increasingly as she declined in the royal favour. The set consisted of embroidered panels, the Histoire de la Paix, between eighteen pilasters, likewise embroidered. It reached from ceiling to floor, comprehending cornice and wainscot and was achieved in a high relief, which attained in some places a depth of five inches, and the flesh of the figures was represented in solid silver. This sort of embroidery was commonly referred to as 'à la façon de Perse'—perhaps another pointer to the oriental flavour of the magnificence of Versailles. There was nothing unusual about fine ladies doing the embroidery for furnishings at that time in France nor in England. Mérigot, in his *Promenade des Jardins de Chantilly*, mentions hangings in the Cabinet des Vues as having been embroidered by a Princesse de Condé, and Celia Fiennes noted of the Countess of Exeter's room at Burghley that 'the hangings are all embroydery of her mother's work very fine'. These were also enriched with silver and gold.

It is not known how much the hangings cost, but when in 1743 the entire *Meuble Brodé* of the Palace was abolished, the melting down of the gold and silver thread realized nearly fifty-two thousand livres. It appears that those of the Salle du Trône or Salon d'Apollon were the most magnificent. 'I inspected them minutely,' recounts Bourdelot, 'and could not withdraw my gaze, though I had in front of me five original canvasses from Italy of the most perfect beauty, and by the greatest masters. Ought one not to go down on one's knees before that Paul Veronese of Our Lord at Cana?'

Bourdelot had a real taste for painting—it reminds one of Horace Walpole's raptures over his father's collection at Houghton—and he kept leaving the ballroom, the same Salon d'Apollon in which the throne stood, to wander back through the apartment and gaze anew at the pictures. He does, however, leave an account of the dancing.

'There were many [ladies] there, both young and beautiful, and scintillating with jewelry; their grace was incomparable. The Princesse de Conti *la Belle* carried off the prize for dancing; all eyes were fixed upon the young Princess. Mlle de Laval was not far from her; towards the end they linked arms; they seemed joined together, as if the two bodies had but a single mind, so perfectly were their steps regulated and timed. But the greatest figure, in which was the centre of all charm, was that of the King. He did not sit on his throne; there were four stools on the edge of the dais; I was surprised to see him sitting there, turning to this side and to that to give an order for the music or for the dance . . . often falling into conversation with the Dauphine. I even saw her dance, and mighty well; she was one of the best dancers in the assembly.'

On these Jours d'Appartement there was not a ball in the ordinary sense of the word, but rather a ballet given by the ladies of the Court. 'Ce ne sont que les dames qui dansent avec la Dauphine,' Mlle de Scudéry explained, 'et cela, joint à son port noble et modeste, lui donne un air de Diane au milieu des nymphes, sans aucun mélange d'hommes. . . . On ne peut rien voir de plus agréable.' The stately movement imposed by music

67

was an important feature of the Court. A special symphony was composed by Lalande for performance during the King's supper, which would have made its ritual almost into a ballet.

Until 1689, when the silver furniture was sacrificed to Louis' military ambition, the Grand Appartement was undoubtedly the most fantastic and sumptuous decorative ensemble in the whole of Europe. It requires an effort to imagine it, particularly when one is actually in the rooms today. Stripped of all their finery they may well appear drab and heavy, and in spite of the great height of the windows they manage to seem dull and ill lit. It was not so with the becoming lustre of a thousand candles. 'Figurez-vous,' exclaimed Bourdelot in his ecstasy, 'quel est l'éclat de cent mille bougies dans cette grande suite d'appartements!' It is the best advice that could be given to a visitor to Versailles today.

The great quantity of candles may be the answer to another complaint often levelled today against the spacious rooms of the *Grand Siècle*, that they were, or rather are, impossible to heat. The candles and crowds together probably made other forms of heating redundant, but in other parts of the Palace the cold was sometimes severe. It is recorded that water and wine froze on the King's dinner-table, and Louis XV was ultimately obliged to abandon his ancestral bedroom on account of the extreme cold.

To the décor of the rooms, and the flattering light of candles, must be added the perfume of flowers, which always abounded within doors, and a constant background of music. Louis had a nice sense of the appropriate, and he controlled every detail of the programme himself. 'I admired the tunes which His Majesty ordered to be sung', concluded Bourdelot; 'they were well selected, moving, and of a neat composition.'

It is easy to imagine the feelings of this quiet, academic man, accustomed, it is true, to the more rough-hewn grandeur of Chantilly, as he drove away from the brilliant Court of which he had been the privileged spectator. The vividness of the impression which it made on him is clear from the liveliness of the account he wrote. In strong relief against the marble and crimson velvet, the silver filigree and gold embroidery, and in brilliant contrast to the more than ordinary splendour of the guests, stands out his picture of the King, 'faisant les honneurs de chez lui en galant homme', magnificently informal against the elaborate setting which he had created for his own person. 'Ce qui plaît souverainement,' concluded Madame de Sévigné in her account of the same year, 'c'est de vivre quatre heures entières avec le souverain, être dans ses plaisirs et lui dans les nôtres.'

FURTHER OFFSHOOTS

1. *Marly*

In June 1679, when the new enlargements to Versailles were in full swing, and the courtyards were filled with the vast cranes and winches used for hoisting blocks of masonry and the Place d'Armes littered with the endless paraphernalia of contractors, a new and important enterprise made its first appearance in the account books. The ground was being prepared for the construction of another royal château between Versailles and St. Germain, and a model had been made by Le Hongre for the building of Marly.

Louis was forty-one that year; he had reached the prime of life and the zenith of his military glory; he had already eighteen years of building experience, and he knew his artists and their measure. It is not surprising that at Marly, where he started with an unencumbered site of his own choosing, he should have produced his masterpiece—'la traduction complète et parfaite de la pensée louis-quatorzième'.

It is important to understand what Louis had in mind when he started. He is often represented as having begun with the intention of building a mere hermitage. 'The King, tired of magnificence and publicity,' wrote Saint-Simon, 'persuaded himself that he wanted something small and sequestered.' But this is unconvincing, because the Trianon de Porcelaine already provided these very requirements. The history of Versailles suggests a more probable motive for this new undertaking. The old Versailles, the beautiful little *maison de chasse* of Patel's painting, had been used as a lodge whither the King could retire from St. Germain with a number of favoured friends and pass a few days of arcadian intimacy; it had been the scene of the most brilliant entertainments, to which invitation had been much sought after. And now the final enlargements were being put in hand which were to make it the permanent home of the Court and seat of Government; Louis needed a new setting for his privileged house parties. In the fullness of time the highest hopes of assiduous courtiers were to be summed up in the customary application: 'Sire, Marly?'

Like most of the King's houses, Marly owed its selection as a site to the Bourbon's love of hunting; three years earlier Louis had bought the land to extend the royal forests, and it appears to have been while hunting that he first came upon the place, 'finding himself in a kind of marsh, where the situation seemed to lend itself to his plan, for he found there a fine vista towards the river, and the place was surrounded by several magnificent woods; its whole aspect determined the King then and there to choose this plot.'

It has been said that beauty is discovered, not created, and it bears witness to Louis' genius that he was able to appreciate the capabilities of the ground. The natural formation was that of a steep re-entrant in the shape of a long horseshoe opening towards the valley of the Seine, and as it were hollowed out of the hillside. The disposition of the buildings was made to conform with the natural lie of the land, the Château proper occupying the focal point of the whole layout, and twelve attendant pavilions, linked by a trellis pergola, lining either arm of the horseshoe. The low ground in the centre was cast into terraces and a series of monumental lakes were contrived, following the line of the main axis.

If this was a hermitage, it was a hermitage in the Grand Style. There were twelve apartments in the actual Château, and twenty-four in the pavilions from the very start, but like all Louis' buildings, Marly expanded. The addition of further accommodation and the leisurely elaboration of the gardens were to occupy

Louis for the rest of his life. In so far as there was an atmosphere of hermitage about the place, it came from the sense of isolation and remoteness. On three sides the high wooded hills enclosed the site; towards the opening of the valley the land fell away, revealing a magnificent prospect towards Maisons-Laffitte and the plain beyond. But although the gardens were thus left open towards the north, their privacy was secured by the skilful use of ground levels. To obtain sufficient space for the Pièce des Nappes, the last of the ornamental waters, the lower gardens had been considerably banked up, and ended abruptly in a high terrace overlooking the Abreuvoir. From the road beyond it was impossible to see into the grounds; it was only to those privileged to enter the precincts that the whole glorious layout of Marly was revealed.

Turning in at the gates, the carriages crossed a circular court flanked by the quadrant arcades behind which lay the stables, and began cautiously the steep descent of the Allée Royale. From this moment the Château was plainly visible, framed between two neat outbuildings and nestling comfortably amid the luxuriant foliage of its surroundings. The impression created was one of extreme richness. The balustrade, with its figures and vases, was brilliantly gilded, so were the frames of the windows; the bas-reliefs which decorated the pediment and the panels above the windows were picked out in gold against a royal-blue; the tall pilasters were of marble, *rouge de Languedoc*, and the whole was underlined with a base of *vert antique*—or so it seemed at a distance; a closer inspection revealed that the entire architecture and decoration of the façades was painted in *trompe l'œil*.

This was true of all the buildings at Marly; the Chapel and Salle des Gardes, flanking the entrance, presented an open arcade towards the forecourt, above which the walls were painted with busts reminiscent of Le Vau's treatment of the Cour de Marbre at Versailles. At the end nearest the Château they each broke forward into a little projection supported on painted caryatides. Answering the Chapel and Salle des Gardes on the far side of the Château were two similar pavilions joined by a wall on which

71

Rousseau painted his celebrated Perspective, after which the building was named. The effect was that of an open peristyle, similar to that created three-dimensionally at Trianon; between its stately rows of columns appeared two long colonnaded wings and a distant prospect of classical landscape. The twelve pavilions reflected either the pilasters and bas-reliefs of the Château or the bust and medallion decoration of the Chapel.

The *Mercure Galant*, 1686, gave the credit for this decoration in fresco to Le Brun, stating that the work was done 'from his designs and under his direction'. But the Comptes des Bâtiments leave no doubt as to who played the major part in the execution. The payment of 74,476 livres to Jacques Rousseau, as opposed to that of 49,495 divided among twelve others, leaves little to the imagination. Rousseau had also distinguished himself in the painting of the Hôtel Lambert, the Orangerie at St. Cloud and the Salle de Vénus at Versailles. After the Revocation of the Edict of Nantes he came to England where he met the Duke of Montagu, for whom he worked, and died in London in 1693. The other painters at Marly seem to have been used merely for hack-work, as the expression 'grosse peinture' suggests. Besides the façades of the actual buildings, the painting was carried into the gardens, where many of the statues were painted in their natural colouring. This was especially true of the birds and creatures which adorned the fountains. The most important items were done by J.-B. Fontenay, 'floral painter', and Desportes, 'painter of animals'.

This external painting made Marly extremely colourful. It is one of the greatest losses of our architectural heritage that so many buildings which used to be polychromed are faded or whitewashed today. To their often garish colouring should be added the spectacular costumes of the people. The Duc de Croÿ, whose memoirs give one of the most vivid pictures of eighteenth-century France, refers constantly to the effect produced by the gorgeous apparel of the Court, and even Madame de Maintenon, usually lukewarm in her appreciation of anything at Marly, drew attention to the same point when she expressed a desire to see all

VERSAILLES IN COURSE OF CONSTRUCTION
A. VAN DER MEULEN

VERSAILLES BEFORE THE BUILDING OF THE NEW CHAPEL
FROM THE HEIGHTS OF SATORY

THE COMPLETED VERSAILLES FROM THE PLACE D'ARMES
PAINTING BY P. D. MARTIN

THE FORECOURTS AND STABLES FROM THE WINDOW OF THE KING'S BEDROOM
DETAIL OF PAINTING BY J.-B. MARTIN

AERIAL PHOTOGRAPH FROM THE WEST

SOUTH AND WEST FRONTS TODAY

LOUIS XIV ENTHRONED.   DETAIL OF PAINTING BY A. COYPEL

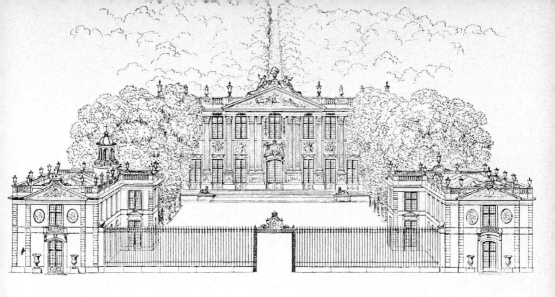

MARLY: THE ENTRANCE FRONT. RECONSTRUCTION BY IAN DUNLOP

MARLY: CHÂTEAU, GARDENS AND PAVILIONS FROM THE NORTH
BY J.-B. MARTIN

THE TRIANON DE MARBRE
BY J.-B. MARTIN

THE MACHINE DE MARLY
BY P. D. MARTIN

THE AQUEDUC DE MAINTENON,
WITH THE CHÂTEAU IN THE
BACKGROUND. LITHOGRAPH BY
I. DE BENARD AFTER GUDIN

THE INSTITUTION OF THE ORDER OF ST. LOUIS SHOWING THE CHAMBRE DU ROI AS IT WAS
AFTER 1701.   BY F. MAROT

THE SALON DE L'OEIL DE BOEUF

the Cardinals there, because their scarlet would answer perfectly with the greenery of the place.

For it was the woodland that was Marly's most distinctive feature. The great trees, shorn and disciplined in their lower members, overflowed in the full luxuriance of their upper branches, presenting the appearance of great plumes. Diderot, writing in 1759, particularly admired their effect, 'the contrast between refined art in the plantations and pergolas, and rude nature in the solid mass of luxuriant foliage in the great trees which dominate and form the background'. It was from this interplay of art and nature that the gardens drew their charm.

Little can be seen today of the gardens of Marly; three of the ornamental waters remain, and here and there a marble statue still cuts its neat outline against the sombre background of woodland. But the strangely beautiful trees are still there, and bear impressive witness to a magnificence long since vanished. Fortunately every detail of the layout is known from three large folios in the National Archives, depicting its final form in 1714. They suggest a cosiness which it is difficult to recapture when visiting the site today; the numerous little closed-in seats and arbours and shady pergolas helped to create that flattering sense of intimacy and exclusiveness which lent its savour to an invitation to Marly.

In the area immediately surrounding the Château everything was closely packed and heavily overhung by high banks and steep woodlands. In each corner was a little Cabinet de Verdure, thickly enclosed by lime trees which sheltered a little fishpond tiled in porcelain and adorned with figures of birds painted in their natural colours. To the south of the Château was the Petit Parterre, from which a noble flight of steps led to the level of the all-encircling pergola, and beyond, continuing the main axis of the gardens, the great cascade known as the Rivière brought its tumultuous waters down the steep avenue from the Reservoir du Trou d'Enfer. Under Louis XV the Rivière, falling into disrepair, was replaced by a grass ride, leaving only the pond called the Déversoir, which had formerly received its waters. This basin remains today, but the panels of red and green marble and the gilt lead figures have gone.

The Rivière raises the question of the authorship of the gardens of Marly. Certain writers have assumed that, since there is no reference to Le Nôtre in the accounts, he had no hand in the design. This, however, is almost inconceivable, and in fact a letter from Cronström, the Swedish ambassador, to Nicodemus Tessin in 1694 mentions the fact that it is 'no longer Le Nôtre who is in charge of the gardens of Marly nor of Trianon; it is M. Mansart'. At the time of the first plan of Marly, Le Nôtre was absent—the plan itself is sufficient evidence that he had nothing to do with it. He had been sent to Italy 'to seek diligently if he might find anything sufficiently fine to be worthy of being imitated in the Royal Houses'. It is reasonable to suppose that Marly profited from the result of his researches until his retirement in 1694. As the first project for the Rivière dates from 1685 it would have come easily within the sphere of his operations.

To the north the windows of the King's apartment overlooked the wider prospect of the lower gardens. On the same contour line as the Château, but set well back on either side, stood the twelve pavilions. One of these was reserved for the Appartement des Bains, and was tiled with Delft porcelain. The other eleven were for the guests, and could be reached by means of a sort of covered way under the trellis pergola. Every pavilion contained two apartments, one on each floor, connected by a tiny oval staircase. One large and one small room, each with a minute anteroom, panelled and furnished in crimson satin, made up the apartment, but it was provided with everything necessary for the comfort of the guest—nightshirt, brushes and combs; packing for a visit to Marly must have been a simple affair.

The pavilions commanded a succession of terraces, each representing a considerable drop in height, and the terraces overlooked the three great ornamental waters, that of the Four Fountains, the vast Miroir, and lastly, the Pièce des Nappes. A wrought-iron balustrade, flanked by Coysevox's celebrated Chevaux de Marly, marked the extremity of the grounds. From here, from a height of some fifteen feet, the visitors could over-look the Abreuvoir and watch, from a detached standpoint, the villagers watering their horses, or let their eyes wander down the valley towards distant St. Germain.

To east and west of the main axis, and behind the pavilions, the Bosquet de Louveciennes and the Bosquet de Marly provided a variety of walks for the guests. The Bosquet de Marly took the form of an elongated U from the *Mail* which was laid out there, enclosing in its rounded end the star-like formation of the Fontaine du Sénat. Many little elaborations, the Salle des Mar-ronniers, the Place des Enfants, Descente du Dôme and Cabinet Sombre, provided a great variety of little arbours conducive to conversation.

The Bosquet de Louveciennes was richer in waterworks. Up nearest the Château, behind the circular arena of the entrance court, was the Amphithéatre, a flight of grassy steps leading from the statue of Hercules to a round pond with a fountain in the middle; alongside of this was the Cascade Champêtre, a miniature version of the Rivière, lined with an alternation of marble statues and gilt vases.

It was devised by Père Sébastien Truchet, one of the odd ecclesiastical figures of the seventeenth century who appear to have interested themselves in almost anything but theology and the affairs of the Church. Originally called to the attention of the King by his successful repair of a watch—a present from Charles II—he became a member of the Académie des Sciences and the friend and associate of the great engineer Vauban; he was more or less attached to the Court, and there is no doubt that he played a considerable rôle in the creation of Marly. For the building of the Cascade he established a little railway on either side, with a pulley wheel which enabled one truck to descend acting as a counterweight to the other which was being pulled up. He also indulged in such varied activities as the construction of a machine for transplanting fully-grown trees and the creation of the 'tableaux changeants' mentioned in the accounts as being in the King's apartment in the Château. One of them was a sort of miniature mechanical opera, the other an animated landscape. Peasants chopped wood, ships circulated upon the water, and Father Sebastien himself came out of a church to salute Louis, who was passing with his hunt. *Madame* describes them in her letter of the 26th January 1710. They sound rather like exhibits on Brighton Pier, but doubtless executed with infinitely greater finesse. What pleased the seventeenth-century mind most was that everything worked 'absolument comme dans la réalité'.

Continuing the tour of the Bosquet de Louveciennes, two parallel walks ran from the Amphithéatre and the Cascade behind the line of the pavilions, at increasingly divergent levels. They crossed first the Bains d'Agrippine; four fountains and a little cascade above, opening out into an octagonal *salle* on the lower level, also adorned with four fountains. Finally both alleys opened out into the last feature of the bosquet, Parnassus, or the Bassin des Muses, which balanced the Fontaine du Sénat on the other side.

The water provided the movement necessary to animate the scene. Sir William Temple, in his treatise *Of Gardening*, drew attention to this need. 'If, according to the newest mode, it be cast all into grass plots and gravel walks, the driness of these should be relieved with fountains, and the plainness of those with statues; otherwise, if large, they will have an ill effect upon the eye.' Marly did not want for water. From the hills around came a steady stream, now regimented into cascades, now flowing smoothly from one basin to the next, all ultimately collected into the Abreuvoir. Great reservoirs high up in the woods behind supplied the fountains which reared their stately columns of water in every corner of the garden. Some of them reached a considerable height—that in the Demi-Lune des Vents exceeding a hundred feet. They could be seen from the road below, playing among the treetops, Tessin wrote to the King of Sweden.

Within doors, Marly was no less original than without; the square ground plan was based on an Irish cross formed by the central octagonal Salon and four radiating vestibules. The corners of the square were filled in with four apartments, each of three rooms, destined for the King, the Queen, the Dauphin and *Monsieur*. Later Madame de Maintenon occupied the Queen's apartment, and *Madame* that of her husband. They were each upholstered in a different colour, red, blue, green and pink. The furniture is difficult to reconstitute exactly. Each apartment had the same furniture, consisting of one bed, two armchairs, twelve folding stools, two cushions, four arrasses and the tapestry hangings, but there must have been other items, for there is mention of the supply of writing tables, cabinets and chests of drawers. Much of the work was of bronze or brass inlay, in the style of Boule, otherwise in marquetry of different coloured woods—'bois de violet, bois d'olivier, bois de lis'. The Cabinet du Conseil had table and stools in green velvet as at Versailles. The upstairs rooms, mostly occupied by the Princesses of the Blood, were also hung with tapestry.

The idea of the Salon, with its four radiating vestibules, may have been inspired by Palladio's Villa Rotunda; it had certain disadvantages as the result of this formation, and it is rare to find any praise for the Salon at Marly from those who were most acquainted with it. Madame de Maintenon led the critics by complaining of the draughts: 'On est battu d'un vent qui fait souvenir des ouragans d'Amérique.' Half a century later Marie-Leczinska was to make the same complaint to her friend the Duchesse de Luynes: 'Yesterday I deserted the Salon; the wind was just as strong there as in the garden.' Moreover, the exact symmetry of the Salon made it possible for a newcomer to lose his bearings. 'Those who are not familiar with Marly', wrote the Duc de Luynes, 'often mistake the side by which they should go out.' The only means of identification was by the south vestibule, which contained the billiard table.

The Salon, which was the room in which Louis entertained his friends, was an elaborate architectural achievement, with fluted pilasters continued above the cornice by Termes. Four glazed doors led into the vestibule, and between them four round-arched windows gave a feeble light to the little cabinets and wardrobes contrived in the angles. On the level of the first floor these windows were repeated to give light to the Terrace, an octagonal corridor which provided means of communication between all the upper-floor rooms. The only direct access to the daylight from the Salon was by means of four *œil-de-bœuf* windows pierced in the dome itself.

This lack of daylight was no great disadvantage, since the Salon was meant for evening use. It opened at six o'clock, when the music began, and the Queen made her entrance. It could be used for every variety of entertainment; there were lotteries, in which the ladies won jewellery and rich stuffs, or there were theatricals, or singing. For this former purpose a portable stage could be erected in a matter of half an hour in one of the vestibules. Sometimes there would be a professional performance of some work by Molière or Baron, sometimes a more amateur show in which many of the Royal Family took part, such as the masquerade given in January 1699 in which the Duc and Duchesse de Bourgogne played Zephyr and Flora; on another occasion the Princesse de Conti sang in a motet composed by that talented musician, the Duc de Chartres. The King, too, had been known to sing with the ladies, accompanied on the clavichord by the Princess de Conti.

But usually the Salon was used for gaming. This was often for very high stakes, and it was the cause of a great deterioration in the Court standards, firstly because it ruined many of the nobles and reduced them to living on their debts, and secondly, because it threw the door open to anyone who was rich enough to lose handsomely. Money and birth were the only qualifications esteemed, and if Louis was not too proud to invite, and even to toady, the wealthy banker Samuel Bernard, he was not too particular either to welcome the Duc de Vendôme, an illegitimate descendant of Henri IV and Gabrielle d'Estrées. Arrogant, gluttonous, cynical and homosexual, he was a man to whom posterity has been reluctant to attribute any virtue; 'filthy in the extreme', was Saint-Simon's verdict, 'and proud of it'. When on campaign it was his unedifying custom to receive his staff officers while seated on the *chaise percée*, often eating his breakfast and dealing with correspondence in the same position. When not at the wars he held Court at Anet, where he and his brother 'faisaient franchement la fête vicieuse'. Yet such a man was invited to Marly on his return from the Italian campaign, and 'no sooner had he ascended into his rooms than everyone, Princes, bastards and all the rest ran after him'. The Dauphin stopped a concert to welcome him, and Louis, leaving his work, came out of cabinet and embraced him several times. The structure of seventeenth-century magnificence was not erected without a scaffolding of stink and corruption.

2. *The Trianon de Marbre*

It was said of Louis that he built Versailles for the Court, Marly for his friends, and Trianon for himself. It would be truer to say that Trianon was built for the Royal Family. The Trianon de Porcelaine had been designed for Louis and Madame de Montespan, and it may have been the desire to be rid of so obvious a reminder of the fallen favourite that moved Louis to rebuild. On the other hand Clagny was a more obvious reminder, and that was allowed to remain. It is probable that the increased size of the Royal Family was the main *raison d'être* of the new Trianon, and possibly the King had outgrown the bizarre taste of the first pavilion.

In the summer of 1687 the little porcelain summer-house was demolished, and Louis' last addition to the dependencies of his palace was put in hand, a building which was to be known as the Trianon de Marbre.

At Marly the architecture was all painted in *trompe l'œil*—the coloured marble, the bas-reliefs, the colonnade of the Perspective, all was painted in fresco. At Trianon the same effect was sought in solid architecture. Real marble plaques and pilasters adorned the walls, real stone carvings surmounted the windows, and a real colonnade united the two main blocks of the building, a happy inspiration due to Mansart's collaborator and brother-in-law, Robert de Cotte. The idea may have been Louis'; it is reminiscent of his instructions for the building of the Enveloppe, where easy access to the gardens from the Court had been desired but not really obtained. A well-known anecdote by Saint-Simon about the building of Trianon testifies to the care with which Louis superintended its construction. He had a sharp eye for detail—'le compas dans l'œil pour la justesse, les proportions, la symétrie'—and he noticed a slight irregularity in one of the windows. Louvois, perhaps anxious to defend the reputation of his workmen, was ill-advised enough to argue the point; measurements were taken, and the accuracy of the King's observation established. The disconcerted minister retreated avowing, according to Saint-Simon, that only another war could save him from disgrace. The war of the League of Augsburg did, in fact, follow shortly after this episode, but it can be safely attributed to other causes, and it did not suffice to consolidate Louvois' position.

By 1688 the new building was finished. Perhaps the fairest appreciation of it comes from the Duc de Croÿ, writing towards the end of the following reign when it was no longer necessary to describe the buildings of the Grand Monarque with uncritical adulation. 'C'est le plus riche et charmant morceau d'architecture du monde,' he wrote, but he added the important qualification—'the view from the entrance to the court is admirable, but the rest does not answer to it.' This is very true, for the façade towards the avenue, giving no hint of the full extent of the whole, suggests a building of a size proportionable to the single storey and Ionic order to which Mansart and Robert de Cotte confined themselves. But seen from the parterre, the Château deploys its monotonous length, interrupted only by the colonnade, turns at right angles to present the fourteen windows of the gallery and its attendant Salon, and finally regains its original orientation in a further façade, all of stone, known from its sylvan setting as the Trianon-sous-Bois. One could easily believe the Trianon-sous-Bois, with its two storeys of windows, its beautifully carved masks and consoles, to be a later addition, somewhat awkwardly joined to the original Château by the gallery; but this is not the case. Trianon was planned and built as a whole.

Another criticism is that the marble is too pale a pink to afford a contrast in tone with the honey-coloured stone of the rest; Nicodemus Tessin, noting all the details of Louis' buildings for possible future reference in Sweden, was the first to notice this slight defect.

Like Versailles and Marly, Trianon played its part in Louis' policy towards his Court. Invitations were given or withheld in order to keep the nobility assiduous in their efforts to remain in the royal favour. The invaluable Saint-Simon reveals how the niceties of etiquette were used to his own discomfiture. When a lady was invited to Marly, her husband accompanied her without need for a personal application, but this did not apply if the invitation was to Trianon. By consistently asking the Duchesse de Saint-Simon to Trianon (the greater honour) and by equally consistently refusing her applications for Marly, Louis was able to convey in no uncertain manner his displeasure with the Duke.

The royal guests were lodged in the two-storey wing of the Trianon-sous-Bois, and here Madame found a lodging to her heart's content. She looked out over the little garden known as 'les Sources', a feature which was unhappily swept away in the replantations of 1775. It must have been a very attractive corner, 'a little bosquet so closely planted that at high noon the sun did not penetrate'. Beneath the trees fifty little springs gave birth to as many rivulets, which formed a diversity of islands, some of them large enough to set table and chairs for a game of tric-trac. The King's private garden was contained in the angle between his lodgings and those of Madame de Maintenon, and thus joined diagonally with the Jardin des Sources. For the rest, the gardens remained largely as they had been during the existence of the Trianon de Porcelaine, the formal parterres soon giving way to the woodland, pierced with long green alleys. There was so great a diversity of walks available that visitors often found themselves in some embarrassment to know which way to proceed. The way was punctuated with little fountains and basins where the intersection of several alleys made a circular clearance in the forest. Their bright, gilded cupids shone among the trees, like the last outposts of art in a landscape which was rapidly merging with its natural surroundings, from which it was only separated by the ha-ha.

On Summer mornings, when there was no council, the King would leave the Palace directly after Mass, and go to Trianon. After dinner, which was at one o'clock, he would work for a little with one of his ministers, but rarely for more than an hour. Then he would hunt. One can picture the meet in the semi-circular forecourt in front of the little Château, and the hounds, with their *valets de limier* and *piqueurs* moving off down one of the green rides towards the ha-ha, followed by the horsemen, and the King in his little open carriage, which he drove himself, using boys as postilions. This equipage was the result of Louis' having fallen from his horse and broken an arm, after which he never followed hounds on horseback.

In the evening there were games to amuse the ladies, often in the form of a lottery for little gifts of jewellery, lace and precious stuffs. Madame de Maintenon drew with the rest, but she always returned her winnings into the pool. Later in the night, perhaps, they would all go down to the canal and embark in the gondolas, or, crowded into the tiny Salle du Spectacle, hear a comedy or a symphony by Lully or Lalande. Supper would be served in the open colonnade looking out over the parterre, and haunted by the still perfumes of the flower garden.

Within doors Trianon presented a suite of interiors which still contain, in their carved friezes, overdoors and panelling, an important souvenir of the *Grand Siècle*, although most of the décor has been tampered with by Napoleon or Louis-Philippe. The historical imagination should try to picture the furnishings of Louis XIV—hangings of red damask or tapestry, in much of which the Chinese taste still lingered. Fourteen rooms are marked in the general inventory as having furniture 'upholstered with Chinese stuffs', and beds were hung with satin 'powdered with flowers and animals from China'. Only the gallery seems to have reflected the majestic style of the parent palace. Its furniture was carved and gilded and covered in crimson damask, with curtains of red taffeta to match. But its real décor came from the set of paintings which lined the walls, twenty-four of them, mostly by Cotelle, representing the chief beauties of the gardens and park.

The paintings on the ceiling of the Grande Galerie at Versailles told of the civil and military accomplishments of the Grand Monarque; those at Trianon commemorated another achievement of which Louis might feel justly proud. As he walked down his gallery he could compare with advantage the successive views of parterres, bosquets and fountains with the state of Versailles as he first remembered it, 'the most sad and barren of places, with no view, no water and no woods'. The twenty-four pictures showed the remarkable alteration which had been witnessed by the last quarter of a century. But the last and loveliest of all the views came not from a picture, but out of the windows of the Salon des Jardins at the end of the gallery—over the parterre, and across the canal to the Ménagerie. No longer could it be said that Versailles was wanting in views, nor in woods, nor in water. This last had been by far the most laborious accomplishment. No one can appreciate the achievement of Louis at Versailles who has not studied the problem of its water supply.

THE PROBLEM OF WATER

With the building of the Enveloppe, the gardens of Versailles began to assume the form which is familiar today, and the new groups of statuary gave the names to the fountains which they still retain. In 1668 the gilt dragon was placed in the basin which it still dominates, while in the following year the Pyramide was erected, to be followed almost at once by the so-called 'Marmousets' of the Allée d'Eau. In 1670 the groups of Latona and Apollo's chariot were positioned at either end of the Tapis Vert, and the next year saw the addition of the Marais and the Théâtre d'Eau. Finally, in 1672, the erection of Marsy's beautiful groups in the grotto, the laying out of the Parterre d'Eau before the Palace, and the installation of a fountain in the Cour de Marbre (both of which Louis desired to play full time) made further, almost impossible, demands upon the hydraulics. This was beginning to present a serious problem.

The water came from the lake at Clagny, from which it was raised by wind or horse pumps of humiliating inefficiency. The engineers, notably Denis Jolly and François Francini, did their best, and a considerable economy was effected by the return of the water from the gardens to the lake. This was achieved by means of a 'moulin de retour' situated somewhere on the site of the present Bassin de Neptune. Although praised by Mlle de Scudéry, the system left much to be desired. Certain fountains, the Dragon, Latona, and the Pyramide, only functioned when Louis was in that part of the gardens. It required a certain nimbleness on the part of the staff to ensure that the right fountain was functioning at the right time, and the overseer, Claude Denis, was liable to fines in case of failure. A letter from Louis to Colbert, dated from Alsace in 1673, suggests that breakdowns of a merely mechanical nature were not uncommon. 'You must arrange for the pumps at Versailles to work properly', he wrote, 'so that when I come back I will find them in a condition that will not exasperate me by their breaking at all times.'

Louis rightly saw that, in the vast formality of the garden which Le Nôtre was creating for his Palace, the movement of water was necessary to avoid the monotony induced by its symmetry. Stillness is a quality becoming to the natural or romantic landscape; the 'jardin français' required to be animated by artificial means. But aesthetic considerations apart, it was not endurable that Versailles, which was already destined to become the permanent monument to the excellence of French artists and craftsmen, and the chief symbol of Louis' supremacy, should remain inferior to the palaces of rival monarchies—and much less of his own subjects—in respect of fountains. Moreover the water, whether from stagnation or from the ordures thrown by the town into the Etang de Clagny, made the place unhealthy unless it was kept in constant motion. Primi Visconti, commenting in 1681 on the foulness of the air occasioned by the excavations, added 'and the waters, which are putrid, infest the atmosphere, so that during the month of August everyone was taken ill, except the King and myself only'. Madame de Sévigné was defeatist in her opinion. 'Kings, by reason of their wealth, can give to the ground a form different from that which it received from Nature, but the quality of the water, and that of the air, are not within their jurisdiction.' The problem of water was a constant worry to Louis, both on hygienic and aesthetic grounds, and it was even considered possible that he would abandon Versailles and 'go and build in a more happy situation'.

But Louis had by no means given up the struggle; indeed, he had hardly even started. 'In a great State,' he observed in his memoirs, 'there are always men suited to any sort of activity; the only thing is to know them and put them in place.' Just as the building of Versailles revealed artists of the first quality in every branch, so the search for water was to bring forth engineers equal to the seemingly impossible task of creating a supply where there was not one. But it was to be a costly and wasteful undertaking, for as Louis grew older, so he grew more obstinate and autocratic, and he applied his ever increasing power with an ever decreasing sense of proportion. It became a point of pride with him to obtain water, and the matter was pushed to ugly excess. There was not only a fantastic expenditure, but an appalling loss of human life.

It is not known what the death-roll was, but it appears that it was considerable. Saint-Simon makes the ominous statement that it was forbidden 'under the severest penalties' to talk of the sick, and particularly of the dead, which the heavy work, and even more the gases given off by the movement of so much earth, were killing. Madame de Sévigné also mentions the 'prodigious mortality' among the workmen, whose bodies could be seen every night being carted off to surreptitious burial.

They were mostly soldiers who were employed on the big works of excavation, the Pièce d'Eau des Suisses being named after the regiment which constructed it, and it is presumable that Louis was no more embarrassed by the casualties at Versailles than by those incurred during the wars; they served much the same purpose. He himself admitted on his deathbed to the future Louis XV that he had often waged war lightly and sustained it through mere vanity. If soldiers were to be sacrificed for such a cause, it is at least not inconsistent that they should be sacrificed for the perfection of Versailles. The *Grand Siècle* was not to be created upon the battlefields alone.

The steady collecting of local supplies was developed parallel with the most fantastic and grandiose schemes for tapping larger resources. One of the most extravagant projects was nothing less than the diversion of the River Loire to Versailles; its originator, Riquet, was on the point of obtaining a two-and-a-half-million-livre contract, when the intervention of the Abbé Picard showed the level of the Loire at Briare to be inferior to that of the Palace gardens.

Picard was an astronomer, and it was he who first thought of applying lenses to instruments of surveying. He was assisted by a Dane, Olaüs Romer, the first scientist to determine the speed of light. To these two men Colbert now turned for help, and their more modest scheme for collecting water from the plateau beyond St. Cyr was the first to be successful. An anecdote in connection with this project will give some idea of the accuracy of Picard's method. The water had been collected in the artificial lakes of Trappe and Bois d'Arcy and was brought along the southern, or far side, of the Heights of Satory, which had to be crossed by means of an underground tunnel. From the lake to the entrance to this conduit was a distance of over two miles, but a decline of only three feet had been allowed for the flow of water. When the canal was filled, it rose to exactly the height of three feet at the entrance to the tunnel—an impressive tribute to Picard's levelling. In 1678 the water finally arrived in the reservoir situated on the roof of the Grotte de Thétis; Louis was present when the taps were opened, and was vastly satisfied with the force with which it flowed.

Picard's success with the Trappe-Bois d'Arcy reservoirs was followed in the next year by a similar work directed by the engineer Gobert. It was a considerable undertaking, 'une entreprise fort hardie', involving subterranean conduits and siphons, sometimes as much as a hundred feet deep, besides bridges, embankments and cuttings. The final link in this chain, the Aqueduc du Buc, had not been completed in 1683 when Colbert died. Louvois succeeded him as Superintendent of Buildings, and had the satisfaction of seeing Gobert's work completed. 'I hope, from the manner in which the works have been constructed,' boasted the engineer, 'that they will last as long as the fame of our master.' His aqueduct remains today in memory of his labours.

Meanwhile Louvois continued the steady elaboration of Picard's original supply-line, extending the network of canals and reservoirs right into the Forêt de Rambouillet and almost as far as Maintenon. Of a total length of thirty-four kilometres covered by this 'lit de rivière', some two-thirds were of solid masonry.

While Gobert, Picard and their successors were establishing this chain of canals and reservoirs, Louis and his ministers continued to entertain hopes of a more spectacular water supply, and it appears that town criers throughout the country invited individuals to submit their ideas and inventions. It may have been in answer to such an advertisement that Baron Arnold de Ville, alderman of Liège, brought before Louis his project for raising the waters of the Seine to the summit of the high ground round Louveciennes by means of a gigantic pump. He had already installed one on his own estate at Modaves, and he brought with him to St. Germain Rennequin Sualem, carpenter, also of Liège, who was the constructor, if not the deviser, of this machine.

A working model was made and tried out in the presence of the King towards the end of 1680; it successfully raised the water to the level of the terrace at St. Germain. A site was selected near Bougival, where a chain of islands divided the waters of the Seine, and in 1681 Arnold de Ville and Rennequin Sualem started the construction of the celebrated Machine de Marly.

Fourteen gigantic waterwheels, each thirty-six feet in diameter, communicated their movement to two hundred and twenty-one pumps working in relays up the hillside, which raised the water to a height of a hundred and sixty-two metres above the river. It sometimes produced as much as five thousand cubic metres of water a day (twenty-four hours). By the 13th of June 1684 the mechanism was completed and tried out, again in the presence of the King. The result being satisfactory, work was started on the aqueduct which was to carry the water to the big reservoirs of Louveciennes and Le Trou d'Enfer, whence it could be conveyed to the gardens of Marly, or of Versailles or Trianon as occasion demanded.

The total cost was between three and four million livres, but there was also a heavy annual bill for maintenance, for, as Nicodemus Tessin noted, it was 'un ouvrage toujours à refaire'. The wear and tear on the brass bearings and the breaking of the chains which relayed the power of the waterwheels to the upper pumps required a constant supply of spare parts, and soon caused a falling off in the efficiency of the machine; nevertheless it was one of the wonders of its age. Contemporary writers noted with astonishment the complexity of its mechanism, and the perpetual grinding of its wheels and crankshafts, but it was claimed that, apart from the constructors, Vauban was the only man who had fully understood it.

Vauban, one of the ablest engineers of his age, was mostly employed on designing the fortifications necessitated by Louis' expanding frontiers, but in 1685 Louvois gave him the task of planning the most gigantic project for obtaining water that was ever actually put into operation. Although a considerable quantity was already available from the sources just described, it must be remembered that there were some fourteen hundred fountains to be supplied, and their use still had to be rationed. Normally only the basins lying nearest to the Château displayed daily, from eight in the morning until eight in the evening. On a special occasion, such as a fête, or the visit of an ambassador or other celebrity, the *Grandes Eaux* were only in full play for three hours at a time. Although on a far more ambitious scale, the fountains at Versailles were still a long way behind those of the Prince de Condé at Chantilly 'qui ne se taisaient ni jour ni nuit'.

Riquet's original idea, however, for bringing the Loire to Versailles had not, it seems, been completely forgotten, and the extension of Gobert's network of reservoirs to the vicinity of Maintenon suggested the possibility of bringing the waters of the River Eure instead. In 1684 La Hire was sent by Louvois to survey the prospect, and reported that the gradients were possible. The most spectacular portion of the works necessitated by this scheme, from Berchères to Maintenon, was put in hand. It consisted of a great embankment, sixty feet high, leading to the aqueduct, where the canal was to recross its own valley within sight of the Château de Maintenon. This aqueduct, most of which can still be seen today, was over five thousand metres long, some seventy metres high, and was to have had three tiers of arcading.

Thirty thousand soldiers were allotted to Vauban for this impressive undertaking, reminiscent of the labours of the Roman legions; discipline, under the Maréchal d'Uxelles, was extremely strict, and Saint-Simon records that even officers were not permitted so much as a quarter of an hour off duty.

During 1685 Louvois made several visits, and assured himself that work was progressing favourably. In July the following year Louis lodged at the Château de Maintenon, and Dangeau noted that the works were well advanced and that success was assured. In May 1686 the King was there again, but for the last time; almost immediately afterwards the troops were withdrawn for service at Neustadt, and the works were never to be taken up again. Eight million livres had been poured into this project when it was abandoned, and it was within a few months of completion. Here, rather than in any of the works of architecture or statuary, would have been a monument worthy to recall the glories of ancient Rome, had it been accomplished. Instead, the gaunt, ruined arches of the aqueduct remain, a noble but melancholy reminder of an Augustan age which just failed to come off.

THE REDECORATIONS OF 1701

The achievement of an adequate water supply left Louis free to turn his attention once more to the interior decoration of his palaces. In the State Apartments of Versailles the Grand Style had found its fullest and finest expression; elsewhere a new development was to set the fashion towards the lighter fancy of the eighteenth century; for just as Louis' reign long outlasted the century to which he gave its greatness, so his ideas advanced beyond the style to which he gave his name.

Towards the turn of the century considerable alterations and reconstructions were carried out in the interior of Versailles. They chiefly concerned the suite of rooms lit by the first-floor windows of the Cour de Marbre, which formed the King's personal apartment ('private' would be the wrong word in talking of Louis XIV).

In the centre of the east façade was the Salon Carré; originally intended as a sort of withdrawing-room to the Galerie, it was built two storeys high and accorded a solid architectural decoration, with white pilasters fluted in gold and a rich cornice and frieze. It was the most important and imposing room in the suite, and doubtless it was this consideration which led Louis to make it his bedroom, for the ceremonial functions of the Chambre du Roi made it necessarily the centre of the life in these rooms. The sun had become the emblem of the King, and since the sun was never seen at a greater advantage than at its rising and at its setting, it was appropriate that the beginning and ending of the royal day should be marked with due decorum. 'Qui n'admire ce bel astre', asked Bossuet, 'qui n'est ravi de l'éclat de son midi et de la superbe parade de son lever et de son coucher?'

The two ceremonies of the *lever* and the *coucher* were of the deepest significance. To Louis etiquette was no mockery, no hollow façade behind which a King might hide his human frailty. He saw in his position the incarnation of the State, a living mechanism which must function with invariable regularity. But beside the obvious convenience of routine there was the peculiar dignity of Monarchy to consider. Voltaire, in his *Siècle de Louis-Quatorze*, states that the Frenchman regarded his King 'as a sort of Divinity', an opinion which is reflected in Louis' memoirs, where he defined God as a Superior Power 'of which our Royal Power is part'. In this context he exacted, and was accorded, a deference not far removed from worship, and the routine acquired thereby a ceremonial significance. Also it achieved the final atrophy of the nobility. Men who found it beneath them to do work of the least utility craved for admittance to the most ordinary details of Louis' private life; the height of honour was to hold the candle to him at the *coucher*.

The Premier Valet de Chambre, a personage who enjoyed considerable influence at Court, slept in the King's room with him. At eight o'clock, having dressed himself, he woke the King. The Premier Médecin and Premier Chirurgien then entered, and Louis' aged nurse, who embraced him, while the doctors satisfied themselves as to his health. At a quarter past eight the Grand Chamberlain was called, and with him those who had the *grande entrée*. He advanced to the bed and drew the curtains, offered the Bible and the holy water, and withdrew; the company followed him into the Cabinet du Conseil. The King recalled them when he had finished his devotions, those who were entitled to the *seconde entrée* were admitted and the presentation of the *robe de chambre* accomplished. When dressed, usually in a brown embroidered suit crossed with the ribbon of the *cordon bleu*, Louis passed, with an inclination of the head, into the Cabinet du Conseil followed by those whose *entrées* permitted them to do so, and gave the orders for the day.

By this time the rest of the Court were assembled in the Grande Galerie waiting for the King to pass on his way to Mass. Here it was possible for anyone to speak to him, the less distinguished being obliged to give previous notice to the Captain of the Guard. It was usually some favour which was requested and it usually received the answer 'nous verrons'.

At some time between midnight and one o'clock Louis retired to bed; again a large attendance awaited him. They were only permitted to be present while he said his prayers, after which a select few remained for the *petit coucher*. This offered another opportunity for speaking with the King, but it was advisable to be brief.

The bedroom also served for certain occasional ceremonies and receptions. An interesting painting by Marot shows the institution of the Order of St. Louis in this room, and gives the best picture of its general appearance at that time. The painting, it must be said, is an anachronism. The Order of St. Louis was created in 1695, and the scene would therefore have taken place in the old bedroom. Marot, however, did not paint the picture until some years after the event, and like so many artists of that time he did not trouble himself with chronological details. The accuracy of his painting of the bedroom is fortunately confirmed by a sketch made by Nicodemus Tessin and preserved in the National Museum at Stockholm.

The bed, framed in a shallow alcove, was the principal feature of the room. It was a stately four-poster, rising to the height of the cornice, and crowned with ostrich feathers at the corners. There were two sets of hangings, one of crimson velvet laced with gold for use in winter, and one of gold- and silver-flowered damask for summer. On either side of the bed hung Domenichino's 'David playing the Harp' and Caravaggio's 'John the Baptist'. There were also two Van Dycks, one of them a self-portrait, another Domenichino and other religious paintings above the cornice. The carvings of the overdoors and the figure of France surmounting the alcove date from 1701 and add considerably to the richness of the general décor. Another feature, specially commanded by Louis, is the fine lace-like carving on the shutters and doors. This was repeated in the

Anteroom and in the two cabinets adjoining the Bedroom and formed a common theme running through the suite.

Besides the *lever* and *coucher* there were other occasions when the King could be seen by the Court and by the public. In the first Anteroom, usually described as 'la salle où le Roi mange', Louis dined at the *Grand Couvert*. To this spectacle the general public was daily admitted, subject to their being decently dressed and not 'of evil countenance'. At Versailles the King ate alone, surrounded by a half-circle of ladies and Princes of the Blood. He rarely spoke, but the silence was rendered dignified by the playing of music in the next room. Two nights before a visit to Marly the ladies were more numerous than usual and got up in the most extravagant fashion. They endeavoured by all permissible means to attract the favourable attention of the King in the hope that they would be selected for the forthcoming voyage; this custom was known as 'se présenter pour Marly'. If a lady was fortunate enough to be selected she brought her husband without further invitation. Unmarried men could also apply, using the form of application prescribed by etiquette: 'Sire, Marly?'

One cannot help being conscious, when reading the accounts of life at Versailles by Saint-Simon, La Bruyère, Madame de Maintenon or the Duchesse d'Orléans, of a great change which came over the Court as the century neared its close. Gone were the gay crowds who had swarmed after Louis on his *promenade des jardins*, applauded the fêtes, complained about the lack of accommodation and rolled wearily back in their great coaches to Paris or St. Germain at the break of day. They may not even have come from purely disinterested motives—*jeunesse du Prince, source de belles fortunes*—but there had been a spirit of freshness, the charm of the unexpected and of unfeigned enthusiasm for the delights which were offered. Now the courtiers had settled down once more to the regular routine of interest and intrigue, of flattery and backbiting, taking the ceremonial side of things for granted and disregarding anything that was not likely to lead to their own advancement. At the beginning of the century François de Sales had written: 'It is a great loss of time to be at

Court, and for many it will mean losing Eternity also.' Now, at the end of the century, La Bruyère could write: 'La vie de la Cour est un jeu sérieux, mélancolique, qui applique.' Even Mlle de Lafayette, formerly so enthusiastic about Versailles, commented on the sameness of everything and every day: 'Always the same pleasures, always at the same hours, and always with the same people.' A cold wind of austerity had chilled the summer landscape, and ominous clouds were gathering on the horizon.

For many who were not distinguished enough to have the *entrée* for the more exclusive functions, much of the day might be spent waiting in the Anteroom outside Louis' bedroom. When this latter was moved into the Salon Carré, the two rooms adjoining it on the south side, the old Bedroom and its Anteroom, were made into one large apartment. This was redecorated, and it was decided to make use of the space above the cornice for a deep frieze. Louis himself determined what the subject was to be: 'jeux d'enfants'. Six sculptors, of whom the best known was Van Clève, worked in a special studio, fitted up for the purpose in the Orangerie, on the realization of this command; together they produced a masterpiece of decorative art. The playing boys form a sort of garland to the ceiling, and their dancing figures and the flowing lines of their scant vestures give an almost Grecian elegance to the room.

Although it was the *œil-de-bœuf* window which gave its name to the room, the playing-boy frieze is of greater significance, for it marks the birth of a new style at Versailles. Unconsciously the Duchesse de Bourgogne was its mother. In 1697 she had come from Savoy as a girl of twelve to all the stale solemnity and setttled routine of Versailles; as Saint-Simon so aptly puts it: 'Elle l'animait tout entière.' Without interesting herself particularly in architecture, she was the source of a great rejuvenation in the heart of the King, which found its expression in the redecorations of 1701. For her the Ménagerie was enlarged to provide a little private residence in the park. Mansart was instructed to draw up plans, and as usual Louis noted his comments in the margin; they are most significant. 'It seems to me that there is something to be changed,' he observed of the decorations, 'that the subjects are too serious, and that there must be youth mingled with what is done.' On another occasion he struck the same note: 'Il faut de l'enfance répandue partout.' That was to be the keynote of the new style at Versailles.

Marie-Adelaïde de Savoie was the granddaughter of Henriette d'Angleterre, and she had the same capacity for enjoying life as her great-uncle, Charles II. Not pretty, but of an inexhaustible vivacity, she had made an immediate impression upon Louis and Madame de Maintenon, and it was in her company, more than anywhere else, that they may be said to have enjoyed a family life together. Although she naturally behaved with decorum on public occasions, she brought a breath of fresh air into the *après soupers* of the Royal Family, disregarding all convention, perching on the arms of chairs, throwing herself on to Louis' lap or climbing on to his knees and embracing him, rummaging among his papers and offering her opinions where they were not asked for. Louis was delighted. The one thing which he had lacked most completely in life, the easy charm of the private home, was brought to him by his little granddaughter-in-law. It made him young again, and brought the vital spark once more into the life of the Palace in which he had immured his Court.

It was at Marly and Trianon that the new influence was mostly felt. Louis had been steadily adding to the embellishment of Marly, but it had been a work of refinement rather than of enlargement. After 1697 the works included some considerable expansion. The Comptes des Bâtiments reveal the years 1699, 1701 and 1703 as those of greatest activity, the total expenditure often surpassing that for the year at Versailles. In 1698 a vast irregular building was added to the old offices, tucked away out of sight behind the Perspective. 'Another block of lodgings is being made here,' sighed Madame de Maintenon; 'Marly will soon be a second Versailles.' Whatever her influence upon her husband, she never succeeded in curbing his passion for architecture.

The Château itself saw a lot of redecoration, which started, typically enough, in the King's apartment. The marble fireplaces and tall mirrors with round arches 'right up under the cornice' were designed by Pierre Le Pautre; the new ceiling in the King's bedroom was typical of the new style, completely plain and centring on a delicate plasterwork rosette, a feature which was to be much used in the eighteenth century.

Within and without the work proceeded at high pressure. *Madame*, astonished to find a wood where she remembered a lake, wrote to describe the scene: 'One would think it was the fairies who were at work here.' The men worked in relays throughout the night, and the coming and going of so many points of light together with the ghostly illumination of the Château certainly presented the strangest spectacle.

In the gardens, hitherto devoted to impressive scenic effects, a lighter note was struck in the creation of the Bois de la Princesse (named after Marie-Adelaïde) and the multiplication of outdoor amusements. The new bosquet, situated between the eastern row of pavilions and the Versailles–St. Germain road, heralded a new style of gardening, for in and out of the straight alleys, which were still *de rigueur*, little tortuous paths wandered with the completest inconsequence, opening unpredictably into Cabinets de Verdure. In one of these a charming little temple was placed to provide shelter in case of rain. It was made up of two semi-circular benches beneath a blue dome supported on marble pillars, and the whole painted inside like trellis-work, powdered with birds and flowers; it was the work of Bellin de Fontenoy, and Louis was so delighted with his achievement that he granted him a special bonus.

Besides the Bois de la Princesse, the installation of a certain number of games may be ascribed to the influence of the Duchesse de Bourgogne. Two courses were laid out for mail, one round the Bosquets de Marly, the other up near the top of the Rivière. Mail is the ancestor of golf. The course was in the shape of a long horse-shoe, edged with boards; one tried to drive the ball round in the minimum number of strokes. More exciting was the Roulette. A steep incline, starting near the Trou d'Enfer at the southern extremity of the gardens, had been equipped with a sort of switchback railway on which ran a toboggan, carved and gilded, in which the Duchesse and her friends could descend at terrifying speed into the valley below.

The high wooded hills of Marly gave a pleasing sense of privacy, and with it intimacy. Here, more than anywhere else, the Royal Family were at home. Racine, one of the first to be asked as a guest, wrote in 1687: 'La Cour y est, ce me semble, tout autre qu'à Versailles.' They collected carp of the most varied colours for the fishponds—the Duchesse de Bourgogne gave them each a name and claimed that they answered to it; they played at mail, or went for a swing on the Escarpolette; they walked up into the forest, or went down to the river to bathe. Indoors the diversions were much the same as at Versailles —concerts, theatricals (in which the family were more often performers than spectators) and the inevitable gambling, which kept them up till the early morning.

As often as not the comparative intimacy of their surroundings and the relative freedom from etiquette brought out the worst in them. Louis himself, growing more tyrannical and selfish with age, showed less of that self-mastery which was so noticeable at Versailles. It seems that his digestion often went wrong; this was not surprising when one reads an account of his diet, for Louis was a prodigious eater. 'I have often seen the King consume four different plates of soups,' wrote *Madame*, 'a whole pheasant, a partridge, a great plateful of salad, some mutton in gravy and garlic, two brave slices of ham, a dish of pastries, and then fruit and preserves.' It is not to be wondered at if his temper was sometimes short. Saint-Simon records his having risen from table and broken a cane across the back of a valet whom he had seen pocketing a biscuit as he cleared away the course; 'these scenes,' he remarked, 'always occur at Marly.' Louis was even known to drop his royal dignity altogether and throw bread pellets at the ladies while at table, and they had permission to return his fire.

The King's example was followed by other members of the family; the Princesses smoked pipes, composed obscene verses, and not infrequently indulged in horseplay, none of it in the best taste. Usually the Duchesse de Bourgogne was at the bottom of the practical joking, and the most frequent victim of her pleasantries was the Princesse d'Harcourt, a 'tall, fat, ugly creature, mightily brisk in her movements, with a complexion like milk porridge and hair like tow, always sticking out and hanging down in disorder like all the rest of her trappings'. On one occasion the avenue to her lodgings in the Perspective was lined with crackers and her porters bribed to abandon her chaise when they started to go off; on another, a squib was placed under her chair in the Salon, and one winter's night the Duchesse de Bourgogne and her suite broke in on the unfortunate lady's beauty sleep, began to pelt her with snowballs, and so continued until 'the nymph swam in her bed, from which the water flowed everywhere, slushing all the chamber'. It is not surprising to learn that 'on the morrow she was sullen'.

Their behaviour did not pass unrebuked. Amid these scenes of senile petulance and juvenile indiscipline moved the dignified figure of *Madame*, carrying beneath her capacious bustle 'the imposing rotundity of a part which shall be nameless'. She observed with rising indignation men remaining covered before the King and seated in the presence of the Dauphin, and the Duchesse de Bourgogne walking arm in arm with her ladies. She might have said quite a lot on the subject, but she contented herself with the remark, 'it no longer bears the slightest resemblance to a Court'.

As at Marly, so at Trianon, the impact of the Duchesse de Bourgogne was immediately felt. Louis fitted up an apartment for her adjoining his own; the Salon Frais was part of it, and seems to conserve in its name the memory of its mistress. The King's own rooms, and those of the Dauphin on the other side of the colonnade, were redecorated along the same lines as those at Marly, and the Royal Family made more use of the little Palace than ever before. Not only Marie-Adelaïde, but *Madame*, the

Duchesse de Bourbon, the Duchesse de Chartres and the Princesse de Conti had apartments here and enjoyed the freedom of the gardens. Directly opposite the Peristyle the trees formed a dark and narrow lane, carrying the dense vault of their branches high overhead. From the far side of the Plafond d'Eau the still surface of the water reflected a beautiful view of the Château in the dark frame of the avenue. From here one could wander by an almost infinite variety of walks back to the elaborate marble Buffet d'Eau and the Jardin des Marronniers at the extremity of Trianon-Sous-Bois.

A party at Trianon was a family affair; it centred inevitably upon the Duchesse de Bourgogne. There would be an opera in the Salle de Comédie—perhaps a work of Lully's, or of the new writer Destouches, who was invited to hear the performance of his *Omphale* at Trianon. Then the room would be converted into a ballroom and Marie-Adelaïde, 'in a magnificent Spanish costume', took the floor with her ladies, partnered by the Duc de Berri, the Duc d'Orléans and the Comte de Toulouse.

It was at one of these family parties, on the occasion of the Duc de Bourgogne's majority in 1695, that Louis made the boast that never in the annals of the Monarchy had the succession been better assured, having a grandfather, father and son all of an age to govern. He spoke too soon. The Grand Dauphin was to die in 1711, the Duc and Duchesse de Bourgogne in 1712, followed to the tomb three years later by Louis himself, leaving the throne to an infant of five years old.

Looking back with this perspective on the family parties of Trianon one sees a certain melancholy mingled with their charm, and it is rather a sad figure that is portrayed by Dangeau sitting in an armchair on the terrace, watching the Duchesse and her suite embark in the little flotilla. Lights dance upon the waters of the canal, as if animated by the bows of the violinists, whose barque has already begun to move in the direction of the Ménagerie. The King leans upon the balustrade watching the dark forms of the gondolas as one by one they slide out and become lost in the shadows; for a while he remains silent, immobile, gazing out into the darkness, and from time to time the voices still reach him with the confused sound of the music, or the ripple of laughter and the splash of an oar in the cold, still air of the night.

MADAME DE MAINTENON AND THE CHAPEL

The rejuvenating effect of the Duchesse de Bourgogne must be set against the austere influence of Madame de Maintenon; for while the younger set were becoming gay and irresponsible, their elders were inclining towards a life of strict religious observance. The religion of a courtier was not necessarily outward and insincere; the letters of Fénelon are witness to the fact; now counselling a duke on the dangers of worldliness, now advising a marquis on the art of meditation, rebuking, consoling, instructing, encouraging, and often revealing that his efforts had not been in vain, he shows that some of the courtiers were genuinely devout.

Of course there were hypocrites as well, and, as always, they were the more conspicuous. Saint-Simon has an anecdote about some ladies who attended evensong punctiliously—provided that the King was there. They sat holding their candles so that the light fell on their faces and enabled them to be identified from the royal tribune. One day Brissac, major of the Guards, played a practical joke on them which was richly deserved; as soon as the ladies were assembled, he ordered the Guards to retire, saying that the King would not be coming. The Guards were turned back by their officers, who were in the secret, but not before the ladies—all but a few whose devotion was genuine—had withdrawn. Presently the King arrived, and was astonished at the smallness of the attendance. 'At the conclusion of the prayers, Brissac related what he had done, not without dwelling on the piety of the Court ladies. The King, and all who accompanied him, laughed heartily. The story soon spread, and these ladies would have strangled Brissac if they had been able.'

Outward forms were becoming compulsory. *Madame*, rebuked

for her Rabelaisian conversation, stuck to her principles of un-puritanical frankness, but the majority followed the example of the King. Nevertheless, the new morality does not appear to have had a lasting effect on the general tone. Critical observers were not impressed by the Court during the last years of Louis' reign. They were difficult years. In 1709 one of the sharpest winters ever recorded brought famine and great suffering to the people, which led to insurrections in Paris. Madame de Maintenon dared not venture out for fear of insult, and pamphlets of the rudest and most blasphemous description were handed about under the very windows of the Palace. The wars with Marlborough, with their humiliating reverses for France, contributed to the general misery and discontent. Such a state of affairs could not be without its repercussions on the Court, and the tension helped to break down the old standards. Ladies took snuff, ignored etiquette, effected a négligée in their costumes, and carried the same slovenliness into their business; 'one fails in all one's duties on principle'. Louis was less often there to rebuke them, retiring more and more into the little rooms of Madame de Maintenon, where he had private concerts, for he was a genuine lover of music, and found consolation in its charms.

Madame de Maintenon, *votre solidité* as he had once called her, acquired a real disgust for the Court. She had been young, she had been beautiful; she had had the freedom of the Salons and of the *beau monde*; she was now in the highest position she could have dreamed of attaining, and it merely left her with 'a terrible void, an unrest, a discontent, a longing to know something else'. Worldly wealth, power and position, once attained, had nothing to offer her; 'je meurs de tristesse', she admitted to a friend, 'dans une fortune qu'on aurait peine à imaginer'. But in the midst of all the gold and glitter of Versailles she had found the pearl of great price, after which 'one has nothing more to find'. She turned, as so many have turned, to God, and received, as so many have received, perfect satisfaction. Uncontaminated by the splendour of the Palace and the debris of the Court around her, she watched over the salvation of the King.

It would be wrong, however, to connect the building of the Royal Chapel with the influence of Madame de Maintenon. She opposed the idea, partly as an extravagance, partly because she thought that the Court would be obliged to abandon Versailles.

It was to some extent the practice of the age to live a humanist and die a Christian; retired mistresses took the veil, and licentious noblemen ended their days in an atmosphere of piety and repentance. In conformity with this pattern, Versailles had to wait for many years after its completion before it received a chapel answerable to its magnificence.

The delay was accentuated by the war of the League of Augsburg, and this had certain fortunate consequences for the architecture of the Chapel. By 1699, when the building was taken up again, Louis had changed his mind upon an important point; the intended material had been marble, the same heavy, brawn-like slabs which decorate so much of the Palace, but having had ten years in which to think it over, Louis decided instead to use the beautiful white stone known as *banc royal*, which gives the Chapel its peculiar charm. There was another advantage from the postponement, for the Chapel benefited, no less than the redecorations of 1701, from the new, lighter style which announced the beginning of the eighteenth century.

On the 8th of January 1699 Mansart had been appointed Surintendant des Bâtiments, while retaining his position as Premier Architecte, seconded by his pupil and brother-in-law, Robert de Cotte, who was to become the chief exponent of the new style. The decorations of the ground floor of the Chapel and the organ case were done after 1708, when Mansart died, under the directions of Robert de Cotte.

Saint-Simon, who was no lover of Mansart, devoted two of his most vitriolic passages to him. 'He had no knowledge of his profession', he states; 'Cotte, his brother-in-law, whom he made Premier Architecte, had no more than he. They obtained their designs and their inspiration from a designer of buildings named L'Assurance, whom they kept as far as possible locked away. Since he had no taste, nor the King either, nothing was ever executed that was beautiful, in spite of the colossal expenditure.'

The Chapel is better evidence of the good taste of Louis and his architects than Saint-Simon's words, for his criticism was by no means an unbiased aesthetic judgement. To the narrow limits of his own standard of values it was insufferable that a mere architect 'of the dregs of the people' should enjoy the entrée to the King's presence when it was possible for a Duke to be kept waiting. Saint-Simon, perhaps more than anyone else, realized the belittling effect of Versailles upon the nobility, and he appreciated it for what it was—'un autre manège de la politique'. He carried his prejudice into his artistic values. This does not alter the fact that he was the source of important information about Versailles, and his open bias lends a relish to his writings.

In particular his spleen was raised by the building of the Royal Chapel, which was in many ways the most original and successful piece of architecture in the whole Palace. 'This horrible excrescence,' he wrote, 'was only built to force the King to comply with Mansart's great project for raising the whole Palace by a further storey.' Since this was never accomplished, the roof of the Chapel, visible on all sides, presented 'the mournful appearance of an immense catafalque'.

Pierre Francastel, who has studied this question, regards the project for increasing the height of Versailles as an alternative to the addition of the two wings, and therefore previous to the final enlargement. It could, in that case, have no relation with the dimensions of the Chapel.

Saint-Simon's judgement is nothing less than a total failure to appreciate the Chapel. True to the traditions of lay and ecclesiastical architecture, it provides the only important vertical accent in this vast layout of horizontal lines. Although the Chapel is made up of purely classical elements, the conception is recognizably medieval in form, having the relative importance of nave and triforium inverted, for the royal tribune was to be on a level with the first floor of the Palace. This placed the King in the same position relative to the congregation as during a coronation at

Rheims. Another medieval effect is the clerestory and roof, with flying buttresses replaced by consoles, pinnacles by statues, and the slender belfry doing duty for the *flèche*. The timbers of the roof differ little in construction from those of a medieval apse.

By 1702 the shell of masonry was complete, and work on the sculpture had started. This was often executed *in situ* after a wax model had been approved and a plaster copy made, either to try the effect or to serve as a guide for the artist to work from. This system helped to produce an astonishing unity of style from a considerable diversity of sculptors. Van Clève furnished twelve models of cherubs to adorn the windows of the first floor, and the execution was then farmed out among the many carvers at work; in the Vestibule, an integral part of the architectural scheme of the Chapel, no fewer than fourteen sculptors co-operated in the carving of the columns and cornice, and the decorations of each of the wall-faces come from a different hand. The unity of style is all the more remarkable considering that the artists ranged from Magnier, of the old school of Le Brun, to young Guillaume Coustou, fresh from the Academy at Rome, and numbered among them such individuals as Van Clève, Le Lorrain and Frémin, First Sculptor to the King of Spain.

But if the individuality of the artist was sacrificed to the unity of the design, no less was the subject-matter of their work regarded as secondary to the decorative effect. The bas-reliefs on the arcading on the ground floor are of a very delicate craftsmanship; seen from the tribunes, they give a pleasing, brocade-like texture to the stone. In fact they represent the Passion of Our Lord, but even those seated close enough to appreciate their form might be excused for overlooking this fact; a cherub showing the purse of Judas suffices to evoke the Agony in the Garden, and a cock to represent the bitter remorse of St. Peter.

One is tempted to compare the Chapel at Versailles with that of Timon's Villa:

'On painted ceilings you devoutly stare
Where sprawl the Saints of Verrio, or Laguerre,
On gilded clouds in fair expansion lie
And bring all Paradise before your eye.
To rest, the Cushion and soft Dean invite,
Who never mentions Hell to ears polite.'

In 1710 the Chapel was finished. On the 25th of April Louis had a motet sung to try the effect of music in it; on the 22nd of the next month he went again, inspected the whole minutely, and had another motet sung. The acoustics of the Chapel are magnificent, and the music which was written for use in it answers admirably to the stately pomp of the architecture and the colourful animation of the painted ceiling. A performance here of Lully's *Plaude Laetare Gallia*, intended for use at the baptism of a Dauphin, or of Lalande's *Te Deum* is an experience never to be forgotten.

At either end of the royal tribune the balcony curves into a little quarter-circle to round off the corners; these projections were used for the accommodation of two little glazed kiosks, 'une lanterne dorée et fermée de glaces' where Princesses who were indisposed could hear the Mass. One of them was always occupied by Madame de Maintenon. They were probably to protect their occupants from the cold; the Comte d'Hézecques, writing of the last years of the *ancien régime*, describes also a larger 'box' which could be erected in the royal tribune—'une charpente dorée, qui en faisait un beau salon'—which insulated the Royal Family from the temperature of the nave.

On the 5th of June 1710 the Chapel was consecrated by the Cardinal de Noailles, and two days later the King attended his first Mass in it. The next day, being Pentecost, the formal procession of the Knights of the Saint-Esprit in their flaming robes fittingly inaugurated the Royal Chapel.

It is perhaps unfortunate that the regulation visit to the Château today should begin with the Chapel. It ought to start with the Escalier de la Reine, which was the ordinary entrance.

The visitor would then pass through the Queen's rooms into the gallery, the Œil de Bœuf and the Chambre de Louis XIV, and from here follow the *chemin du Roi*. Every day Louis went from his bedroom into the Cabinet du Conseil, entered the Grande Galerie, and passed right down the imposing enfilade of the Grand Appartement to attend Mass in the Chapel. Every room was a profusion of coloured marbles, gaudy hangings, silver furniture and gilt decorations. The doors of the Salon d'Hercule were thrown open, and the King passed into the Vestibule of the Chapel. . . .

The contrast is astonishing. In place of the heavy marble, the pure, cream-coloured stone and delicate play of light on the carvings create an entirely different atmosphere, cool and refreshing; it is as if one has cast off the colourful paraphernalia of Royalty. But if colour is the attribute of Royalty, that of Divinity is light, and the tall windows, open colonnade and pale stone of the Chapel make the fullest use of this element. The side windows of the ground floor give but a feeble illumination to the nave, but those of the apse, where the arcading curves into a graceful ambulatory, provide, by contrast, a dramatic lighting to the altar. Gilding, conspicuously absent from the rest of the Chapel, is used also to focus attention on the sanctuary, and to conduct the eye thence, by way of the organ case, to the brilliant profusion of the painted ceiling—the Promise of Redemption. It would be a fitting note on which to end the tour, for the Chapel marked the completion of the Palace.

It would have been a wonderful experience, between 1710 and 1715, to have made an ascent in a balloon from the Place d'Armes, for it is only from the air that the whole Grand Design could be taken in at once. Contemporary artists appreciated this necessity, and J.-B. Martin has left a bird's-eye view of the completed Versailles which may be compared with that painted by Patel more than fifty years previously. By a happy chance, Patel showed the Court arriving at an apparently deserted Château, whereas Martin depicts a procession of coaches departing from a Palace evidently teeming with human life. The crowd swarming round the entrance to the Petit Escalier du Roi is perhaps the most significant feature of Martin's painting.

It is the most perfect portrait of Versailles. The artist has set himself to tell us the whole truth. His accuracy is scrupulous but his detail is never obtrusive. He shows to its full advantage the long, regular, ever widening procession of the forecourts—the complex, many faceted construction of the roof. He respects the colour scheme, a bright array of brick and stone and slate and gilded lead, which, Sir Christopher Wren had noted, 'makes it look like a rich livery'.

He has drawn his axis obliquely, thus masking the asymmetry of the Chapel, which stands like a miniature Cathedral, its golden belfry riding high above the rooftops of the Palace. Behind these he allows a glimpse of the long, uninterrupted outline of balustrade and vases, suggesting the more princely architecture of the garden fronts.

From the increased altitude of Patel's viewpoint, the whole layout of the gardens would have appeared behind—to the left the Orangerie, swelled to a gargantuan size, and beyond it the Pièce d'Eau des Suisses, lying like a silver mirror beneath the sombre woodlands of the Heights of Satory; to the right, the smaller but more ornate ensemble of the Bassin de Neptune and the Allée d'Eau. Behind the Château an elaboration of parterres gives place gradually to the regimented plantations of the lower gardens, with white marble colonnades and kiosks gleaming through the trees, and here and there a stately fountain raising its crystal column above the foliage. Below these lies the great cruciform canal, with a gay flotilla riding its waters; the huge brigantine, flying the Royal Standard and decked with an awning of blue and silver, four chaloupes in red, blue, green and yellow, and the violet of the Neapolitan felucca presenting a very glorious spectacle to the eye.

But the imagination is not answerable to the law of gravity; it must soar to greater heights if it is to comprehend the whole of the Grand Design. At a more considerable elevation, when the features and contours of the park appear as a plan reduced to a scale that would include not only the Ménagerie and Trianon, but the town of Versailles, the Château de Clagny and more distant Marly, a new feature of the countryside would become apparent: the great chain of reservoirs linking Marly to Versailles, Versailles to Rambouillet, and Rambouillet to the valley of the Eure, and collecting water from the hills on either side to contribute to the embellishment of a royal garden.

The interior of the Palace offered a scene no less imposing, revealing a noble unity of design and an astonishing richness of furniture; everywhere it seemed as if Midas had run his fingers over the decorations, leaving them of sparkling gold.

And yet there was something lacking.

The whole character of the place had been one of growth, a character which gives the study of Versailles the interest, almost, of a biography. But like so many things on this earth, it proved more enjoyable in the getting than in the possessing. It had been Louis' ambition to possess a palace which would be without rival in Europe. He had achieved it, but the happiest moments in his life had been when that ambition was yet unattained; once Versailles was completed, his interest slackened, and wandered off down the avenue that led to Trianon, or over the distant hills to Marly. It had been his ambition to possess a brilliant Court, but the most brilliant moments had been those of the first fêtes when his political structure was still in the making. The finished product seemed only to testify to the truth of La Bruyère's words: 'A healthy mind acquires at Court a taste for solitude and retreat.' They testify to the truth of the paradox that nothing fails like success.

How different was the Versailles of those last days! And yet it was chiefly different in that it remained the same. Change and development had been the keynotes of its history; now they were silent. Only the seasons now brought their successive changes to the trees and hedges of the gardens, clothing their naked branches with a light veil of foliage and making the avenues cool and shady for the ensuing summer; but to no purpose. In vain did the autumn succeed the summer, covering the plantations with her gold and umber mantle, 'comme une vieille tapisserie de château'; but spring held no promise and autumn no enchantment since the death of the Duchesse de Bourgogne. That had been the bitterest blow to Louis, 'la seule grande douleur de sa vie'. But it was more than that. It was the end of the *Grand Siècle* at Versailles. 'Tout est mort ici,' sighed Madame de Maintenon; 'la vie en est ôtée.'

Pitifully reduced in numbers, the Royal Family continued to assemble, as it always had, in the Cabinet des Perruques after supper. *Madame*, delighted to be admitted to the inner sanctuary of a Court which she had always criticized with malevolence, now joined the circle, and the old Maréchal de Villeroi, veteran of Louis' campaigning days, came too and sat with them in the gathering gloom of the evenings. Then the musicians in the next room would fill the air with the light strains of Lully, and almost imperceptibly the conversation drifted into reminiscence, and they talked on into the night of the fêtes of the old days and the *Plaisirs de l'Ile Enchantée*.

IV

Versailles in the Eighteenth Century

ON THE 1st of October 1715 Louis XIV died at Versailles of a gangrene in the leg. Right until the end he showed that self-mastery which had been so remarkable a feature of his life, and he died, as he had lived, in the midst of a full Court, true to the principles of publicity which had made his reign so spectacular.

Publicity was an art studied in its finest degree by the seventeenth century; the magnificent spectacles to which all were admitted; the elaborate fireworks which all could enjoy; even some of the most domestic occasions in the King's life were accessible to the humblest bourgeois who could dress decently and hire a sword to gain admittance to the Palace. It was as if Versailles were a royal museum in which the person of the King was the chief exhibit, and in some ways more truly open to the public than it is today. The gardens and the great reception rooms were open to all, and it is astonishing to read in the memoirs of the times the number of thefts that were committed, of brass taps and lead pipes taken from the fountains, and even gold braid cut from the curtains of the Galerie, and all removed under the very noses of the Suisses who guarded the Palace.

These soldiers had certain orders to observe; no one of disreputable appearance was to enter (although there is abundant evidence that many did), a gentleman was not to offer his arm to a lady (except in case of infirmity), a lady might not have her train carried, a gentleman might not enter with a stick in his hand, a monk not at all. The restrictions, however, were enforced with great tact.

It sometimes happened that a countryman, up to see the sights of the Court, penetrated into the Œil de Bœuf, attracted by the distinguished crowd in *grand habit* and *cordon bleu* that was gathered round the fireplace. If the warning given by the Suisse at the door, 'passez, Monsieur, passez dans la Galerie', was not heeded, another Suisse, under pretext of looking to the fire or adjusting the curtains, would take the offender aside and explain his error, thereby sparing him the humiliation of a public dismissal.

Connoisseurs of art were given access to the magnificent private collection of the King, which was housed in the rooms lying along the north side of the Cour de Marbre on the first floor. These rooms were known as the Cabinets du Roi, and their names suggest their purpose; there was the Cabinet des Perruques where the King was powdered after the *lever*, the Cabinet du Billiard, Antichambre du Petit Escalier, Cabinet des Tableaux, Cabinet Ovale and Petite Galerie, and lying inside these, the little Cabinet des Curiosités. Beside their private use, these rooms housed most of Louis' art treasures and he was very agreeable to the admission of those who were interested. The Abbé Bourdelot obtained admission through his friendship with Bontemps, the Premier Valet de Chambre and a person of considerable influence at Court. 'He had me conducted into the Petit Appartement du Roi,' writes the Abbé, 'which is none the less large, magnificent and sumptuous.' The pictures, which were arranged according to the artists' names, were provided with curtains, which were drawn for his inspection. Guides were at hand to instruct him as to the exhibits, and he was all the time in his usual transports of admiration.

It is essential to bear this publicity in mind when approaching the study of Versailles and Louis XV, for he came to dislike it, and his dislike is clearly reflected in his alterations to the Palace. During the fifty-odd years of his residence he was to change the appearance of the interior so as to make it largely unrecognizable as that of Louis XIV, and, but for want of money, he would have changed the exterior also. He did not, however, move into Versailles until 1722, and the period while he lived at Vincennes and the Tuileries is one of great interest to the historian of art. For seven years the great Palace stood unused, the comings and goings of a host of small fry serving only to accentuate the emptiness of the State Apartments. In summer the public roamed in the gardens, until the mists of autumn rising from the canal shrouded the building in their mysterious veil, the wind swept the fallen leaves across the gravel walks and alleys, and a thousand shuttered windows stared blankly out over the naked trees and statues of Le Nôtre's garden.

People even talked of pulling the Palace down, or of transporting it piecemeal to St. Germain; to many it seemed to be dead. But it was only sleeping, and during its sleep Versailles was, in fact, active in the effect which it was producing, during these very years, upon the architecture of Europe. Along the banks of the Rhine, and in the remoter kingdoms of Würtemberg and Bavaria, new and ever-larger palaces were rising from the ruins of the wars of the previous century, and their builders looked to France for their model.

For during the Regency foreign princes did not cease to visit Versailles. Peter the Great lodged first in the Queen's apartment, then in those of Madame de Maintenon at Trianon. He had the fountains played, inspected the machines 'with an astonishing attention', and expressed himself well satisfied with what he had seen. He took back with him to Russia the French architect Le Blond, who supplied the designs for Peterhof. German princelings, making that indispensable accomplishment of their education the *Kavalierstour*, prolonged their stay in France as far as their means would permit them, and formed their taste in the galleries of Versailles and Meudon and in the gardens of Marly, Trianon and St. Cloud. 'A young man,' said Frederick II, 'passed for an imbecile if he had not stayed for some time at Versailles.' On returning to their own lands, the battleground of Europe for the past hundred years, they tried to reconstruct their little principalities and duchies on the grand lines of the French monarchy. Not only did French become the official language of their Courts, but their clothes, their food, their music, all had to be French if it was to be considered in good taste; every Court had its French artists to adorn it, and the Prince sought relaxation in the arms of a French mistress. The attempt to ape the magnificence of Louis XIV often led to absurdity. 'It has always been their misfortune,' complained *Madame*, 'that the Germans not only imitate the French, but they always go twice as far as we do here.'

Most particularly was this influence felt upon the Rhine, among the small Catholic states on the French frontier whose ruling families were often connected by marriage with the Royal House of France. The historic capitals of the Palatinate, Cologne and Trèves were abandoned, and at Mannheim, Bonn and Coblenz electoral palaces arose upon foundations almost as extensive as those of Versailles. French architects were in demand, and where they were not to be had, French models were copied, so that each Residenz had its Trianon, its Grotte de Thétis, its Bassin d'Apollon after the manner of its prototype. Robert de Cotte, First Architect to the King, furnished designs for Bonn, Brühl and Poppelsdorf for the Elector of Cologne, and a palace for the Prince von Thurn und Taxis in Frankfort, while in Strasbourg his episcopal palace for the Cardinal de Rohan was to bring a knowledge of the Grand Style to the uttermost confines of France.

The French influence was spread also through the works of Boffrand, whose magnificent Château at Lunéville for the Dukes of Lorraine shows clearly, in the progression of its wings towards the town, the inspiration of Versailles.

German architects were not slow to follow suit, and one of the most interesting of their 'mushroom palaces' was the work of Maximilien von Welsch. Built for Lothar von Schönborn on a site dominating the confluence of the Rhine and the Main, it bore the name of La Favorita, but Lothar himself usually referred to it as 'Petit Marly'. The Elector's *Lustschloss*, with its fantastic baroque staircase peopled with an entire orchestra in stone, already existed at one end of the garden, and was placed too near the river to permit its use as the focal point of the proposed layout, so at 'Petit Marly' the position of the château proper was occupied by a magnificent orangery. The narrowness of the site (or was it of the Elector's fortune?) permitted only six pavilions, but otherwise the dispositions were only slightly altered, and added to their own attractions the advantages of a prospect comparable only with that of St. Cloud or Meudon.

The later addition of the *Porzellanhaus* recalls the obvious prototype of the first Trianon. There were, in fact, several examples of this type of decoration in Germany, the most notable being, perhaps, the summer dining-room at Brühl, near Bonn, and the kitchen at Amalienburg, in some ways the most charming of garden pavilions, where the Delft panels bear a close similarity with those of the Trianon de Porcelaine.

But it was not merely architects who were attracted by the foreign markets or expelled as Protestants by the Revocation; with them went painters, cabinet-makers, iron-workers and other craftsmen. England profited by the arrival of a number of Huguenot workmen, of whom Jean Tijou is perhaps the most celebrated on account of his beautiful wrought-iron work. In architecture, Robert Hooke, who built the first Montagu House 'in the French pavilion way', gave impetus to a modest attempt to introduce ideas from over the Channel which found its highest expression in the second Montagu House (somewhat improbably attributed to Puget) and in Boughton and Petworth, both of them magnificent houses whose architects are unknown. At Montagu House the team of interior decorators, Rousseau, La Fosse and Jean-Baptiste Monnoyer, created a décor which drew from Walpole the sincere confession 'qu'on ne peut aller plus loin en fait de peinture'. In gardens the style of Le Nôtre enjoyed a considerable vogue until it was largely effaced by the school of Lancelot Brown.

One of the rallying points of the Huguenots was the salon of the Duchesse Mazarin at Chelsea. Here they met another French exile, the philosopher Saint-Evremonde. Saint-Evremonde was in close touch with Ralph, Duke of Montagu and with a certain

Dr. Sylvestre, who seems to have played an important part in directing the cultural activities of the Duke. The French gardens at Boughton could compare favourably with those of Chantilly or St. Cloud.

The influence on style exerted by these Huguenot craftsmen, together with the direct impact of Versailles upon Bavaria and the Rhineland, helped to make France in the eighteenth century what Italy had been in the Renaissance—the cultural centre of Europe. 'Who could have told,' asked Montesquieu, 'that the late King had established the greatness of France by building Versailles and Marly?'

On the 15th of June 1722 the Court returned to Versailles. The town had suffered from the absence of the Royal Family, and as the procession of coaches rolled out from the Avenue de Paris into the Place d'Armes, they were greeted by almost the whole population. It was expected that the glories of the Court of Louis XIV would be renewed, and a special firework display had been arranged. But in this the bourgeois were disappointed; the Regent 'not judging it convenient', the firework display did not take place; nor, with relatively few exceptions, were the fêtes of the *Grand Siècle* to be resumed.

The change came gradually and, to begin with, the great tradition in architecture was maintained, and the finishing of the Salon d'Hercule—already planned by Robert de Cotte—in no way suggested the destiny which the next forty years were to reveal in the interiors of Versailles.

The Salon d'Hercule, the link between the Vestibule of the Chapel and the Grand Appartement, not only continued the style of Louis XIV but surpassed much of it in excellence. The twin pilasters, rising between stately round-arched windows to support a heavy, richly carved and gilded cornice, show Robert de Cotte to be the pupil of Mansart; only the fireplace with its carved scrollwork suggests the style to which Louis XV was to give his name. But it was the ceiling which gave the Salon d'Hercule its special lustre. This heroic conception, the Apotheosis of Hercules, was the work of a humble postilion's boy,

Antoine Le Moyne. 'Il n'y a guère dans l'Europe,' wrote Voltaire, 'de plus vaste ouvrage de peinture que le plafond de Le Moyne, et je ne sais s'il y en a de plus beau.' Cardinal Fleury considered that it made the rest of the painting in the Château seem dim by comparison. Le Moyne spent three years in achieving his masterpiece, and it was not until the 26th of September 1736 that the finished work was revealed. 'That day,' wrote Nonnotte, 'the King, going to Mass as was his wont, looked at the work of Le Moyne with an expression which announced the good fortune of the painter.' On his return he stopped again to look at the ceiling, and created its author his Premier Peintre then and there.

But it was not, as was anticipated, the beginning of a glorious career for Le Moyne, for within a year he had taken his life, the unhappy victim of a morbid delusion that he was being persecuted. Nor did the inauguration of the Salon d'Hercule in any way foreshadow what was to be the future of Versailles from an artistic point of view; rather was it to prove the last variation upon a noble theme. By this time Robert de Cotte was dead, and the Duc d'Antin, Directeur des Bâtiments since 1708, was to follow him to the grave in a few weeks. In another, obscurer portion of the Palace work had already begun in which the true style of Louis XV was revealed. The future lay in the hands of a young man, Ange-Jacques Gabriel.

THE PETITS CABINETS

High up under the roofs of the Palace, round the little courtyard known as the Cour des Cerfs, Louis began, as early as 1727, to construct a network of cabinets, linked by narrow galleries and little winding stairs. Here were tiny libraries of the neatest invention and the most elegant design, and a bathroom with bedroom attached in which the young King could relax after his ablutions; above was a workshop fitted with a lathe where he worked ivory under the direction of Mademoiselle Maubois; there were still-rooms and a bakery where he made chocolate and sweetmeats, not without the expert assistance of the *pâtissier* Lazur; there was a terrace garden with trellis screens and a little aviary.

Here, with a small circle of intimate friends, Louis could shut himself off from the heavy formality of the Court, before which he only appeared on those occasions which etiquette demanded. This twofold existence made him a somewhat elusive figure to his contemporaries. 'Everything becomes more and more

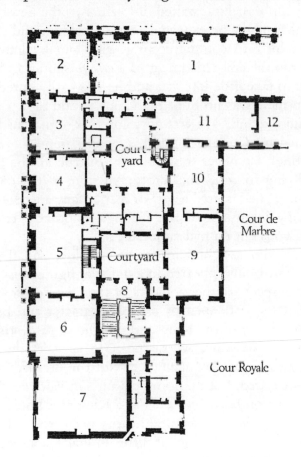

THE PETITS CABINETS OF LOUIS XV

1 Grande Galerie (*below*); 2 Salon de la Guerre (*below*); 3 Chambre du Trône (*below*); 4 Chambre du Lit (*below*); 5 Salle du Bal (*below*); 6 Oval staircase from first floor; 7 Libraries; 8 Galerie de la Géographie; 9 Salle-à-Manger; 10 Petite Galerie; 11 Salon de Jeu

dependent on the character of the King,' wrote d'Argenson, 'and his character becomes even more problematic.'

Historians have found themselves in the same perplexity as d'Argenson; they range between two extremes represented by Michelet on the one hand and Pierre Gaxotte on the other, and the same diversity of opinion is to be found among those who knew the King in person. To those who only saw him in his official capacity, Louis was stiff and awkward and had no conversation; ambassadors waited in vain for the few gracious words which might be expected to terminate an audience, and the Queen took to communicating with him by letter rather than undergo the embarrassment of a conversation. In his work he seemed to take little interest, and he was easily bored; on the days when there was no hunt the Court would say: 'Le Roi ne fait rien aujourd'hui.' He was not, however, a man to be disregarded. Madame Campan found his manner imposing and even disconcerting. 'He never took his eyes off you all the time that he was talking to you,' she wrote; 'in spite of the comeliness of his features, he inspired a sort of fear.' Many anecdotes reveal him as quite insensible of the feelings of others, 'comme un enfant qui vous fait du mal en jouant'.

To those who saw him in his private life, and these were extremely few, Louis appeared in a different light. Most interesting in this respect are the memoirs of the Duc de Croÿ and the Duc de Luynes, both men of reliable character and belonging to the inner circles of the King and the Queen respectively, and of Dufort de Cheverny, whose position as valet de chambre gave him an intimate acquaintance with the life of his master. 'Un Roi,' he stated, 'est un homme pour son valet de chambre.'

This distinction between Louis as a King and Louis as a man is underlined by the architectural history of his reign. His whole delight was in the creation of little intimate apartments and little isolated houses. In the privacy of the Petits Cabinets he shed that awkwardness and aloofness noticed in the State Apartments; 'at supper in the Cabinets,' Luynes relates, 'he is, so to speak, like an ordinary individual.' The most important of his early creations was the Château de Choisy-le-Roi; those who had the privilege of following him here on his frequent visits saw him in his most informal mood; 'this ease in society was more evident at Choisy than anywhere else,' continues Luynes in the same passage, 'il est presque comme un seigneur particulier qui fait avec plaisir les honneurs de son château.'

If boredom was his chief enemy, he was capable of sustained enthusiasm and considerable application where his personal interests were concerned—as huntsman, botanist and architect. The real power of Madame de Pompadour, which enabled her to retain her supremacy long after she had ceased to be Louis' mistress, lay in her ability to keep him interested and amused, and she admitted that he was only really happy with his architectural designs spread on the table before him.

It was to the Petits Cabinets that the young Gabriel would bring the drawings, sometimes beautifully decorated and bound, to lay before his royal master. It was in this way that the true style Louis-Quinze came to be created.

The rooms were decorated with delicately carved panels painted in a distemper known as 'Chipolin' and finished in a *vernis Martin* with the gloss and freshness of porcelain. This was the most typical feature of the new style; gilding was either banished or confined to the frames of pictures and mirrors, and its place was taken by soft colours. 'Les peintures couleur d'eau, petit vert, jonquille, lilas, gris de perle, bleu de Prusse font la gaîté des appartements.' There was no heaviness and no over-charging with ornament, the effect being built on the nice balance between the plain surfaces and the finely carved detail of the frames. The mouldings were gracefully turned, their arches breaking into delicate scrolls that curled in upon themselves and blossomed forth into a spray of tiny flowers, or become lost in a lace-like rosette at the foot of each panel. There was grace, lightness and refinement in every room, but none of the restlessness and fantasy of the more exuberant rococo.

First to be built were the libraries; they were ranged round the north side of the Cour des Cerfs and formed a little suite of four rooms, of which one, the Galerie de la Géographie, was little more than a corridor equipped with 'very beautiful maps' mounted on spring rollers. The carved decorations were almost confined to the window recesses, but of course the books themselves, 'très bien choisis et très bien reliés', formed an important part of the whole scheme, and where space did not permit of the genuine article, the walls were lined with the backs of books specially ordered from the Sieur Collombat, the Court bookbinder. Ten large folios bore the legend 'Descriptions de Pays Inconnus'; even the titles of these fictitious volumes were chosen with care and with humour for the young King. In light mood also were the dogs' heads in the panelling of the Cabinet Doré, which connected the libraries with the Grand Appartement, and the twenty-four stags' heads which gave its name to the Cour des Cerfs.

In 1764 these libraries were dismantled, and a new one constructed in the attic above the Cabinet du Conseil. This room retains today one peculiar feature which recalls the habits of Louis XVI. In the window lying nearest to the frontispiece of the Cour de Marbre there is a circular hole in the glass; this was made for the reception of Louis' telescope, through which he used to watch the arrival of visitors to the Court as they came up the Avenue de Paris.

On the opposite side of the Cour des Cerfs from the libraries, and overlooking the Cour de Marbre, was the Petite Galerie, sometimes called the Galerie des Petits Cabinets to avoid confusion with Louis XIV's Petite Galerie on the first floor. The five dormer windows provided a feature of which Gabriel made the happiest use, creating thereby a series of delightful panelled recesses, which are still to be seen, but the gilding dates from the days when this formed a part of the apartment of Madame du Barry. Originally the panelling was painted 'de différentes couleurs tendres' but later, in 1764, Piganiol de la Force noted that the painting was 'couleur d'or'. The wall opposite the windows was decorated with six paintings representing scenes of big game hunting by Boucher, Lancret, Van Loo, Parrocel, Pater and

Troy, which formed the most important decoration of the Galerie. They can be seen today in the Musée de Picardie at Amiens; they are violent pictures, both in the scenes depicted and in the colours used, and must have sorted ill with the daintiness of the panelling.

Next to the libraries on the east side of the Cour des Cerfs was the Salle-à-Manger. The atmosphere of this room is admirably suggested by the two pictures ordered for it in 1735 and now in the Musée Condé at Chantilly—the Déjeuner de Jambon by Lancret and the Déjeuner d'Huîtres by Troy. Historically, the Dining-room was the most important of the Petits Cabinets, for it was the scene of the intimate supper parties for which they were, above all, famous. The only really detailed accounts of these parties comes from Croÿ, and they are most interesting; it seems that he was half expecting to become involved in some orgy which did not, in fact, take place. He was influenced, no doubt, by the uninformed opinion of the Court, for those who could not obtain admittance referred to the Petits Cabinets as 'rat's nests', grotesquely exaggerated the cost of their construction, and formed any ideas they pleased as to what went on there. In fact the only reproach to the King's conduct that comes from a reliable source is a mild one. 'In the early days of the Cabinets,' Luynes noted in July 1743, 'the suppers were extremely long; there was a lot of champagne drunk. For the last two or three years this custom has been greatly changed; the King does not drink any more.' Both Luynes and Croÿ make it quite clear that the intimate suppers were partaken of in an atmosphere of harmless and homely decorum.

It is amusing to read the account of Croÿ's first supper; he was torn between the desire to be admitted among the élite and the fear that by so doing he might be obliged to compromise his moral integrity. Invitation was much sought after, and extremely difficult to obtain by those who did not follow the King to hounds, for the suppers were always held on the days when there was a hunt. Croÿ tells of the elaborate precautions he had to take to have the King reminded of his presence. Invitation at that time could virtually only be obtained through Madame de Pompadour, and the list, either compiled or approved by her, was brought to Louis on his return from the chase. Those who hoped to be asked presented themselves at the door of the Cabinet du Conseil. Louis marked off the names of those to be invited, which were then read aloud by the *huissier*, and one by one the guests made their way into the Cabinets.

'On entrait à mesure par le Petit Escalier,' recounts Croÿ, 'et on montait dans les Petits Cabinets. J'y soupai donc pour la première fois à Versailles.' One can imagine the thrill of climbing the little oval staircase and finding oneself in this inner sanctuary of the Court. 'The Dining-room was delightful, the supper enjoyable, without restraint. We were only served by two or three Valets of the Wardrobe, who retired after placing all that was necessary before each of us. The King was easy and gay, but always with a certain grandeur which one could not overlook; he did not appear in the least shy, but very much at home, talking very well. . . . We were there for two hours with great freedom and no excess.' After dinner the company moved into the Salon de Jeu and played until about one o'clock. 'Ainsi se passa la première fois que je soupai dans les cabinets de Versailles,' concluded Croÿ. He was relieved to find that he had been able to partake of the life of the inner circle 'sans rien faire de mal' and determined to do whatever was necessary to obtain admission from time to time, resolving all the same to do so 'without too much abandon, so as not to be carried away by the torrent'.

There was also a little Salle-à-Manger d'Eté on the very top floor, level with the roof garden. On summer evenings the King and his guests would sometimes go up on to the roof and walk round behind the balustrade. 'For some time,' relates Luynes, 'he has been going up on to the roof of the Château and walking with those who have the honour of dining with him right to the end of the new wing, and from there right to the end of the Aile des Princes.' It is the most fascinating walk in the whole of Versailles. The view of the gardens and park was not the least attraction of these midnight expeditions; one can imagine the warm smell of lilac and lime trees and the still darkness of the plantations, cut here and there by the pale luminosity of water or the dim outline of a parterre. Over the courtyards they could look down into the illuminated windows of the sleeping palace, and sometimes Louis would make surprise visits to his courtiers. 'He has been several times to converse with Madame de Chalais,' continues Luynes, 'by a window which opens on to the roof, and with Madame de Tallard by the chimney.'

It is possible that this taste for rooftop communications was inspired by Chantilly. Guests were lodged here in the attics of the Grand Château, to which the chief means of access was by the windows. 'Je fus étonné d'arriver chez moi par les fenêtres,' wrote Croÿ after his first visit; 'le lendemain je fis avec admiration le tour en dehors des attiques dans les ballustrades. . . . C'est la plus belle chose que je connaisse, et la plus singulière.' Louis had stayed at Chantilly in 1722 and again in 1724, and he may have been struck by this unusual attraction. More often the evening after a supper party was spent at the tables of the Salon de Jeu, which occupied the angle of the roof at the east end of the Petite Galerie. One end of the room was rounded into a graceful semicircle, and the panelling painted an off-white with the mouldings in a tender green. After supper the King and his associates retired into this room; Louis made the coffee and served it himself to avoid the constraining effect of servants, and the company settled down to a party of comète, cavagnol or tric-trac. Everyone was permitted to sit, and the evening passed without formality until the King, with a gay 'allons, allons nous coucher', gave the signal to retire. The ladies made their reverences and departed, and the men descended to present themselves in the ordinary way for the *coucher*.

For sixteen years Louis continued to sleep in the bedroom of his great-grandfather, in spite of the impossibility of heating so lofty an apartment. The cold at Versailles could be severe, and Louis found it necessary on some occasions to pass into the Cabinet du Conseil and warm himself before going through the ceremony of the *lever*. But he did not like doing this too often, because it entailed waking his personal servants before the usual hour. 'Lorsque je me lève avant que l'on soit entré,' he told Luynes, 'j'allume mon feu moi-même . . . si je passais dans mon cabinet, il faudrait appeler; il faut laisser dormir ces pauvres gens, je les en empêche assez souvent.' There was a certain simplicity and modesty about Louis which did not exclude consideration for others, and which often makes him an amiable person to read about.

When he was ill it was his custom to have his bed made up in the Cabinet du Conseil for the warmth and convenience which it afforded, and this may have given him the idea of making a new bedroom for his personal use.

During the voyage of the Court to Compiègne in the summer of 1738 the first of the old cabinets of Louis XIV, on the north side of the Cour de Marbre, was enlarged and redecorated by the sculptor Verberckt, and equipped as the Royal Bedroom. The panelling survives today intact, but the character of the room has been somewhat lost by the disappearance of the bed, balustrade and pillars from the alcove. The latter were in the form of palm trees whose undulating branches enclosed the upper half of the recess.

Here it was Louis' practice to sleep, but first he held the *coucher* in the official bedroom and laid himself solemnly in the ancestral bed; when the company had withdrawn, he got up and went and slept in his real room until, in the morning, it was time to get back into the official bed and receive the entrées for the *lever*. Etiquette, in fact, was becoming a mere hollow shell behind which the King led, as far as possible, a private life of his own. The two bedrooms bear out Madame Campan's words: 'Séparer Louis de Bourbon du Roi de France était ce que le Monarque trouvait de plus piquant dans sa royale existence.'

THE PETITS APPARTEMENTS

The new bedroom brought Louis down, so to speak, on to the second floor of the Château, and it was here, in fact, in the suite of rooms formerly called the Cabinets du Roi, that most of his day was spent, whether attending councils, giving private audiences, dealing with correspondence or arranging the details of his hunts. Every room is filled with memories of him, and their decoration provides some of the finest examples of the style to which he gave his name. As he grew older, his interest in the Petits Cabinets declined, and in 1766 they were made over to the widowed Dauphine, Marie-Josèphe de Saxe, but from 1738 onwards the remodelling of the first-floor rooms pursued its leisurely course.

If Etienne Martin was the artist whose name is chiefly remembered in connection with the Petits Cabinets, Verberckt and Rousseau established their reputations in the creation of the Petits Appartements, as the first-floor suite came to be known. For these rooms, larger in scale and accessible to a wider public, were accorded a more princely decoration in white and gold, according to the fashion of the age.

In 1751 the former bathroom with its adjoining bedroom was cast into one to give a private dining-room for the suite. The supper parties were growing too large for the Petits Cabinets, and could no longer be held on the top floor. The new room, decorated *à la moderne* and hung with pictures of Comus, presented a simple rectilinear panelling which might well seem to be of a later date. Croÿ again leaves an account of the supper which he attended here on the 24th February 1756. There was a vast crowd hoping for admission, many of them huntsmen, but Croÿ had his application backed by Madame de Pompadour and seconded by the Princes de Tingry and de Soubise, who had the advantage of being on the spot when the selection was made. This time thirty-three names were called, and the company seated at two tables.

The *soupers de chasse* continued in the next reign, and are amusingly described by the Comte d'Hézecques, who also gives details of the furnishings of that date. The King's golden dinner service was exposed in glass cases round the room. It does not all of it appear to have been in the best taste, and contained such absurdities as a gold enamel hen, almost life-sized, sitting on a basket in which fresh eggs were placed. More attractive is his description of a chest of drawers so contrived that each drawer, on being opened, caused a little tune to be played upon an organ concealed within the body of the piece. Besides these details, Hézecques noted the effect produced by this system of selection upon the courtiers. 'A neuf heures,' he relates, 'un huissier, ouvrant la porte de l'Œil de Bœuf, proclamait le nom des élus qui se glissaient avec orgeuil dans l'appartement, tandis que les reprouvés allaient chez eux cacher leur dépit et manger tristement leur repas.'

Under Louis XV the supper parties were frequently followed by amateur theatricals, a form of entertainment for which the King's associates seem to have been more than commonly gifted. Madame de Pompadour, however, whose voice was sweet and melodious though not strong, contrived to outshine the rest. A little company was formed with its rules and regulations (it is noticeable that, whereas the gentlemen players were fined for the least unpunctuality, the ladies were given a quarter of an hour's grace) and placed under the direction of Moncriff, Lecteur to the Queen, and La Vallière. In January 1747, when a performance of *Tartuffe* was given, Luynes noted 'there were very few spectators . . . in all only fourteen persons'. Often Louis invited his family, and it is evidence of the Queen's acceptance of the *ménage à trois* that she sometimes joined the party.

Performances were given in the Petite Galerie; not the one on the second floor described in the last chapter, but that on the first floor, which had formed a part of the original cabinets of Louis XIV. This room, however, had certain inconveniences as a theatre, and in the following year Luynes describes a new portable stage, which could be put up in a matter of twenty-four hours, contrived by La Vallière in the spacious well of the Escalier des Ambassadeurs.

This staircase, much admired in the previous reign by reason of the magnificence of its marbles, the excellence of its paintings and the heroic scale of its proportions, was falling, like so many monuments of the Grand Style, into disfavour. It was practically only used for the ceremonial processions of the Saint-Esprit. It was for such spectacles that Versailles had been designed; first came the Petits Officiers, then the Grands Officiers, then the Chancellor of the Order, in rochet and violet cape, immediately followed by the novices in their short coats. Those who had already been admitted to the Order were gorgeously arrayed in silk trunk hose and stockings, their tunics crossed with the blue riband, and wearing the long robe of blue velvet embroidered with tongues of fire and doubled with ermine, upon which lay the golden collar from which hung the dove which was the emblem of the Order. Le Brun's staircase was a worthy theatre for such pageantry, but it was no longer in keeping with the spirit of the reign. It was a different sort of theatre that Madame de Pompadour interested herself in, and as early as 1748 the staircase was doomed to destruction. It would be wrong, how-ever, to connect the disappearance of this majestic piece of architecture with the whims of a pleasure-seeking mistress. La Vallière's construction could be put up without any damage to the fabric. The demolition of the staircase was part of Gabriel's project for rebuilding the whole of the entrance court.

The ordinary access to the Petits Appartements was from the Escalier de la Reine, on exactly the opposite side of the Palace. To avoid the considerable detour of using this, a small staircase, known as the Petit Escalier du Roi, was contrived on the east side of the Cour des Cerfs. Descending this, the King crossed the Salle des Gardes on the ground floor and found himself in the Cour Royale, where his coach normally awaited him.

It was just as Louis was descending the steps which led from the door to the level of the courtyard, on the 5th of January 1757, that Damiens, pushing his way suddenly through the crowd, struck him with a hunting knife just below the right ribs. In the glare of the flambeaux it was difficult to see what was happening; the King himself was not at first aware that he had been wounded. 'Duc d'Ayen!' he gasped, 'on vient de me donner un coup de poign!' At the same time the Maréchal de

Richelieu called out: 'Qu'est-ce que c'est que cet homme avec son chapeau?' Damiens, profiting from the confusion, had time to re-enter the crowd by the hole through which he had made his abrupt sortie, before the King, who had clasped his hand to his side, saw that it was covered with blood and called out: 'Je suis blessé! Qu'on arrête cet homme, et qu'on ne le tue pas!'

Louis, though not seriously injured, was convinced that the dagger was poisoned and that he would die, and the Petits Appartements became a scene of tense emotion, and were thronged by the innumerable figures of the Court, whose function, usually confined to the State Rooms, now brought them into the more restricted space of the private suite. Louis, however, did not die. His huntsman, Lasmartes, predicted right when, on examining the wound, he said: 'Ce n'est rien, Sire, dans quatre jours nous forcerons un cerf!'

Louis XV, perhaps more than any other of his family, was a mighty hunter, and under him the Chasse Royale assumed a new aspect. The heavy mounts of the previous reign were replaced by English thoroughbreds, and the speed of the pursuit was greatly increased. It was not unusual for the King to force three animals in the same day. Also, under the influence of the Marquis de Dampierre, the musical accompaniment of the chase began to assume its picturesque form. Louis, lethargic and bored by the functions of Royalty, showed himself an energetic and intelligent organizer where his favourite sport was concerned.

'Le Roi fait véritablement un travail de chien pour ses chiens,' d'Argenson noted; only the personnel of the hunt seemed to escape his attention. One day, relates Cheverny, after a more than usually exhausting pursuit, the King was about to get into his coach to return to Versailles.

'The King called Lasmartes with his harsh voice, by which he could be distinguished among a hundred thousand.

' "Lasmartes," he said, "are the hounds tired?"

' "Yes, Sire, fairly tired."

' "Are the horses tired?"

' "Yes, I think so."

' "Nevertheless," continued the King, "I will hunt the day after tomorrow."

'Lasmartes remained silent.

' "Do you hear, Lasmartes? I will hunt the day after to-morrow."

' "Yes, Sire, I have heard every word, and what I don't like is that I always get inquiries whether the horses and hounds are tired, but never the men." '

It was possible to talk to the King in this way; Luynes, whose respect for Royalty was unquestioning, admitted that 'one was often tempted to forget that he was the master'.

There is one room in Versailles which particularly recalls the passion of Louis XV for the chase, and that is the little anteroom opening on to the Cour des Cerfs, called the Antichambre des Chiens. Besides having, in its four decorated overdoors, the only survival of the original cabinets of Louis XIV, the room is remarkable for the beauty of its frieze representing a hunt. This was appropriate enough, for it was from this room that Louis would depart, by way of the Petit Escalier, to partake of his favourite pastime.

The Antichambre was also used to accommodate a number of hounds which were fed by the King and thus got to know him personally. They were lodged in little cubby-holes in the wainscoting, which have unfortunately disappeared. La Martinière describes the room as being thus equipped, and from his description it would seem to be an arrangement similar to that in the first anteroom at Amalienburg, the delightful little hunting lodge built by the French architect Cuvilliès in Bavaria. The care which Louis bestowed upon his hounds did not escape the notice of d'Argenson: 'It shows that the King has imagination and a feeling for order, method and detail when it is necessary.'

It was the general opinion at Versailles that Louis XV was almost incapable of work; indeed, he appeared to some to be wholly frivolous. 'Il était fort adroit à faire certaines petites choses futiles sur lesquelles l'attention ne s'arrête que faute de mieux,' wrote Madame Campan. In particular he had perfected the art of decapitating an egg with a single backhand stroke of the fork, and regularly performed this feat at the Grand Couvert. Nevertheless, Louis had his serious side, and not only where hunting, botany and building were concerned.

It was frequently noticed that the Prince de Conti, armed with a portfolio stuffed with papers, and sometimes accompanied by a secretary, ascended the Petit Escalier and entered the Arrière-Cabinet unannounced. Here he remained for a long time closeted with the King. D'Argenson and Luynes were both equally mystified: 'Everybody is asking what is the subject of this work; it seems that nobody knows.'

The secret negotiations concerned Louis' foreign policy, mostly the affairs relative to Poland, to whose throne Conti aspired. They have no relevance here, but it is significant to notice the interest and the ignorance of the Court. Perhaps the same curiosity is revealed in Croÿ's account of the supper party quoted above. After the meal the guests assembled in the last room of the first-floor suite, the Cabinet Intime; the door was open, and Croÿ could see into the Arrière-Cabinet. The room seemed to be filled with books and instruments, and there were some lovely flowers. 'I would have loved to have rummaged about in all that for a few hours,' concluded the Duke; doubtless he was not the only one who would have appreciated an intimate acquaintance with this secret apartment.

The normal scene of Louis' official work, however, was the Cabinet du Conseil, which dates in its present form from 1755, when it was enlarged at the expense of the adjacent Cabinet des Perruques, and completely redecorated. The previous room had been furnished with a rich profusion of red velvet; five armchairs and ten folding stools covered in brocade 'à grand dessin', and for the King a couch upholstered in crimson velvet. The council table was covered in green velvet braided with gold. The room, lit only by two windows from the Cour de Marbre, was somewhat obscure and to give it more light it was accorded a decoration of mirrors something like that of the adjoining gallery.

The accounts for the year 1755 reveal the progress of the work of redecoration, and also the proportion of work done by the sculptors Verberckt and Rousseau. The former received only 1,000 livres, the latter 21,000. The ensemble of the decorations, then, can safely be attributed to Rousseau.

It is interesting to enter the Cabinet du Conseil from the Galerie and to compare the two styles. In the paintings of the gallery ceiling Le Brun tells of the achievements of Louis le Grand; the frontiers expanded, the arts encouraged, order restored to the finances. We pass into the Cabinet; the symbolism here is reduced to three small gilded panels, on each of which is carved a group of boys, playing with scales, mirrors and dogs—to represent Justice, Sincerity and Faithfulness, the qualities demanded by the King of his ministers. Others are depicted with such warlike or marine instruments as are best calculated to suggest the purpose for which the councils might be held. The general effect of the room is rich, and the detail charming, but it is hardly a worthy treatment of so lofty a theme. Indeed, the whole change from the Grand Style to that of Louis XV may be seen in the process which demoted the deities of Le Brun to the playing boys of Rousseau.

Although the King's bedroom was, in the ceremonial sense, the centre of the Palace, the Cabinet du Conseil was, in fact, the central room in the King's life. It is interesting to note that in Gabriel's project for rebuilding this part of the Palace, the Council Chamber was to be the architectural centre of the layout.

Here the King worked with his ministers and held his Conseil d'Etat, Conseil des Dépêches, Conseil des Finances; here foreign Princes and Ambassadors were granted audience and new Cardinals received their hats; here the engagements of members of the Royal Family were negotiated, and the marriage contracts signed. Here both Madame de Pompadour and Madame du Barry were first presented to the Court, and it was on his way out of this room into the Galerie that the Cardinal de Rohan was arrested after the *dénouement* of the affair of the diamond necklace. In his daily life Louis used this room for the ceremony of the *débotter* after hunting, and for giving the orders for the day after the *lever*; from here he regulated his family and his household, and wrote much of his correspondence.

When the busy day was done, and the ministers had taken their leave and departed, and the King and his associates had withdrawn to the intimacy of the Petits Cabinets; when the tall shutters had been closed, exposing momentarily a further profusion of gilded ornament to the flattering light of the candles which now began to twinkle in every window of the great Château, and a comfortable fire glowed in the marble fireplace, the real occupant of the Cabinet du Conseil assumed his vacant possession.

Enthroned on a cushion of crimson damask, placed carefully in the centre of the hearth, Louis' cat, a beautiful white Angora 'd'une grosseur prodigieuse, très doux et très familier', accepted without question the regal state to which it appeared to have been born. One of Dufort de Cheverny's most informal anecdotes of life at Versailles tells of an unworthy violence done to the dignity of this stately creature.

One day when Louis had retired to the cabinets, Cheverny and Champcenezt, valet de chambre at that time, poured spirits of wine on the animal's jaws, and were amusing themselves with its antics when, in the middle of a loud peal of laughter, the King came into the room 'comme une bombe'. Everyone immediately sprang to his place, assuming an innocent and grave demeanour as best he could; the King demanded the reason for their hilarity. 'Nothing, Sire,' lied Champcenezt, 'it was a story we were telling.' At this moment the cat resumed its mad gyrations, to the discomfiture of all present; they had no alternative but to make a clean breast of the affair; Louis' face darkened. 'Messieurs,' he said, 'je vous laisse ici, mais si vous voulez vous amuser, j'entends que ce n'est pas au dépens de mon chat.'

In reading the memoirs, particularly of Cheverny and Hézecques, one is sometimes struck with the likeness of Versailles to some vast and expensive school; Louis at least showed himself an indulgent and understanding house-master.

Strictly speaking, the Cabinet du Conseil did not form a part of the Petits Appartements. These were all on the north side of the Cour de Marbre. It appears that under Louis XV they were not accessible to the public as they had been in the previous reign, but under Louis XVI they were again opened. Nevertheless they retained throughout their history the aspect of show-rooms in which the King's best pictures and *objets d'art* were exhibited. Hézecques speaks of the 'multitude of figures in porcelain' copied from statues of Louis XIV's generals which were to be seen here, and of the rich furnishings; 'the rarest pieces were accumulated there, besides a whole host of other curiosities'. Today the Petits Appartements present the finest interior decorations of the whole Palace, but the rooms are largely empty, and it requires an effort of imagination to furnish them again with all their exquisite appointments.

Next to the Bedroom is the Cabinet de la Pendule, which received its present form in 1760. It is important to note, however, that much of the decoration dates from the former Cabinet Ovale, which was constructed in 1738 at the same time as the Bedroom. Verberckt, in making the extra panels for the new rectangular room, copied his former style exactly. This was the result, often perplexing to art historians, of the economy observed in Marigny's department. Whenever possible he ordered the re-use of old material. The extracts from his correspondence with Lécuyer about new work, printed in the next chapter, will show why he had a preference for the old. The plan of the Cabinet de la Pendule has Marigny's notes in the margin: 'How much will it cost if we use all the old, and what there is in the workshop?'

The most notable piece of furniture in this room was the astronomic clock, from which it took its name. The clock, designed by Passement, made by Dauthiau, and ornamented by Caffieri, showed not only the hour, but the day, the month, the year and phase of the moon. It was surmounted by a crystal globe in which the planets performed their revolutions according to the system of Copernicus. Louis XVI, also a lover of things mechanical, used to stay up in his room until midnight on New Year's Eve to see the complete change recorded on his clock.

Beyond the Cabinet de la Pendule was the Cabinet Intime, occupying the corner overlooking the Cour de Marbre and the Cour Royale. It appears to have been Louis' favourite room; in 1741 Luynes describes him as being 'almost always in the cabinet which is beyond the Cabinet Ovale'. Its former decoration, still intact at the time that Luynes wrote, was of pilasters with richly carved wainscoting and hangings of crimson damask braided with gold, forming a background to some fine paintings —Raphael's Holy Family, two Holbeins, one of Erasmus and one of Thomas Cromwell holding a little cross, among others. Here also stood the magnificent desk built for Louis by Riesner, which can be seen today at the Louvre, and of which a copy, made for Sir Richard Wallace, is in the Wallace Collection.

In 1760 this room was redecorated by Verberckt and Rousseau, the latter only doing two of the overdoors. The panelling is of exceptional merit and represents one of the most perfect examples of the style in the Palace. The carved medallions are enlivened by playing boys, whose appearance here is so charming and carefree that it is possible to forgive their intrusion into the Council Chamber.

The room served many different purposes, as may be inferred from the diversity of names accorded to it by the memorialists of the Court. It served as a dining-room, gaming-room or study; Cheverny refers to it as the 'Cabinet Intérieur' or 'Cabinet Intime'. Perhaps the latter is the best name, for the room is forever associated with the most moving scene recorded of Louis' private life, the funeral of Madame de Pompadour.

It was fixed that the cortège was to leave Versailles at six in the evening; etiquette forbade the presence of the King. Outside was raging a fearful tempest, and the rain lashed incessantly against the windows of the Palace; alone with his valet de chambre, Champlost, Louis had shut himself up in the Cabinet Intime, and was standing on the balcony which looks out over the Place d'Armes and the Avenue de Paris. 'Il garde un silence religieux,' wrote Cheverny, 'voit le convoi enfiler l'avenue, et, malgré le mauvais temps et l'injure de l'air auxquels il paraissait insensible, il suit des yeux jusqu'à ce qu'il perde de vue tout l'enterrement.' He turned and re-entered the room; two large tears stood on his eyelids and ran down either cheek. 'Voilà les seuls devoirs que j'ai pu lui rendre,' was all that he could say.

MADAME DE POMPADOUR

For twenty years Madame de Pompadour had occupied without question the most important position at Versailles. It has not been possible to confine reference to her to a special chapter; her influence was everywhere, but in Versailles itself there is very little today that can help to recapture the atmosphere of her presence.

It is possible to visit her old apartment, a suite of rooms occupying the top storey over the Grand Appartement, but the whole is deserted and dirty, the walls have been coated with a displeasing grey distemper, and only a carved mirror frame or the gracefully turned proscenium of an alcove remain to evoke the memory of their former decoration. One can still mount up, by a dark, cramped staircase, into the little box which served as a room for her maid, Madame du Hausset, and from which she overheard and recorded her mistress's conversations with the King, but it is not possible even to reconstruct from the accounts of the period what delicate shades of *vernis Martin* may have adorned the walls, and one can only guess at the elegant profusion of beautiful furniture, pictures, porcelains and other *objets d'art* with which the rooms were filled. Only the view from the windows retains its original appearance, giving an enfilade right along the Aile du Nord and a close-up of the eight statues over the colonnade marking the Vestibule to the Chapel, or an aerial view of the Parterre du Nord, with its bold geometrical shapes outlined in flowers, and the neat rows of conical yew trees overhung by the dense mass of the plantations.

The apartments had originally belonged to the Duchesse de Châteauroux, and combined the attractions of their prospect with the convenience of their communication with the Petits Cabinets. So attractive did she find her rooms, that she often went for days on end without ever quitting them.

They had been made more easily accessible by the installation, in 1743, of a lift, the famous 'fauteuil volant' or 'machine des Petits Appartements' devised by the ingenious Sieur Arnoult. This was not, as a matter of fact, the first lift to be installed at Versailles. Dangeau, writing in 1691, mentions that the Prince de Condé had a lift installed at Chantilly, another in the Palais Bourbon and a third in his apartment at Versailles. Sébastien Locatelli mentions an even earlier instance in the Palace at Turin in 1664 which was hoisted and lowered by means of a green silk cord. It was worked by a counterpoise, and only required 'two fingers' to manipulate it. 'This machine,' he said, 'is covered with green velvet, bordered with gold and fringed. Oh, what a pleasing invention!'

The Bourbons took an almost childish delight in mechanical things—a taste which was typical of their age. Another example was the 'table volante' at Choisy-le-Roi, which was copied, or rather improved upon, at the Petit Trianon. Louis was also interested in science, and had his laboratory in the room directly over the Salle d'Apollon; that is to say, beyond the suite accorded to Madame de Châteauroux, through which he had to pass, conveniently enough, to get to his work. There had always been laboratories in the Petits Cabinets, notably on the very top floor, level with the Salle-à-Manger d'Eté and the roof garden. Louis also interested himself in the art of distillation, as the names of these apartments suggest—'laboratoire où le Roy distille' and 'Cabinet de distillation du Roy'.

In 1745, soon after the death of Madame de Châteauroux, the

THE CHAPEL

'MADAME', THE 2ND DUCHESSE D'ORLÉANS
BY H. RIGAUD

MADAME DE MAINTENON
BY J. B. VAN LOO

FÉNELON.   BY VIVIEN

THE DUCHESSE DE BOURGOGNE
DETAIL OF PAINTING BY P. GOBERT

LOUIS XV.   BY DROUAIS   MARIE-LECZINSKA.   PASTEL BY Q. LA TOUR

CABINET DE TRAVAIL DE LOUIS XV WITH THE BUREAU BY RIESNER

MADAME DE POMPADOUR.   BY BOUCHER

THE SALLE-À-MANGER DES RETOURS DE CHASSE

CABINET DE MADAME ADELAÏDE

ROOFSCAPE OF VERSAILLES FROM ABOVE THE QUEEN'S APARTMENT.
THE DORMER WINDOWS TO THE LEFT ARE THOSE OF DU BARRY'S ROOMS

THE MAIN AXIS OF THE GARDENS FROM THE ROOF

TWO OF LOUIS XIV'S DÉCORS DESTROYED BY LOUIS XV
(*above*)   THE APPARTEMENT DES BAINS

(*below*)   THE ESCALIER DES AMBASSADEURS
            MODEL BY M. ARQUINET

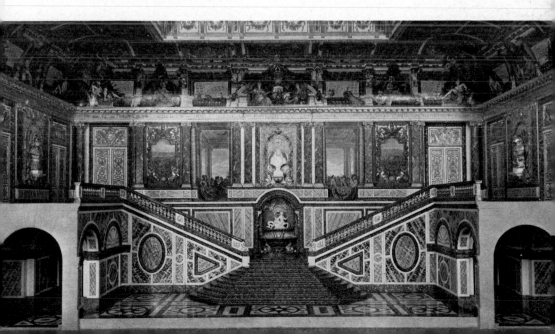

THE PAVILLON FRANÇAIS, INTERIOR

Court began to be aware of a new direction taken by the roving eye of the King. There had been many *bals masqués* that season, and the King had taken good care to preserve his incognito. 'All the masked balls,' noted Luynes, 'have given rise to new rumours of the King's love affairs, and principally of a Madame d'Etioles, who is young and pretty.' She was a great deal more than this. She was a person of great wit and taste, and alive with enthusiasm. She was not burdened with any of the usual inhibitions of the Court, and this was what made her most attractive to the King. Above all, she was intelligent, in an essentially feminine sort of way. She very soon discovered that Louis' greatest interest was in architecture—an interest which they had in common—and she exploited it systematically. The building operations during the period of her supremacy would fill a book; they also came near to emptying the treasury. They included the Châteaux of La Muette and Saint-Hubert, the Petit Château at Choisy, hunting boxes at Le Butard, Saclay and Fausse Repose, besides the Pavillon Français and the Petit Trianon. There were also considerable alterations to most of the royal palaces. In 1752 Choisy-le-Roi doubled its size, during the next ten years Compiègne was almost wholly reconstructed, and a vast new wing was thrown out along the south side of the Cour d'Honneur at Fontainebleau.

For Madame de Pompadour herself, the Château of Crécy-Couvé was bought in 1746, and in the next two years 700,000 livres were spent on its decoration. In 1748 La Celle St. Cloud and the Hermitage at Versailles were added; the following year saw the building of another Hermitage at Fontainebleau, and 1754 of one at Compiègne. Even with these the Marquise did not feel herself adequately lodged. Crécy-Couvé was too remote, La Celle St. Cloud too small. In 1748 was started a more spacious residence near Meudon, the Château de Bellevue. 'C'est un endroit délicieux pour la vue,' she wrote in 1751 to Madame de Lutzelbourg; 'the house, although very big, is manageable and charming, without any sort of magnificence.' It was sold to the King in 1757, when Madame de Pompadour installed herself

F

instead at Champs. Four years before her death, she had acquired Ménars in Touraine, which was destined for her retirement.

In 1752, eight years after her installation at Versailles, Madame de Pompadour, ceasing to be the mistress of the King, was granted precedence as a Duchess and descended to the ground floor of the Palace. This was an honour hitherto reserved for the Princes of the Blood. 'I will not be able to occupy it until after Fontainebleau,' she wrote to Madame de Lutzelbourg, 'because it will all have to be put in order.' It was, of course, inconceivable that she could occupy the rooms as they were.

The new suite was on the former site of Louis XIV's Appartement des Bains, and during the reconstructions an octagonal marble cistern was discovered, which Madame de Pompadour installed as a basin in her new garden at the Hermitage, near the Bassin de Neptune. In Louis XIV's reign the Appartement des Bains had formed an important and imposing suite of rooms, occupying the north-west corner of the ground floor of the Palace. 'Cet appartement,' wrote Piganiol de la Force, 'efface tout ce qu'on nous raconte de la magnificence des bains des anciens.' Luynes makes an interesting comment on the cistern— it was 'for bathing several persons in at once, as was then the custom'. One is reminded of Pepys' disgust at the practice of bathing—'methinks it cannot be clean to go so many bodies together in the same water'. In Louis XV's days the standard of hygiene was much improved. His own bathrooms always were equipped with two baths, one for soaping and one for rinsing.

The work to be undertaken on the new apartment was considerable, involving nothing less than the complete reconstruction of this part of the Palace, but there were only six months available for its completion. 'On attaquera tout à la fois,' wrote Le Normant de Tournehem, Madame de Pompadour's uncle, who had received the charge of Directeur Général des Bâtiments. For some time the work went forward at full speed, being carried on by night as well as by day. But as the time for the return of the Court from Fontainebleau approached, the situation became more and more critical, and to make matters worse, there was difficulty over the finances. 'I cannot conceal from you,' wrote Lécuyer to Le Normant, 'that they are absolutely without funds.' Verberckt was having to pay out wages at the rate of three hundred livres a day, while 37,812 livres were still owing to him from 1747. Guesnon, charged with supplying panelling for the rooms, was little better off. Of fifty thousand livres owing to him, only four were paid, and he was obliged to borrow at interest to keep his workshop open. On top of everything, Madame de Pompadour announced her intention of returning a week earlier than she was expected from Fontainebleau. 'Il faut faire l'impossible pour que cela soit prêt,' was all that her uncle could order.

Although she undoubtedly fanned the flame, Madame de Pompadour cannot take the entire blame for Louis' expenditure on houses. He had a natural inclination that way. In 1737 Luynes had noted 'the King continues to show a taste for building'. In the following year he gives some interesting figures about the finances. 'The ordinary upkeep of the Royal Houses, combined with the annual expense of the King for his Household, amounts to about twenty-five million livres a year.' The Army List for a year in time of peace he estimates at just twice that sum, and the royal revenues he puts at somewhere round two hundred and thirty million gross, but of course about half this went to the Fermes Générales.

The difficulty was that there was no Colbert to provide for the King's extravagance. Versailles had, under proper control, contributed to the greatness of Louis XIV; his vast expenditure had at least created a priceless collection incomparably housed, and had established the supremacy of France in the world of art; under Louis XV the money only too often served for the distraction of his own boredom or the satisfaction of the whim of one of his concubines. In the fullness of time Versailles was to play a not unimportant rôle in the downfall of the Monarchy. To the already overburdened vessel of the nation's finances, the Comptes des Bâtiments now imposed an all but intolerable strain:

in addition to the incessant demands of the King and his mistresses upon the Exchequer, the steady task of upkeep and redecoration of the private suites of courtiers as well as general repairs of the most urgent nature were claiming the attention of the unfortunate Marquis de Marigny and his Contrôleur, Lécuyer.

The upkeep of the apartments of the Grands Seigneurs was at Louis' expense, and he was fairly liberal in according repairs and redecorations. D'Argenson was exaggerating, however, when he wrote 'nobody is refused who asks for some adjustment of their apartments at Versailles, mirrors, panelling, fireplaces, etc.'. The accounts show that, while such grants were being made almost daily, they were confined to more or less necessary repairs. The Duc and Duchesse de Chaulnes obtained a grant of only 811 livres, 'His Majesty having considered it expedient only to accord the purely necessary repairs'; the Comtesse de Maulde received only 600 for 'alterations and adjustments', it being understood that any further expense would be borne by the Countess herself. These examples are drawn at random from the accounts.

As to general repairs, the correspondence between Lécuyer and Marigny is full of references to the pressing need for restoration on the one hand, and the utter inadequacy of funds on the other. All work having been held up by the war, the situation, by 1757, was becoming desperate. 'Lécuyer thinks he ought to renew his remonstrances,' reported Marigny to the King, 'on the imminent ruin of this house.' The Orangerie was in the most immediate danger, as well as the marble surrounds to most of the basins in the garden. The cupola over the Chapel was in a dangerous condition, and was imposing a strain on the timbers of the roof by reason of its immense weight. The Aile du Gouvernement (today the Aile Gabriel) was sadly in need of repair, 'all the timber being entirely rotten'. Faced with the difficulty of restoring this part of the Palace, Louis decided in favour of reshaping the entire entrance front in a style more in keeping with the garden fronts. This idea had been in the background for a long time, and had received the approval of Voltaire at any rate on aesthetic grounds. Blondel even went so far as to describe the architecture of the Cour de Marbre as 'semi-Gothic'. The 'Projet Gabriel', however, although it embraced the whole entrance side and more, only resulted in the rebuilding of the Aile du Gouvernement, for the royal finances were by no means equal to tackling so vast an enterprise. On the 21st of June 1773 Gabriel wrote to inform Marigny of a revolt among the workmen employed on the new wing, whose pay was six weeks in arrears. It was not until after the Revolution that the opposite side of the courtyard received symmetrical treatment.

In 1769, when work was in hand on the Salle du Spectacle and the rooms for the Dauphin were being redecorated, the situation was, if possible, worse. 'All the contractors for these parts,' wrote Marigny to the King, 'are in the deepest discouragement.' Two hundred out of some two hundred and fifty workmen had been withdrawn from the Salle du Spectacle; the agent supplying the panelling for the Dauphin's rooms refused even to begin work before he received payment. It was not without cause that Marigny complained to the Abbé Terray of the 'misère des Bâtiments du Roi', and wrote in despair to the Comtesse de Noailles, Dame du Palais to the Dauphine: 'For the last eighteen months I have hardly had the disposition of a single penny for the relief of a throng of wretches who are dying of hunger, and to whom, at the moment, wages are due for a year and a quarter.'

Although he was sometimes badly informed on the subject, and prone to exaggeration, d'Argenson had not been far wrong when he predicted 'buildings are bringing desolation to the country and will be the ruin of it'.

THE PETIT TRIANON AND MADAME DU BARRY

The embarrassment and despair of the administration contrasts strangely with the sound workmanship and carefree elegance of the buildings; that contractors should be prepared to undertake such work without immediate hope of payment suggests an attitude towards Royalty and privilege which is almost beyond the reach of our imagination today. Voltaire gives a hint of it when he writes: 'The majority of Parisians, born during the reign of Louis XIV, regarded a King as a sort of divinity.' With a fine indifference to material difficulties, which they regarded as the concern of underlings, Louis and Madame de Pompadour went on to create one of the architectural masterpieces of all time—the Petit Trianon.

It was not until the death of Madame de Châteauroux that Louis really 'discovered' Trianon. Tired of his restless wanderings from one royal house to another, he found, as it were, on his own doorstep the accommodation which suited him most. Here his own apartment communicated directly with that of Madame de Pompadour. She was not slow to exploit his new interest in the place.

In 1749 the Duc de Luynes noted a new hobby of the King and his mistress: 'The King and Madame de Pompadour have been amusing themselves by collecting pigeons and poultry.' They were to be found everywhere, at Fontainebleau, at Compiègne, on the rooftops of Versailles; now they were to have a home of their own, situated to the north-east of the Jardin du Roi at Trianon. By November Luynes was able to report that the 'New Ménagerie is almost finished'. The 'New Ménagerie' is a somewhat grandiose name for what was, in fact, a farmyard. The hen-coops and pigeon-houses were supplemented by the addition of cow-houses and sheep-pens, and surrounded by a little garden, the architectural focus of which was a little pavilion in the shape of an Irish cross, which was one of Gabriel's most charming inventions.

A rotunda with a frieze of farmyard scenes supported by eight Corinthian columns opens by four tall windows on to the gardens, and between the windows four small doors lead each into a tiny room which forms, on the outside, one of the limbs of the cross. The rich relief and sculptural effects of the skyline

are typical of the period; there is nothing to suggest the new
style which Gabriel was to create, twelve years later, within a
hundred yards of this pavilion. One of the little rooms, the
boudoir, was accorded a brilliant white and gold decoration,
in keeping with the central rotunda, but the other three were
kept plain, being destined for kitchens and service.

On the opposite side from the farm buildings was a little
summer-house called the Salon Frais. Its lines were continued
on either side by a trellis arcade, and it boasted some fine carving
from the chisel of Verberckt; two of his panels are to be seen
today in the Petit Trianon on the north wall of the Anteroom,
for the Salon Frais fell into disrepair during the latter half of
the century and was dismantled. It had served for occasional
refreshment on summer evenings, while the larger pavilion
could be used for supper parties, games and music. Perhaps the
most typical picture, however, is that given by the Duc de
Croÿ: 'The King was very fond of plans and buildings. He took
me into his pretty pavilion in the gardens of Trianon, and
observed that that was the style in which I ought to build. . . .
He worked on his drawings for a long time himself with
M. Gabriel.' It may have been in this way that the Petit Trianon
itself came to be designed.

Besides architecture, however, Louis had another hobby,
which was botany, which he began to cultivate about this time,
and which was to develop into a sincere and sustained interest.

Real enthusiasm is nearly always contagious, and Louis had
the good fortune to meet, through the introduction of his friend
the Duc d'Ayen, a real enthusiast for horticulture, one Claude
Richard. Described by Linnaeus as 'the ablest gardener in
Europe', Richard had sacrificed everything to become the pro-
prietor of a botanical garden at St. Germain in which he had
formerly been employed, and had made it one of the wonders
of his age. To this garden Louis made several visits, and he
never failed to come back with his coach filled with its produce
to offer to the Queen and the ladies on his return.

In 1750 Richard received the title of Jardinier-Fleuriste to the

King, and with it sole charge of the new garden at Trianon; but he imposed one condition—he was to receive his orders only from the King in person. The cultivation of strawberries was Louis' first interest, a taste which is to be found reflected in the decoration of the Dining-room of the Petit Trianon. All the different existing sorts in Europe were assembled, and before long Louis was able to offer the produce of Richard's researches to his Court. 'One had to eat them in his presence,' noted de la Gorse, 'praise them and find them delicious if one desired to pay court to him effectively.'

From the cultivation of strawberries, Louis passed to a more scientific inquiry into diseases which affected corn, and from that to a classification of plants. This latter research brought a new personality into the gardens of Trianon, Bernard Jussieu, some-times known as the 'Newton of botany'. Jussieu was a person calculated to please his sovereign, being utterly indifferent to any consideration of interest which might accrue from his royal connection. Not the least attraction of the rapidly expanding garden was the simple, straightforward manner in which Louis could converse with his gardeners, who felt, in their turn, that they could treat him as a man and not as a King.

The constant presence of the King in this part of the garden was a sufficient pretext for the construction of a little house on the site; the planning of such an enterprise was always a favourite amusement, and Louis, Madame de Pompadour and Gabriel together produced a design which, by the simplicity of its conception, the purity of its line and the delicacy of its ornament, is at once the first and finest example of the classical revival, usually labelled Louis-Seize. Without and within the treatment is entirely new, and it is difficult to believe that the Petit Trianon was planned by the same trio that designed the Pavillon Français.

Simplicity is the keynote of the Petit Trianon, but simplicity is nearly always deceptive. It is not to be achieved without a fault-less taste backed by a lifetime of experience, and it presupposes a perfect command of technique. Gabriel, in designing the façades, appreciated nicely the variety of texture possible in the fine, honey-coloured stone. A rusticated lower storey, fluted pilasters and a delicately chiselled entablature set off the contrasting smoothness of the undecorated wall surfaces, and the same effect is achieved in the well of the staircase, which is treated as exterior architecture, almost as if it had been intended for a little court-yard open to the sky. A subtle use has been made of the drop in the ground level to obtain a pleasing variety by presenting two façades of two stories and two of three. The north and west fronts have the basements masked by a terrace and *perron* whereby the rooms are approachable directly from the gardens; the more imposing height of the entrance front is balanced by the low outbuildings which enclose the court. The original orientation being towards the Pavillon Français, the west front was accorded the richest treatment, the columns being in full relief and making an impressive play of light and shade in the evening sun; only towards the east, where the windows over-looked the rows and rows of frames of the botanical garden, has Gabriel omitted all decoration; it is no fault of his that this less interesting façade should now command one of the major perspectives, towards the Temple d'Amour.

The entrance, upon the south side, gave direct access to the stone staircase, where the cold, severe architecture is relieved only by the graceful sweep of the wrought-iron banister. To the left was the inevitable Salle des Gardes, and to the right, the Billiard Room; otherwise the whole of the ground floor was devoted to offices.

The first floor was arranged to provide a tiny reception suite, anteroom and two dining-rooms overlooking the Jardin Français, and a Grand Salon de Compagnie facing towards the north. A narrow passage, lit by the windows which help to give the staircase well the appearance of an open courtyard, connects these rooms with the private suite, the Cabinet du Roi (later the Queen's bedroom) and a botanical library. These were very small, low rooms, and provided with an *entresol* with the King's bedroom, cabinet and anteroom above. The rest of the bedrooms were on the top floor.

The interior decoration reflected the original purpose of the building, a centre of botanical research, and is almost wholly floral. The beautiful lilies in their circular wreaths which decorate the panels of the Grand Salon, the swags and drops over the arched pier-glasses, and bunches of roses in the Cabinet du Roi are carved with an accuracy and a precision which had to pass the scrutiny of a botanist King, and in the festoons of fruit which appropriately adorn the panels and marbles of the Dining-room, the strawberry is given a prominent place. Unfortunately the original painting, a delicate water-green, with the reliefs picked out in white edged with gold, has disappeared under a dirty whitewash.

Besides serving as the centre of Louis' horticultural interests, the Petit Trianon was designed for privacy. Even the presence of servants placed an unpleasing restraint upon the intimate circle of the King, and in the Dining-room the tables were constructed after the manner of the already celebrated *table volante* of the Petit Château at Choisy-le-Roi, only they were worked by a system of counterweights 'far superior to that of Choisy for the simplicity of the mechanism'. The tables were accompanied by four side-tables known as *servantes* or *postillons*, and when the next course was ready to be served, they descended through the floor into the kitchens and were replaced by a metal rose. The tables once loaded, the petals of the rose opened out and slid into the flooring, and the tables reappeared in their former positions. They were the invention of Loriot, and were exhibited in Paris in 1769 at the Louvre.

For the paintings which were to form the overdoors to the reception suite, Cochin was ordered by Marigny to select subjects and to designate artists suitable to execute them. 'It is in this *maison de plaisance*,' he wrote to Marigny, 'that the King keeps his most beautiful flowers. I have therefore tried to get subjects for the overdoors into which flowers can be worked.'

Trianon was ready to be used in August 1770. On his return from a visit to Louveciennes Louis slept there for the first time; but Madame de Pompadour was not with him; she had only lived to see the shell of the masonry completed, and it was her successor, du Barry, who was to share with Louis the delights of his new residence.

Madame du Barry, the last of Louis' mistresses, was the pretext for the last major redecoration of the Petits Cabinets, which was carried out during the voyage to Compiègne in 1770. These rooms have recently been restored to the state in which Madame du Barry used them. They are most interesting as evidence for the eighteenth-century taste for bright colouring.

The Petite Galerie was divided into two, forming a bedroom to the west—immediately over the King's bedroom—and a Grand Cabinet to the east. The original Dining-room reassumed its former function, and the room next to it became the Ante-room, after which was the Bathroom.

The décor of *vernis Martin* was replaced by gilding in the Bed-room and Grand Cabinet, and in the Library. But the inner rooms overlooking the Cour des Cerfs have been restored in their original colours and varnish. The Cabinet de la Chaise—a term which began to be replaced about this time by 'Lieu à l'anglaise' or 'chaise anglaise'—was a real water-closet, with a marble pan and *bidet*. It was painted yellow with light blue mouldings. The Bathroom was in the same colours, and equipped with a porce-lain stove to warm it, and, as usual, two baths. The Anteroom was in lilac on a yellow ground, a contrast which is particularly effective for the fine, rather Chinese motif of the frieze. Most charming of all is the Dining-room, in emerald-green on a white ground. The walls are treated in an extremely simple rectilinear design, which gives a sense of elegance to an uncomfortably low apartment. By contrast, the two window embrasures retain the lace-like carving of the earlier décor.

Du Barry's library, a room with rounded corners and con-taining a recessed alcove like a bedroom, has a white and gold design, recently freed from a thick grey distemper. The little rosette on the ceiling of the alcove is perhaps the most exquisite piece of carving in the whole of Versailles. It is still a charming room, but the imagination must fill the shelves with the books, beautifully bound in red morocco and stamped with du Barry's arms, now to be seen in the Town Library at Versailles. The furniture also must be imagined. The rooms were filled with almost miniature furniture of mahogany and satinwood, rosewood and ebony, decorated with bronzes and ormolu and plaques of porcelain. These were sometimes floral and decorative and sometimes in the form of miniature paintings copied from Watteau and Van Loo. Of particular interest was the 'piano anglais' in the Salon built by Clicot. It had adjustments to represent flute and flageolet, lute and cymbal, and was made of rosewood and ormolu with blue and white mosaics.

Like all royal mistresses, Madame du Barry had both admirers and denigrators among the Court. Anyone who was a member of the circle of the young Dauphine, Marie-Antoinette, detested her.

Palewski, in an interesting study of the royal hunt, records an unexpected meeting between the King and his mistress and the virtuous Duc de Penthièvre. The *rendez-vous de chasse* was at Saint Hubert, but the provisions had gone astray, and the royal party were overtaken by nightfall before they had eaten. 'Suppose we go to the Château of our cousin, the Duc de Penthièvre?' suggested the King. Du Barry demurred for a while, for Penthièvre was a man of the most upright character, and would not willingly have received her under his roof, but Louis insisted, and the party proceeded to Rambouillet. They were met by the Duke in a cook's apron, saucepan in hand; he was in the middle of preparing soup and a ragoût for the poor of his estate. His charitable habits secured him from violence under the Revolution, but his daughter-in-law, the Princesse de Lamballe, was too closely associated with the Queen's circle to escape.

Du Barry, though she too ended on the scaffold, acquired some of the Duc de Penthièvre's virtues. 'Madame du Barry,' wrote the Comte d'Hézecques, 'was much loved at Louveciennes, and did a lot of good there.' Hézecques is borne out by the witness of du Barry's accusers. Item fourteen of her indictment bears the note: 'She has always been protected in the most scandalous manner by the administrators of her district, and still is.'

There is little record of the life led at Trianon by Louis and du Barry; the privacy for which the house had been so carefully designed appears to have been well respected. In 1772 Louis ordered the building of a little Chapel, for, although he had given up the practices of Confession and Communion, he always continued the habit of attending Mass. It was part of the etiquette of the Court that he should, but at Trianon etiquette was never very strictly observed. The building of the Chapel may have sprung from deeper desires.

The Chapel cost 68,500 livres. The Petit Trianon itself only cost 861,456 livres, and the buildings of the Ménagerie, Pavillon Français and the expenses for the botanical garden added in, the round figure comes to about one million four hundred thousand livres over a period of twenty-five years.

It was here, in the spring of 1774, that Louis began to feel the symptoms of the smallpox which was to bring him to his grave. He did not want to leave his little house, but his physician, La Martinière, insisted that he should be moved, while it was possible, to Versailles; he was wrapped in a cloak, thrown hurriedly over his nightshirt, and bundled into a coach to be driven back, shivering with fever, to the great Palace. It was not seemly that a King of France should die at Trianon.

THE QUEEN. MARIE-LECZINSKA

The brilliance of Pompadour and du Barry, together with the scandals and intrigues of their followers and their enemies, have combined to distract attention from the fact that from 1725, for almost the first time since the Court was established here, Versailles had a Queen. Although she enjoyed no influence at all, and ambitious courtiers and courtesans could afford to ignore her altogether, she was respected by all, and placed, as by common consent, beyond the range of that mud-slinging which was as common in the corridors of the Palace as in the gutters of the town. Quiet, unobtrusive and stately, Marie-Leczinska is only saved from dullness for those who can appreciate the radiation of her religious devotion and charity, to which sterling qualities she added a lively sense of humour. 'Nobody in the world,' wrote the President Hénault, 'has a better sense of the ridiculous.' But she was more than a virtuous woman; she was a Queen. 'This same Princess,' continues Hénault, 'so good, so simple, so sweet and so affable, carries herself on State occasions with a dignity which commands respect.' In her private life, lived in the little cabinets behind the Queen's apartment, she was modest and unassuming; passing into the State rooms, 'elle redevient la Reine, et conserve dans la Cour cette idée de grandeur telle que l'on nous représente celle de Louis-Quatorze'. It was only in her part of the Palace that the true traditions of the French monarchy were upheld.

One of the few really nice people who have ever lived in the royal apartments of Versailles, Marie was the only, much cherished daughter of Stanislas Leczinski, sometime King of Poland. The flood tide of victory which attended the early career of Charles XII of Sweden had raised Stanislas to a throne, but the receding waters had left him high and dry, with the rank and outlook of a monarch, but the prestige and financial resources of an exile. At the Hôtel Weber, a modest private residence at Wissembourg, he kept his shadow Court, entertained occasionally by his more prosperous neighbours, the Cardinal de Rohan and the Maréchal du Bourg, and living on an irregularly-paid pension from the King of France, and an ever-decreasing hope of regaining his throne.

As a King, Stanislas was remarkably unsuccessful; to compensate, he was the best of fathers, and his home in exile was lit up by the happy relations which existed between the ex-King and his daughter. She was brought up by him on solid religious foundations based on practical charity, and she was encouraged in a taste for reading, music and painting. Her natural qualities were early tempered with the endurance of adversity and disappointment, but her endowment was not such as to give any very bright matrimonial hopes.

One morning, however, her father had burst into her room at

Wissembourg, his face radiant and excited. 'Oh! my daughter!' he had exclaimed, 'let us fall on our knees and thank God!' 'What, Father,' answered Marie, 'are you to be recalled to the throne?' 'Heaven has granted us more than that,' replied her father. 'You are to be Queen of France!'

It was indeed true; party and political considerations, which were more involved in the rivalry between the House of Condé and the House of Orléans than with the welfare of the State, had brought about this sudden change in the affairs of the exiled family. It may well be that the gratitude with which she accepted this unlooked-for crown caused Marie to carry it with such dignity and such distinction during the forty-three years of her life at Versailles.

It was not destined to be a joyful existence. Too ready to find pleasure in what she knew to be her duty, Marie had fallen in love with her handsome young husband; 'la Reine aime le Roi à la fureur,' wrote Stanislas, who was the only man to know Marie at all intimately. But she was not made to inspire similar affections in Louis' heart. In contrast with the easy familiarity and confidence which existed between herself and her father, her relations with the King soon degenerated into indifference on his part and timidity on hers. Too nervous to say anything of importance to him, she took to communicating with her husband by letter. Louis was inevitably the centre of Court intrigue, and it was the business of the little cabals of Versailles to provide him with a mistress who would serve their interests and bring them into power; in the end they were successful, but Louis was not finally to relapse without a 'day of dupes'.

In 1744 Louis went on campaign, leaving the Queen in possession of Versailles, her written application to follow him having been turned down on the ground of economy. On the 9th of August he was taken seriously ill at Metz; on the evening of the 14th, Marie, who was in almost hourly communication with d'Argenson, learnt that the situation was becoming critical. Not only was the King's life almost despaired of, but the salvation of his soul was in peril, for Madame de Châteauroux had followed him to Metz and his confessor refused to grant him absolution while she remained in the town. Louis, still under the influence of his mistress and her astute uncle Richelieu, remained impenitent. That night Marie knelt alone at the balustrade of the Royal Chapel at Versailles; so far her urgent entreaties to be allowed to join her husband had been ignored, but this time her prayers were answered. The next day she learnt that the King had given in to his confessor; Madame de Châteauroux had been sent away; it was agreed that the Queen should advance as far as Lunéville. With all possible haste her equipage took the road along which she had made her first triumphal progress to Fontainebleau, and once more she received the acclamations of the people, to whom every stage of her journey seemed symbolic of the much-hoped-for reconciliation between herself and the King. At each relay courtiers were despatched to Argenson; 'au nom de Dieu obtenez-moi la consolation de le voir'.

Arrived in Metz, she was summoned to the presence of the King, whom all supposed to be dying. The reconciliation was complete and sincere. To Marie he had confessed: 'Je vous ai donné, Madame, bien des chagrins que vous ne méritez pas; je vous conjure de me les pardonner.' But he had gone further than that; he had sent for Madame de Villars to find out whether he had really received the forgiveness of his wife, and once, seeing her friend and confidante, the Duchesse de Luynes, in his room, he had bidden her approach his bed, and repeated his apologies for his treatment of her mistress.

The next day, to the surprise of all and the unspeakable joy of Marie, there was a considerable improvement in the King's health. The doctors declared that he was out of danger. Popular rejoicings knew no bounds, and it was on this happy occasion that Louis received the name which he was not destined to retain, 'Louis le Bien-Aimé'. The public knew little of the power of those evil influences to which he was subject, and of which the Duc de Richelieu was the most assiduous agent. It is possible also that the authorities of the Church went a little too far in rubbing in their moral.

On the 7th of October Marie set out from Lunéville to return to Versailles, while the King left in the opposite direction to rejoin his troops. Once more the road was lined with enthusiastic crowds, and the air was filled with frantic cheers for the King and Queen; the people rushed from all parts to see the great berline with its gilt scrolls and proud blazons making its cumbersome way along the roads; they little imagined that it contained the most unhappy woman in France. The same day that she had left Lunéville she had written the most heart-rending letter to Argenson. 'Pleasures, even the most innocent, were not made for me; I no longer look to find them in the world.' The King had relapsed into indifference as he had recovered in health, and she knew now that her cause was lost forever. 'I melt as I write; I do not know what I am saying to you; I only know that I am speaking from my heart, and my heart is in agony.' Her last and dearest hope, to accompany Louis to Strasbourg and share with him the joyous reminiscence of her first tremendous welcome there, had been turned down with the curt, humiliating phrase, 'ce n'est pas la peine'.

From that time on, Marie settled into a melancholy existence, resigned to the infidelity of her husband, though not ceasing to love him. Curiously enough, the coming of Madame de Pompadour improved their relationship; perhaps Louis' happiness, Pompadour's tact and Marie's resignation combined to effect this. 'The King has carried his attentiveness to the Queen to the point of noticing an old inkstand which the Queen has been using for some time,' observed Luynes in December 1746, 'and he sent her another very beautiful one.' It was not inkstands, not even little attentions that Marie longed for, but the thought was a kindly one. It very possibly came from Madame de Pompadour; she had a sharp eye for such details, and a genuine desire to please the Queen.

If Marie was denied the pleasures of living in happy union with her husband, she at least had her friends and her children, though the latter belonged more to the State than to herself. The over-doors in the Queen's bedroom were a constant reminder of this fact. The subject chosen for Troy's painting was 'la Gloire s'emparant des Enfants de France'; they were *Enfants de France* before they were her children, and Marie, obedient to the etiquette of the Court, was to be deprived of most of her family.

The Dauphin, brought up like his father by the Duchesse de Ventadour until the age of seven, was handed over to male tutelage on the 15th of January 1736. The Comte de Châtillon, governor, and the Évêque de Mirepoix, preceptor, and their assistants were present in the Cabinet du Conseil. 'Sir,' said the King to Châtillon, 'into your hands I commit that which I hold most dear.' Then, turning to the Dauphin, he added: 'You will obey Monsieur de Châtillon as you would obey myself, and never forget the care taken by Madame de Ventadour.' At this the Duchesse, unable to restrain her tears, made as if to retire, and the little Dauphin ran after her, but was intercepted by Châtillon. He and Fleury accompanied the young Prince back to his own apartment on the ground floor, where they found the blinds down, a miniature stage erected, and the curtains ready to go up on a marionette show. The official winds were at least tempered to the royal lamb. 'The Dauphin behaved himself on this first day,' noted Luynes, 'with all the courage and all the reasonableness you could imagine.'

The other children who survived were all girls, and these, with the exception of Madame Adelaïde, were sent off to the Abbey of Fontevrault in Touraine to be educated in less expensive surroundings than Versailles. Adelaïde was the most colourful personality of the family. At an early age she had conceived the extravagant project of exterminating the English by the simple expedient of inviting all the men to sleep with her—an honour she was convinced they could none of them refuse—and strangling them one by one. She was also artistic and an accomplished musician. Happily the Music Room in her beautiful suite of apartments at Versailles remains intact. Verberckt's rich decoration with the two lovely drops of musical instruments and other motifs recalls the evening in 1763 when Mozart came and played to the Princess. She was herself no mean performer on the violin, but it is perhaps more in keeping with her tomboy character that she could sing bass nearly as loudly as her brother. The royal children frequently visited their parents, and Luynes noted that they were very shy in the presence of their father, but very much at their ease with the Queen.

Among Marie's friends the most notable were the Duc and Duchesse de Luynes. A grandson of Dangeau and friend of Saint-Simon, Luynes is the memorialist *par excellence* of the reign, and if he lacks the literary ability of his more illustrious fore-runner, he compensates by the scrupulous accuracy of his chronicle. Described by the President Hénault as 'the most estimable man in the world', he was one of the few at Versailles who were above those considerations of interest which under-mined the morals of most of the Court. His second wife became the Queen's dearest friend, and as often as the King supped in his Petits Cabinets, Marie went down and supped with the Luynes in their apartment.

Her greatest joy was to go and visit them at their country house, over the hills behind the Heights of Satory, and a little too far away for Marie's liking. It is not at Versailles that the memory of Marie-Leczinska is most easily evoked, but here at Dampierre, a plain but pleasing château which displays its courts and gardens snugly beneath the gloriously wooded hills of the Vallée de Chevreuse and conceals behind its sober façades a rich and charming decoration.

Today Dampierre appears neglected; there are no flowers on the parterre and grass has invaded the paths and courts and over-hangs the moat. The little pavilion on the island, where Marie loved to go and play at cavagnole, is suffering a humid disinte-gration and casts a somewhat mournful reflection in the waters of the canal. Here perhaps Marie and her friends could relax and forget their positions, but at the Château etiquette was not for-gotten. On one occasion the Dauphin had to refuse to offer the napkin to his mother so that the honour might pass to their host. Nevertheless, despite the formality of outward appearances, the friendship was deep and sincere. When the Duchess got smallpox, the Queen could not sufficiently express her anxiety, nor the Luynes their appreciation of it. 'Have done with all expressions of gratitude,' wrote Marie, 'it is quite simple to feel deep concern for those one loves, and quite natural to love those who are lovable.'

Another member of their set was the Cardinal de Luynes, a man of genuine, if simple piety and of an endearing absence of mind. His sermons were directed with unerring aim at the vices peculiar to the Court—no other vices being known to him. The standard of behaviour in the Chapel left much to be desired. The Marquise de la Tour du Pin tells how the ladies who followed the Queen to Mass were met at the doorway of the Salon d'Hercule by their *laquais* armed with huge red velvet sacks fringed with gold. As soon as the Royal Family had entered, they dived into the galleries to left and right of the Royal closet and scrambled for the seats nearest to the King. Their *laquais* then arranged the velvet sacks about their knees and feet and tucked their trains in beneath the pews. By the time they had opened their Missals the Celebrant had usually reached the Gospel.

It was this sort of conduct which moved the Cardinal de Luynes to eloquence. 'How is it that luxury follows you to the very steps of the altar? How is it that these cushions and sacks of velvet covered with fringes and tassels precede your arrival at the Temple of the Lord?' Unfortunately, having composed this tirade for the Court, he read it, in a moment of total abstraction, to an entirely bucolic congregation. 'Quittez, quittez ces habitudes somptueuses!' he urged the bewildered peasants, who were as innocent of the irreverence imputed to them as they were ignorant of the articles which he described. The story got round, Madame Campan informs us, and so amused the Court that titled ladies used to get up early to witness these strange miscarriages of zeal.

*

In the Queen's apartment at Versailles—the suite of rooms overlooking the Orangerie and corresponding to the Grand Appartement on the north side of the Palace—the memory of Marie-Leczinska is somewhat eclipsed by that of her successor, Marie-Antoinette. Nevertheless, the decoration of the Queen's bedroom dates almost entirely from 1736. It was thus the first big room to be altered under Louis XV, the King's apartment remaining untouched until two years later. Being the first venture in the new style, it raised the inevitable protest from the die-hards. 'What could be more august,' asked Saint-Yves, 'than the King's State Room at Versailles? Seeing it, one could almost fancy oneself in the midst of Ancient Rome. . . . Those who are charged with the decoration of the Queen's would have done better to have copied exactly what has just been destroyed. Our moderns, prodigal in ornament, are but indifferent decorators.' Such protests come from most receding generations. In fact, however, the royal workshops had shown that they could match the Grand Style in the construction of the Salon d'Hercule; now they established their independence of the Louis-Quatorze style in the creation of the Queen's bedroom, which was to make the name of Verberckt. It is today one of the most beautiful parts of the Palace, and thanks to the work of the late Conservateur, M. Mauricheau Beaupré, is hung with a facsimile of the last *meuble d'été* made for it at Lyons under Marie-Antoinette.

Tall mirrors, placed between narrow panels which take to some extent the place of pilasters in the decorative scheme, answer each other from opposite sides of the room, between the doors and the alcove. The uprights of these mirror frames are in the form of palm trees, whose foliage curls in at the top to hold an oval picture, surmounted by a winged crown. The whole alcove was hung with tapestry and enclosed behind a balustrade. The space behind this was known as the 'ruelle' (literally, a 'little street') and was used for private receptions. 'Les jours que le Roi soupe dans ses cabinets,' wrote Luynes, 'la Reine s'établit dans la ruelle de son lit avec M. le Dauphin, Mme la Dauphine, et la conversation est extrêmement gaie.'

Luynes also describes the furnishings in the summer of 1743; there were two armchairs and a few stools, and the tapestries all in a white Touraine silk enriched with painting and embroidery, the design centring on a large vase 'which makes a very beautiful effect'. The bed, he noted, was not the traditional four-poster, but the newer style called *à la duchesse*. This description is of a *meuble d'été*. Each *meuble* would only be used for a few years and then replaced, the old set being the perquisite of the *dame d'honneur*.

The oval frames which formed the upper part of the mirrors contained portraits of the King and Queen, and a picture of Stanislas was similarly placed between the windows.

Here Marie lived most of her life as Queen, wife and mother. Here, more than anywhere else in the Palace, the old etiquette of the Court was punctiliously observed. A single example will show how careful Marie was to accord to everyone their little distinctions. There was always likely to be trouble about the seating arrangements, and Princesses had to make sure that the right number of the right sort of chairs and stools was available for their receptions. Duchesses had what was called the 'droit du tabouret', that is to say, the right to sit, on certain occasions, on a sort of stool, known as a tabouret, in the royal presence. M. de Châtillon, governor to the Dauphin, was made a duke in 1736, and his wife was presented to the Queen. Marie was at this moment on her feet and about to go to the comedy, but she tactfully sat for a few moments to enable the new duchess to enjoy her privilege. These little details, which may seem fatuous enough today, had to be observed minutely, for great offence might be caused by their neglect.

Even in childbirth—a public event, which took place in the State Bedroom—Marie-Leczinska did not forget the petty rights of her ladies. During the birth of Madame Louise she called the Duchesse de Rochechouart to her side. 'I think you would find it embarrassing,' she said, 'to hold my hand; I know, all the same, that you have a right to.' She had, in fact, given her hand to the King. When she heard that it was yet another girl she said to him, somewhat pathetically: 'Je voudrais souffrir encore autant et vous donner un Duc d'Anjou.' Their second son, the Duc d'Anjou, had died in infancy.

The great rooms of the State Apartments were the scene of these exacting public appearances at which Marie never failed to uphold the dignity and the great traditions of the Royal Family, so frequently neglected by her husband. She did, however, lead her own private life apart from the gaze of the curious, but it is difficult to reconstruct today, for the décor has been replaced.

Behind her State Rooms she had constructed her own series of Petits Cabinets—by all accounts equal to those of the King for charm and delicacy of ornament. Here it was her custom to retire for two hours every day. Her time was given up to music, painting and reading poetry, or devoted to her little hand press on which she printed prayers and maxims for distribution among her friends. There were three little oratories and a bathroom behind the Grand Cabinet, where only the Duchesse de Luynes dared to disturb her mistress.

The decoration of most of these rooms was of wood carved by Verberckt and painted in natural colouring and finished with *vernis Martin*. Sometimes the panels themselves were painted with Arcadian landscapes framed in trellis arches. The effect can still be seen in the tiny boudoir which separates the cabinets from the Antichambre du Roi (the State Dining-room), but these panels, which have suffered from the application and removal of a coat of whitewash, were originally in the little rooms of the Dauphine on the ground floor. There was a Petite Galerie which was painted in *vernis Martin* in 1740; there was a Grand Cabinet Vert with a niche embellished by the carver Roumier; there was the tiny Cabinet des Poètes used as a library for the Queen's favourite form of reading, and a bathroom decorated with porcelain tiles.

The largest room, known usually as the Grand Cabinet Intérieur, was rich in floral carving, painted in natural colouring and enclosed by a coved ceiling painted with trellis-work perspectives and dotted with birds and flowers.

Some of the painting of the Queen's cabinets came from her

own hand. According to Madame Campan, there was a professional artist to help the Queen, who not only mixed the colours and dipped the brush, but told his royal pupil exactly where to apply each touch; 'plus haut, plus bas, Madame; à droite, à gauche', and then, when she had gone, he repainted the whole thing. Madame Campan was certainly never present on these occasions, and the value of her evidence may be doubted. When the panels came into the possession of the Comte de Noailles (whose wife, as *dame d'honneur*, had a right to the furniture of her mistress on her death) he complained to Marigny that the cabinet had 'no other virtue than that it was painted by the Queen'. He did not wish to be put to the expense of adorning his house with indifferently painted Chinamen being converted to Christianity by indifferently painted Jesuits. For the pious Marie-Leczinska, while following the fashion for chinoiserie, had gratified her religious taste by depicting the conversion of China. On the whole it seems likely that the panels were mostly by her own hand.

The taste for little apartments was as typical of the eighteenth century as theatrical grandeur had been of the seventeenth. Nevertheless it would be wrong to suppose that the large-scale receptions and fêtes dear to Louis XIV were altogether eschewed by his successor. In fact there were many brilliant fêtes during the reign of Louis XV, but none so magnificent in scale as those given at the wedding of his grandson to the Archduchess of Austria, Marie-Antoinette, which was also the occasion of the last important addition to Versailles, the Salle de Spectacle or Opéra.

The project was an old one; as early as 1748 Gabriel had brought out his designs comprising the elegant new façade, whose simple rectilinear proportions and stately attached portico are reflected in the waters of the reservoir. But it had to wait many years before it was completed. The custom had been, when any really large-scale entertainment was given, to rig up a ballroom for temporary use. For the marriage of the Dauphin (Louis XV's son) an apartment of unequalled splendour had been constructed in the Grande Écurie; and now in 1767 the marriages of the Dauphin's children were looming on the horizon and disquieting the royal exchequer. To improvise four successive entertainment rooms and to have nothing to show at the end for the expense was monstrous, and Papillon de la Ferté, Intendant des Menus Plaisirs, addressed a memorandum to the King urging the completion of the theatre of the reservoirs. The undertaking, costly though it would be, might almost be regarded as an economy, since it would put an end to the constant expense of temporary structures.

In March 1768 the King ordered a model from Arnoult, and promised to see about providing funds. This was certain to be the greatest difficulty, and Gabriel had advised the selection of Parisian workshops, the contractors of Versailles being at that time 'weighed down by the misery and debts which they had incurred in the service of the King'. As the result, the job was given to Pajou, whose workshop behind the Louvre became at once a hive of activity, functioning every day, Sundays and Saints' days included, and during the nights as well. To obtain these working conditions he was obliged to pay the least of his employees twelve livres a day. He was a rash man to advance his own money on a royal building; in vain he wrote to Marigny begging to be put 'in a position to satisfy his artists, become his creditors'; the correspondence on these accounts continued right up to the Revolution.

It was not, however, an extravagantly conceived design, for the architecture is almost entirely of wood painted to resemble a marble called *Sérancolin*. The colour scheme is one of the most successful at Versailles. The marbling is achieved in a warm salmon pink against a background of dark grey-green known as *verd-verd*, both of an infinitely subtle variety of tone and lavishly enriched with gilding. Contrasting with this is the cold, bright cobalt of the silken hangings and the more sombre blue of the patterned velvet upholstery.

The auditorium, in the shape of a truncated ellipse, is encircled by a colonnade which breaks into a graceful apse above the

Royal box. Each bay of the colonnade is backed by a mirror, and each mirror reflects, and thus completes, a half chandelier which hangs against its surface. The rest of the house is lit by fourteen great chandeliers suspended on blue silk cords. They are each of them five foot high, and each contains ninety-six crystal pendants. In the apse is an even larger one, eight foot in height and with more than three hundred pendants. Its erection over the Royal box was no easy matter. It took eight men to lift it, and a special scaffolding had to be constructed for its hoisting. These chandeliers, Croÿ noted, were left illuminated throughout the performance, thus 'lighting up from below a superb ceiling, they produced the most admirable effect'.

Painted by du Rameau, and representing 'Apollo preparing crowns for those illustrious in the arts', the ceiling reflects the dominant theme of pink and blue which is continued in the smaller ceilings above each of the bays of the colonnade. By Gabriel's express instructions, du Rameau was charged 'to decide on all the tones and mixtures of colour that need to be observed in order to create an all-embracing harmony'.

The proscenium, crowned by an impressive heraldic achievement, is squarely framed in a colossal order, enclosing the first two tiers of boxes on either side. The stage was fully equipped with all the elaborate machinery required for theatrical productions of that date, but it could also be made to join up with the auditorium and thereby form a single unit. The scene could be set to reflect the amphitheatre, the floor of the pit jacked up level with the stage, and the whole opera house transformed into one enormous ballroom.

'I saw this room,' writes the anonymous author of a *Description of Versailles in 1837*, 'lit with a hundred thousand candles; the mirrors, the chandeliers, the beautiful paintings and the gilding produced a wonderful effect.' The phrase 'a hundred thousand candles' is an exaggeration, but there were certainly more than three thousand candles in use for a full illumination. The effect is beautifully captured in the watercolours of Moreau le Jeune, of which one, representing the auditorium, is here reproduced.

On the 16th of May 1770 the Dauphin and Marie-Antoinette were married in the Chapel at Versailles, and at 9.30 that night the *Festin Royal* inaugurated the celebrations. In the Salle de Spectacle the floor had been laid down, and a table with covers for twenty-two was set in the middle, and surrounded by a balustrade. A hundred and eighty musicians were accommodated on the stage, and the Court, in the scintillating glory of full dress, occupied the boxes around. The Duc de Croÿ, as usual, went into raptures over the new room: 'For a whole hour I did not tire of admiring it from all sides; seeing it, one was tempted not to regret the two and a half million which it cost, and the more so because it did away with the necessity of building anew on each occasion.'

One of the most striking features of Croÿ's account is the stress which he lays on the dresses and the illuminations. Without these scenic effects, Versailles may well appear a dull and lifeless backcloth. At the wedding the Chapel had been filled to its utmost capacity 'so that one saw only a solid mass of gorgeous dresses'; the lovely costumes, the beautiful white stone of the Chapel, and the sunlight streaming in through the tall windows moved the Duke to rapture. 'It was one of the finest things one could possibly see; above all, the sun brought out its full brilliance.'

In the evening the Galerie des Glaces formed the setting to the gaming, and again the same impressions struck him. 'Everything had been lit up, and the dresses showed with a greater lustre by their light. It is astonishing how it shows them up, and brings out the gold and silver, just as daylight tones them down.' This must always be remembered about gilding; it is meant to be seen by candlelight.

On the second day of the celebrations the Salle was restored to its shape as an opera house, and the Court assembled for a performance of Lully's *Perseus*. Two hundred guards assisted to work the machinery and act as walkers on, and Heinel and Guimard danced in the company. *Perseus*, unfortunately, was a complete failure. Although it had been revised by Jolivau and was produced 'with all its pomp and all its magnificence', it was an essentially sad opera and inappropriate to the occasion, as could be seen by the 'general expression of boredom on every face'.

To compensate for the dullness of *Perseus*, the firework display and illumination of the park, two days later, were perhaps the most magnificent ever seen at Versailles. A wonderful impression is given in Moreau's sketch; starting from the extremity of the canal, where the *Temple du Soleil* fixed the view, the lights run round the entire perimeter, while the ships, also brilliantly illuminated, provide an element of movement to the scene. In the foreground the area surrounding the Bassin d'Apollon is lined with arcades and obelisks of light and appears to be a solid mass of humanity. There were some two hundred thousand admitted that night to see this never-to-be-forgotten spectacle. Years after the Revolution, when the English traveller Nattes visited Versailles his guide still remembered the wonderful impression of that evening: 'This immense park, illuminated through all its extent, was far more brilliant than when lighted by the sun in all his splendour. The waters in their varied falls reflected in a thousand ways the effects of the illumination; some, falling from a great height, seemed to shed torrents of light, while others, elevating their streams high in the air, appeared to descend in a shower of fire.' It was impossible for him to do justice to the scene; there were so many things which 'at the same moment dazzled the eye and astonished the mind'; in vain did he string together the details he had noticed, 'all that you read of Fairyland would give but an imperfect idea of the reality'.

The fireworks, too, had surpassed anything of the kind that had ever been seen. The Court saw the display from the windows of the Galerie; the curtains were drawn back and the magnificent spectacle of the illuminated parterres revealed. To those without, the lighting up of the gallery windows—a lovely sight at any time—meant that the climax of the evening was approaching, and one can imagine with what pleasurable expectation they watched for the King to give the signal for the fireworks to start by hurling a flaming lance from the central window. Nor was the display unworthy to terminate the week's rejoicings. 'It was concluded,' wrote Nattes, 'by a *Giranda* of twenty thousand rockets, which by its prodigious detonation and the immense blaze of light, produced the effect of a terrific eruption of a volcano.'

LOUIS XVI AND MARIE-ANTOINETTE

On the 10th of May 1774 the young couple who were the centre of all these rejoicings became King and Queen of France. 'M. le Dauphin et moi,' wrote Marie-Antoinette to her mother, 'sommes épouvantés de régner si jeunes.' Their succession, however, was the joy of all France, and in particular of the younger generation at the Court, who had, for the most part, little respect for the stately tradition which was their heritage, 'happy to scoff at the outmoded ways, the feudal pride and grave etiquette of our fathers,' wrote Ségur, 'anything that was long established seemed to us tiresome and ridiculous.' The works of Lully were brought up to date, those of Molière condemned as 'in exceedingly bad taste'; the gardens of Le Nôtre were found insupportable, and the Palace of Le Vau and Mansart ripe for reconstruction. The numerous projects for rebuilding Versailles—far more revolutionary than Gabriel's—showed as little appreciation of its architecture as understanding of the financial condition of the country; the pursuit of pleasure was as devoid of responsibility as of sense of values. 'As for us, the gilded youth of France,' wrote the Comte de Ségur, 'we walked upon a carpet of flowers which covered an abyss.'

It was a theme to which he constantly returned. 'Jamais réveil plus terrible ne fut précédé par un sommeil plus doux et par des songes plus séduisants.'

Most of the memoirs of this reign were written retrospectively. Looking back on the last days of the *ancien régime* across years darkened by bloodshed and exile, it seemed to many that it had been a golden age; their writings have evidently acquired some of the gilt of nostalgic reminiscencces, but they are more interesting to read than the chronicles of disputed etiquette of the previous reigns. Thanks to their more human approach, the picture seems to come into sharper focus for the final scene. A landscape is never so vivid as in the last hours before the sunset fades.

*

Despite the new atmosphere, life at Versailles seems to have continued very much the same. Chateaubriand, after his presentation in 1787, made the significant remark, 'Louis XIV était toujours là.' In the State Bedroom, now hung with purple and gold brocade and lit with porcelain candelabra, the ceremony of the *coucher* continued in all its splendour. 'At eleven o'clock,' wrote the Comte d'Hézecques, 'the service and the Court arrived. Everything was prepared; a magnificent gown of gold brocade and lace; on an armchair of red morocco, the nightdress of white silk embroidered at Lyons; the shirt, wrapped in a piece of taffeta; on the balustrade, a folded cushion of cloth of gold on which were laid the nightcap and the handkerchiefs. By their side the slippers, of the same stuff as the gown, were placed near the Pages of the Bedroom, who leant against the balustrade.' A loaf, two bottles of wine and some iced water, known as the 'en-cas', were placed in readiness. Elderly courtiers, such as the Prince de Soubise and the Duc de Penthièvre, continued to make their low obeisance before the royal bed, even in the absence of the King. So greatly was this holy of holies revered that the customary precedence in going out of a room was reversed, it being the greater honour to remain a moment longer in the royal presence.

The King was still addressed, and then only by his intimate friends, in the third person; 'le Roi a-t-il fait une chasse heureuse?' 'le Roi n'est-il plus enrhumé?' He continued to eat in public at the Grand Couvert 'with a good humour which it did one good to see'. It was still the height of honour to hold the candle to him at the *coucher*. Men of the highest esteem and character, such as the Maréchal de Broglie, were seen to colour with disappointment and indignation if they were denied this distinction, 'so incomprehensible is the heart of man, which includes such petty foibles alongside of the highest qualities'. Versailles, as an institution, had been largely responsible for this degradation of the nobility.

The little sartorial distinctions which had intrigued the Court in its earliest days continued to enjoy their vogue. Those invited to Trianon wore a red coat embroidered with gold; for Compiègne the uniform was green; for Choisy, blue. It was more distinguished to be asked to hunt a stag than a roebuck, and the braiding of the uniform showed what sort of animal one was entitled to pursue. A *débutant* was only allowed to follow the first run of the day.

Among the crowds which jostled in the anterooms and thronged the passages of Versailles were many characters who formed an odd contrast with the finery of the courtiers. Such a man was Capitaine Laroche, concierge of the Ménagerie; vulgarly bespangled with jewels and gold braid, he made his punctual attendance at the *coucher* almost insupportable by reason of his extremely unhygienic habits; 'jamais sanglier dans son bouge ne laissa échapper d'odeurs aussi fétides'. In vain did the pages try to discourage his presence by chucking his wig up on to the top of the bed; he had come forearmed with a new one in his pocket.

Another grizzly character who rubbed shoulders with the élite was the doorkeeper of the Royal Anteroom. 'This fat Swiss,' relates d'Hézecques, 'vegetated behind an enormous stove in the Œil de Bœuf, where he ate and digested his food under the noses of Dukes and Princes. At night he unrolled his little bed in the Grande Galerie, and could claim to be the most sumptuously lodged man in France.'

But if the stately ceremonial of Louis XIV continued together with a certain amount of the dirt which had always accompanied it, the habits of privacy of his successor survived as well. Louis XVI also liked to sup in the comparative intimacy of the

Petits Appartements, and it appears that he did himself uncommonly well. 'It must be admitted,' wrote Séguret, 'that it would be difficult to carry the art of gastronomy to greater lengths.' He also liked to walk upon the rooftops of the Palace and watch arrivals in the courtyard below; he also had scientific and mechanical interests, and established a forge in the Petits Cabinets; here he amused himself by learning the trade of a locksmith. According to Hézecques his work showed little evidence of real ability or long apprenticeship in this art, but it was not unknown for the King to be found on his knees before one of the doors of the Palace, picking the lock.

The King, in fact, was one of the contrasting elements in his Court. Awkward and clumsy in his manner, shifting uneasily from one foot to the other during a conversation, and usually at a loss for anything to say, he moved with his heavy lumbering gait 'like a peasant waddling behind his plough' amid the elegance of his Court. Like all his predecessors on the throne, Louis was a great huntsman and an excellent shot. Between his accession and the end of 1787 he had shot 189,251 birds including swallows, and had killed 1,274 stags. In his journal he hardly mentions any other preoccupations. It is strange to read his entry for the 14th of July 1789; he had not hunted that day and he put down the single word 'rien'.

Louis was not attuned to his times. He never understood the Revolution. He never understood his Court. While they were going into ecstasies over Beaumarchais he remained faithful to Molière, but his real taste was for tragedy, and he knew most of Racine by heart. He was interested in history and geography and was a great reader. It is not inappropriate, then, that his first alteration to Versailles was to build himself a large and elegant library on the site of one of Madame Adelaïde's former rooms.

It is an impressive testimony to the versatility of the artists that the Library—the noblest room in the Louis-Seize style at Versailles—should have been designed by Gabriel and executed by Antoine Rousseau, who were two of the greatest exponents of

THE PETIT TRIANON, ENTRANCE FRONT

THE PETIT TRIANON, GARDEN FRONT

THE BASSIN D'APOLLON AND CANAL ILLUMINATED FOR THE WEDDING OF LOUIS XVI AND
MARIE-ANTOINETTE

LOUIS XVI.   BUST BY HOUDON   MARIE-ANTOINETTE.   BUST BY LE COMTE

THE BIBLIOTHÈQUE DE LOUIS XVI

MARIE-ANTOINETTE.   BY MME VIGÉE LE BRUN
THE PORTRAIT WHICH CAUSED A SCANDAL IN 1783

THE REPLANTATION OF THE GARDENS, 1775
BY HUBERT ROBERT

THE BELVÉDÈRE

ILLUMINATION OF THE TEMPLE D'AMOUR. ENGRAVED BY NÉE AFTER THE WATER COLOUR BY THE CHEVALIER DE L'ESPINASSE

ILLUMINATION OF THE GROTTO AND BELVÉDÈRE.   BY CHÂTELET

THE BOSQUETS DE TRIANON

the previous style. It was the last work either of them was to do for Versailles.

Rousseau's ornament is restrained and exceedingly subtle. The rounded corners of the room are relieved with drops representing the great diversity of subject-matter in the Library shelves— globe, telescope, Roman sword, shepherd's hat, books, which vary from the *Henriade* to the works of Bossuet, and the masks of Comedy and Tragedy, all joined together by a network of flowers and ribbons. Other floral drops, of the most delicate design and the most exquisite workmanship, mark the divisions between the bookshelves, while the centre of each case is surmounted by a gilt bas-relief, on the one side Apollo leaning on his lyre, and on the other France receiving homage from the arts. The greatness of France in the world of art and letters was a fitting subject for the symbolism of Versailles, and Louis peopled his Library with Sèvres statuettes of the great authors of his country—La Fontaine, La Bruyère, Racine, Boileau. Here, surrounded by the images of a glorious past, Louis loved to sit, at a little desk drawn up into the window recess so that he could look out on the people who came and went about their business in the courtyards of his Palace. Behind him, the vast mahogany table, made of a single piece of wood, was littered with books and papers. It was his favourite room, and it is still one of the few rooms in the Palace which have that 'lived-in' look which distinguishes a house from a museum.

On the other side of the Château, in the old State Rooms of Marie-Leczinska, lived the new Queen and her ladies, their towering head-dresses and unwieldy trains imposing upon them a stately deportment and an odd, distinctive gait by which a lady of the Court could always be identified. They never raised the foot off the ground, and appeared thus to glide rather than walk, and they managed their gorgeous costumes with an impressive ability. 'It was a great art,' wrote Madame de la Tour du Pin, 'to be able to walk in this vast apartment without catching the train of the lady who preceded you. You had to avoid ever raising the foot, but to let it slide along the parquet flooring—

always highly polished—until you had crossed the Salon d'Hercule.' Those who were to be presented at Court took special lessons in this, and the standard was extremely high. 'Les dames de la Cour avaient en tout cela,' remarked d'Hézeques, 'une adresse admirable.'

It was among the ladies, then as always 'wondrous fond of place', that etiquette had found its stronghold. 'I will content myself with remarking,' wrote d'Hézecques, 'that the ladies have always been more difficult over etiquette than the men.' Nevertheless it was to be a woman who helped to undermine the structure of the French monarchy by attacking this most conspicuous of its bulwarks. The old etiquette had not been invented to no purpose. It was the necessary complement to a Monarchy which was based on a presupposition of the inequality of man. 'Strip the Prince of the glory with which he is surrounded,' observed d'Hézecques, 'and he will be no more in the eyes of the populous than an ordinary man.' Perhaps the most penetrating observation on the subject comes from the Comte de Ségur. 'The French,' he wrote, 'in spite of the light-heartedness with which they are reproached, or perhaps even because of this light-heartedness, soon cease to respect the authority of those who govern them once they see them without the garb of gravity'.

One of the objects of the old ceremonial had been to present the Royal Family to their subjects, who had free access to Versailles, in as imposing a light as possible. Anyone who was 'cleanly dressed' could watch the Queen dining on certain days of the week. 'This sight,' says Madame Campan, 'was the delight of provincials.' Up at Versailles for the day, they were able, if they were quick, to see the Queen served with the entrée, and then rush off in time to see *Mesdames* at dessert. The people enjoyed the pomp and pageantry of the Court, always provided that there was not a shortage of bread. Although economically the country was ripe for revolution, the Royal Family still had a great deal of prestige to lose. It is odd to read in a publication entitled 'la Maison du Roi' of 1789 of 'this attachment which borders on fanaticism (*enthousiasme*) which the Frenchman has for his King, of the effect of which all those who did not witness the return of Louis XV after his illness at Metz can only form a very imperfect idea'.

Marie-Antoinette, although opposed by nature and upbringing to solemnity and representation, was by no means devoid of natural majesty, and she stood out in clear relief against the already brilliant background of the ladies of the Court, 'as a great oak in a forest dominates the trees around it'. She was also endowed with considerable personal charm. D'Hézecques tells of one of her minor conquests, a certain M. Castelnau, Deputy of Bordeaux, who was so overcome by her charm that he spent the whole of his life at Versailles never missing an opportunity of seeing his Queen. 'Tout son bonheur consistait à voir la Reine, et sa vie se passait dans la Galerie de Versailles.' A single instance would prove nothing; the world has always its eccentrics, and few pretty women have not their silent and unseen admirers. But the accounts of Marie-Antoinette's charm are too numerous to be discredited; the only pity is that she reserved them for so small a circle; wisely bestowed, her favours might have been a useful stay to the tottering fabric of the *ancien régime*. As it was, she alienated both the public and the Court by neglecting her duties towards them and concentrating on living the sort of life she wanted to live with the friends of her choice.

Young, irresponsible, but knowing her own mind and determined to get her own way, Marie-Antoinette was not at this stage able either to return the ponderous affection of her husband nor to maintain the tradition of her predecessor in upholding the etiquette of the Court. Her initiation was perhaps unfortunate; she was placed under the tutelage of her *dame d'atours*, Harpagon, Comtesse de Noailles. This lady had much the same effect upon the Queen as an inflexible and puritanical governess might have upon a spirited child; instead of instilling her excellent principles, she provoked reaction. 'She had no outward attraction,' wrote Madame Campan, 'her deportment was stiff, her look severe; she knew her etiquette backwards.' The stately, but seemingly pointless ceremonial of the Court was not enhanced in the

Queen's eyes through being associated with this old Gruffanuff—
Madame l'Etiquette, as she called her.

Madame Campan relates a typical example of the Countess'
insistence on *minutiae*. 'One day the Queen was receiving someone or other—I think they were newly presented—and I was
near the bed with the ladies-in-waiting. Everything was in order,
or so, at least, I supposed. Suddenly I noticed the eyes of Madame
de Noailles fixed upon mine. She made a little sign with her head.
Her eyebrows were raised, lowered, and raised again. Then she
began to make little gestures with her hand. I had no doubt from
this dumb show that something was not *comme il faut*.' Completely mystified, Madame Campan looked about for a possible
cause for her discomfiture, but the Countess' consternation only
increased. 'The Queen noticed all this and looked at me with a
smile. I found some means of getting close to her, and she said
in a low voice "undo your pinners or the Countess will die of it".
All this agitation was caused by two pins which were holding
up my pinners. The etiquette of costume prescribed for this
occasion "barbes pendantes".'

One other instance will suffice to show how irksome were the
duties expected of a Queen of France. When she dressed in the
morning, her chemise was handed to her by her *dame d'honneur*.
If, however, any Princess of the Blood was in the room at the
time, the *dame d'honneur* handed the shirt to the senior one
present, who in turn handed it to the Queen. One day, when the
dame d'honneur was about to pass the shirt, there was a scratch
on the door—one never knocked on the doors of the Royal
Family—and the Duchesse d'Orléans entered. The shirt was
immediately placed in her hands, but she had hardly had the
time to take off her gloves when there was another scratch,
and in came the Comtesse de Provence, who ranked senior;
but the Duchesse d'Orléans could not give her the shirt; she
had to hand it back to the *dame d'honneur*, who passed it to
Madame. During all this the Queen was standing shivering with
cold and muttering through clenched teeth, 'c'est odieux!
Quelle importunité!' These little rights and precedences, of

course, only affected the Court, but they were jealously guarded.

Marie-Leczinska respected them, as has been shown, even in childbirth. This was no doubt the worst ordeal which confronted a Queen. In the great bedroom a special bed was prepared near the fire, for it was December when Marie-Antoinette was brought to bed of her first daughter, and screens had been erected to keep off the multitude of onlookers—'the crowds of sightseers who rushed into the room'. They even climbed on to the furniture to get a better view of the proceedings; 'one could fancy oneself in a public place,' wrote Madame Campan. It was on this occasion that Louis broke open the window 'with a force which only his love for the Queen could have given him', for the Queen was in danger of suffocation and the Princesse de Lamballe had fainted. Marie-Antoinette's reactions to this public delivery are not recorded, but perhaps her attitude towards royal motherhood can be sensed in her words when first she saw her infant daughter: 'Pauvre petite, vous n'étiez pas désirée, mais vous ne m'en serez pas moins chère. Un fils eût appartenu plus particulièrement à l'état. Vous serez à moi; vous aurez tous mes soins, vous partagerez mon bonheur et vous adoucirez mes peines.'

Although her tardy motherhood brought Marie-Antoinette to a more responsible outlook on life, it did nothing towards reconciling her to her public existence. In future the royal children were brought into the world before a small and select audience only, and the family was another pretext for the Queen to live her own existence in her Petits Cabinets.

The major works of reconstruction date from 1779. The first room to be altered was the Library, but this did not arise from any particular desire to read on the part of the Queen. 'Apart from a few novels,' wrote Besenval, 'she never opens a book.' Perhaps on account of her lack of interest in their contents, many of the volumes in her library were false, the Court bookbinder, Martial, having provided a selection of decorative backs to ornament the shelves.

The Méridienne, a little octagonal room with a niche for a day-bed, was mostly decorated with mirrors, for it was here that

Marie-Antoinette came to try on her new and often preposterous coiffures, chose her jewels and the materials for her dresses and held her interminable conferences with her dressmaker, Rose Bertin. An album was kept with samples of the materials of all her costumes, and was brought to her each morning. She marked with a pin the choices for the day, and the dresses were then brought up from the Garderobe.

The decoration of the room was designed by Mique and executed by the brothers Rousseau, sons of old Antoine Rousseau whose last work had been the King's library. It recalls their only work at Trianon, the little boudoir behind the Queen's bedroom. The delicate patterns carved on the panels have all the precision of the bronze *appliqués* on the glasses and mirrors; they incorporate peacocks and flowers, hearts pierced with arrows, and dolphins, the latter, of course, referring to the fact that since the 22nd of October 1781 France had an heir to the throne. His birth was the signal for an outbreak of rejoicing which almost restored the waning popularity of the Queen.

In 1783 the largest of the rooms, the Cabinet Intérieur, was redecorated and became known as the Cabinet Doré. The decorations were in the very latest style, and would almost pass for *Empire* were not their date fully attested by the accounts. The eight large panels, which form the greater part of the decorative scheme, are richly embellished with gilt carvings in which figure winged sphinxes, displayed eagles and smoking braziers, suggestive of a later date. Here stood the Queen's harp and harpsichord, used when Marie-Antoinette sang with Grétry and Madame Vigée Le Brun. Here were held private audiences, and from here, relates Madame Campan, Lauzun was expelled with an indignant 'sortez, Monsieur!' after which the Queen gave orders that he was never to be admitted again. It was commonly rumoured that Lauzun had been over-gallant in his address to the Queen.

Marie-Antoinette was not at all an easy person to work for. She never appreciated the difficulties created by her whims. When she first started work on the Petits Cabinets the Comtesse de Noailles had ordered plain shelves by way of an economy. Marie-Antoinette had intended a more elaborate décor with glazed bookcases enriched with carving. When she saw the shelves she ordered them to be destroyed in her presence. One scents a little of her antipathy to *Madame l'Etiquette* in this outburst. The financial situation was as bad as it had been under Pompadour. 'In a workshop of sixty workmen,' wrote Heurtier to Angivillier, 'I have never been able to get together twenty.' Marie-Antoinette had her Appartement des Bains in the *entresol* beneath the Cabinet du Conseil. One day she ordered the complete destruction of the Bibliothèque de Madame Sophie, and the workmen toiled late into the night to remove the stucco. Next day came a further order from the Queen demanding the preservation of the old decorations! 'Il y a de quoi perdre la tête,' wrote the exasperated Heurtier.

The royal children were lodged with the Governess, the Princesse de Guéméné (later replaced by the Duchesse de Polignac), at the extremity of the Aile du Midi, where the Dauphin had a little compound railed off where he played at gardening with his father. In this part of the Château also was situated the Pavillon de Provence, inhabited by the King's eldest brother, the future Louis XVIII. Although there was no particular affection between the Queen and *Madame*, the Royal Family used to have its reunion here in the latter years of the reign. *Madame*, arriving from her beautiful little Pavillon de Musique at Montreuil, her coach filled with flowers from the garden, was a devotee of the rural life, and followed the fashion in having her own little Hameau just outside the gates of Versailles. She caught birds there in a net, which were converted into soup for the royal soirées. The doors remained closed, and servants retired after placing the dishes on the table, but the occasional bursts of laughter revealed to those outside that the Royal Family were passing an agreeable evening.

A significant difference between Louis XVI and his wife was that his Petits Cabinets were open to the public, in the best Versailles tradition, at any time when he was not using them, but Marie-Antoinette's remained rigorously private. Arthur Young visited Versailles, not for the first time, in 1787, and was struck by this difference. 'In viewing the King's apartment, which he had not left a quarter of an hour, with those slight traits of disorder that showed he *lived* in it, it was amusing to see the blackguard figures that were walking uncontrouled about the Palace, and even in his bedchamber; men whose rags betrayed them to be in the last stage of poverty. . . . One loves the master of the house who would not be hurt or offended at seeing his apartment thus occupied if he returned suddenly. This is certainly a feature of that *good temper* which appears to me so visible everywhere in France. I desired to see the Queen's apartment, but I could not. Is Her Majesty in? No. Why then not see it as well as the King's? *Ma foi. Mons., c'est une autre chose.*'

The Petits Cabinets were the scene of most of the family life of the Queen, but unfortunately she was not contented with such domestic pleasures as could be obtained within the context of her official existence. She wished to have the privacy of an ordinary individual. 'In my cabinets and at Trianon,' she told one of her ladies, 'I will enjoy the comforts of private life, which do not exist for us unless we have the wit to procure them for ourselves.' How little she understood the world she lived in! Nothing was to bring her more unhappiness than her pursuit of these plain, homely pleasures. She cannot have known much of her Court if she really supposed that no one would take advantage of her most innocent desires.

Mercy, reporting the matter to Vienna, gave a good appreciation of it: 'Those who approach sovereigns have always some ambitious plans in their minds, or some end in view, either for themselves or for their friends, and the smaller the number of persons who obtain almost exclusive access, the more insistent are their intrigues, the more difficult to clear up, and by consequence, by far the most dangerous. A great Court ought to be accessible to a great many people.'

In 1777 Versailles was almost abandoned. How Louis XIV would have been surprised and dismayed at the Versailles of his descendant! The number of inmates had greatly decreased. In 1756 Blondel quoted two hundred and twenty-six private apartments in the Palace. By 1781 the figure had dropped to one hundred and eighty-eight. Imperceptibly, the nobility were losing the habit of coming. Mercy informed the Empress that 'want of occasion to pay one's court would end by reducing both the habit and the desire'. The facts indicate that he was right. 'Versailles,' wrote the Duc de Levis, 'that theatre of Louis XIV's magnificence, was no more than a little provincial town to which one only went with reluctance, and from which one made one's escape as quickly as possible.'

Since the death of Madame de Pompadour Versailles could not be said to have occupied its predestined position as the cultural centre of France. It became instead a costly fiasco. The Duke of Dorset, who was English ambassador at the time, made a note on the extravagance in one of his despatches. 'Their Majesties, the Dauphin, and the rest of the Royal Family, are removed from Fontainebleau to Versailles. The expense attending these journeys of the Court is incredible. The Duc de Polignac told me that he had given orders for 2,115 horses for this service. . . . Besides this, an adequate proportion of horses are ordered for the removal of the heavy baggage.' Calonne, he mentions, was obliged to borrow to meet this expense.

It was typical of the new Court that it did not like Marly. Exactly fitted to the needs of Louis XIV, it was even less adaptable than Versailles to the fashions of his successors. Apart from the *entresols* put in by Louis XV, and the suppression of the Rivière, it had remained practically unaltered. 'Everything there,' wrote Madame Campan, 'seemed to have been created by the magic power of a fairy's wand'; the painted decorations and abundant ornament made it all look rather like a scene from an opera. After dinner the Court went out in their light carrioles to drive in the park, where the trees had now reached a prodigious height. Nevertheless, some of the fountains still raised their crystal columns above the treetops, and the sparkling cascades and silvery sheets of water contrasted deliciously with the sombre background of woodland. But only Madame Campan appears to have appreciated its beauty.

The Salon was still overcrowded and the stakes at *pharaon* were higher than ever. Any rich financier could come and play, but of course he would not be accorded an apartment and was dubbed a 'polisson'.

During her first stay, Marie-Antoinette went up at three in the morning with a numerous attendance to the Grand Belvédère to see the sun rise. Unfortunately the King did not accompany her, and the incident, somewhat inexplicably, gave rise to the first calumnies against her name. The same voyage saw the arrival on the scene of a character who was to cast an ominous shadow across the life of the Queen—the jeweller Boehmer, already occupied with the creation of his fabulous diamond necklace.

Had Marie-Antoinette lived the public life expected of a Queen of France it would have been much more difficult for these malignant rumours to get the footing they did in the popular imagination. In particular they were stimulated by her almost secret life at Trianon.

THE QUEEN'S GARDEN

The gardens at Versailles, at the beginning of the reign, still preserved their form and appearance from the days of Le Nôtre. Louis XV had done little more than keep them up, and that somewhat inadequately. Le Normant de Tournehem's report on the 'dépérissement général' in 1750 had been ignored; that of Lécuyer seven years later had resulted in certain repairs, but apart from the creation of a little playground for the Dauphin, to the north of the Parterre de Latone, there had been little alteration.

The gardens of Le Nôtre, however, were exposed to a very different threat than mere destruction by the elements; they were becoming unfashionable.

Fashion is only too often bred of a desire for novelty. 'Il n'y a que la nouveauté qui puisse frapper les hommes,' wrote the

Vicomte d'Ermenonville, himself the author of one of the first
landscape gardens of France, 'ce qu'il y a de plus nouveau, c'est
la nature.' It was the general complaint that the gardens of the
humanists had relied too much upon artificial effects and left too
little to the workings of nature. Moreover, ideas were beginning
to change as to the purpose for which a garden should be
designed. In 1752 Blondel had described the layout of Versailles
as 'better suited to set forth the magnificence of a great Prince
than to offer to the mind a peaceful walk and a retirement conducive to philosophy'. Now philosophers were beginning to
play a more important rôle in French history than Princes, and
they often interested themselves in questions of taste.

Already such expressions as 'heureuse négligence', 'piquante
bizarrerie', and 'beau désordre' were beginning to creep into the
vocabulary of gardening, and the new, easy landscapes of England were contrasted favourably with the symmetry and *ordon-
nance* of the French school. These criticisms did not pass
unchallenged; Argenville, in the preface to his rather tedious
Voyage Pittoresque, launched a lively counter-attack to Laugier's
chapter on gardening. The attacks on formalism were redoubled.
'Le Nôtre,' wrote Ermenonville, 'massacred nature; he invented the art of surrounding himself, at great expense, with a
belt of boredom.' The only trouble was that nature had not
been massacred. During the last hundred years nature had been
steadily enriching the work of Le Nôtre in her own inimitable
manner, giving a nobility and a grandeur to the woods which
were not of man's making. The gardens had become, in Delille's
phrase, 'chefs d'œuvre d'un grand Roi, de Le Nôtre *et des ans*'.

It was at this moment of mature perfection that the trees were
destined to disappear. Outwardly magnificent, the bosquets of
Versailles contained a large quantity of dead wood. This may
have been the result of Louis XIV's method, learnt from the
gardener of the Prince of Nassau, of transplanting trees of an
already considerable size. Nicodemus Tessin had included in his
drawings of Versailles a sketch of a 'machine pour transplanter
des arbres'; it was known more familiarly to the workmen as

'the Devil', on account of its immense strength, based on the principles of the lever and the pulley wheel. It had enabled the gardens to be stocked with trees often attaining to four or five feet in circumference. By the reign of Louis XVI many of these trees were dead, and it was decided that it would be best to cut them all down and proceed with a general replantation.

The felling of a noble wood is a profoundly moving spectacle, and the destruction of the venerable trees of Le Nôtre did not pass unmourned.

Few people have ever appreciated the gardens of Versailles more wholeheartedly than the Duc de Croÿ. He knew when and where to enjoy them; he was prepared to walk to the far side of the Pièce d'Eau des Suisses, 'où le coup d'œil du fond est admirable', or to get up early and see the sun rise upon this princely scene. On the morning of the marriage of the Dauphin and Marie-Antoinette, when the last great illumination of the gardens was receiving its final touches and the landscape was resplendent in all the freshness of a spring morning, he mounted by means of the Petits Cabinets on to the roof of the Palace. It is by far the best viewpoint from which to enjoy the gardens. 'I do not believe that anything in the world has equalled the beauty of that sight, the effect of which was greatly enhanced by the freshness of the new-born leaves,' he wrote, *'c'est de là qu'il faut voir Versailles!'*

The cutting down of the trees was a blow which staggered him; he could hardly bear to revisit the place. 'I did not dare look that way in the gallery; they had been so beautiful when I last saw them, and my heart bled for them.' Nevertheless he was too sincere a critic not to recognize the interest now given to the works of statuary; 'all the marbles in the garden being visible at once, a superb ensemble was revealed'. The appearance of the park denuded of trees is shown in two pictures by Hubert Robert in the collection at Versailles. Two years later Croÿ again noted that the naked gardens, seen by the light of the rising sun, made 'a most imposing show'.

What was most satisfactory to him was that the replantation

was following the broad outlines traced by Le Nôtre. It had been decided that Versailles was too vast a conception and too public a place to respond to ordinary country-house treatment. Faced with the possibility of reshaping the whole on lines more consistent with contemporary taste, Louis and his advisers found that the original layout was best preserved.

Certain improvements and simplifications were introduced within the framework of the old design, and use was made of the botanical researches carried out in the gardens of Trianon. Trees were planted in accordance with the nature of the soil, and a note of variety obtained by the introduction of a few foreign species. Planes, maples, pines and cedars broke the monotony of the serried ranks of chestnut and lime.

Some of the features of the old garden disappeared in the re-plantation, in particular the labyrinth. 'It has never been the King's intention to restore the labyrinth,' wrote Angivillier to Rosset in September 1782. 'His Majesty preferred a private garden planted with trees and flowering shrubs, mostly exotic species; this was executed some three or four years ago, and is beginning to produce a most agreeable effect.' This royal enclosure, whose winding paths centre on a plantation of tulip trees, is sometimes known as 'the Queen's Garden'. Today it has lost the atmosphere of privacy which once distinguished it, and its chief interest lies in the memories which it evokes of the affair of the diamond necklace; one August night of 1784 the Cardinal de Rohan, dupe of Madame de la Motte, came secretly to this garden and accepted as the gracious words of his Queen the rehearsed speech of the woman Oliva.

Another important change was the creation of the Bains d'Apollon. The statues, originally ordered for the Grotte de Thétis, had been tucked away—'dumped rather than placed'—in the part of the garden lying directly north of the Parterre de Latone, sheltered under three little gilded kiosks of slightly oriental aspect. The model for one of them is exhibited today in the rooms of Madame de Maintenon. Mique and Hubert Robert were invited to submit designs for the re-formation of this plot to provide a setting worthy of the statues. Models were made, and the design of Hubert Robert accepted; being a painter who already saw classical architecture through the eyes of a romantic, he had achieved the more picturesque result. The cost of its execution was estimated at 180,000 livres, but public opinion, with its fatal taste for exaggeration, put the figure at one and a half million.

The big *Rocher*, sculptured slightly to suggest Grecian architecture, opens its cavernous mouth to contain the statues, which appear strangely dwarfed by their situation; a cascade finds its inconsequent way down the face of the rock and fills a pool at its foot. There is certainly none of Le Nôtre's formality here, but Hubert Robert has not come appreciably nearer to nature. Nothing could be more patently artificial. 'On ne peut bien imiter les rochers,' wrote Delille, 'pas plus que tous les grands effets de la nature.' The new Bains d'Apollon broke the lines of Le Nôtre's plantations without adding particularly to their charm. Nature, however, always strictly impartial, was as kind to Hubert Robert as she had been to Le Nôtre. The trees grew magnificently round the ridiculous grotto and screened it from the windows of the Palace. No longer offensive to the general layout, the Bains d'Apollon provide an amusing surprise to the visitor, but it is possible to walk all over this part of the gardens in summer and remain unaware of their presence. It was not at Versailles that the *Jardin Anglais* was to show its charm.

One of the first acts of Louis XVI on ascending the throne had been to give the Petit Trianon to the Queen. She was delighted to have a place of her own. The staff were put into her own livery—red and silver—and the orders signed in her name. When she put up instructions, some years later, in the park of St. Cloud, signed 'de par la Reine', it caused a scandal: the Queen of France had no authority but that of her husband. At first, however, the public was pleased to hear of Louis' gift of the Petit Trianon; it was a refreshing novelty to have a King whose only mistress was his wife. More shrewd, and always

well informed through her minister, Mercy, the Empress Maria
Theresa foresaw the possible danger of such a playground to
her frivolous young daughter. She wrote urging her to a responsible view of her position: 'that the King's charming first
present may not provide occasion for too large expenditure, let
alone for dissipations.'

There was little scope in the actual building for expensive
alterations, for it was already perfect. The tiny boudoir behind
the Queen's bedroom, added in 1787, is the only decoration in
the new style. It was in the gardens that Marie-Antoinette was
to realize her mother's worst fears and to earn herself the name
of 'Madame Déficit'. On the 2nd of July 1774 Mercy reported
to the Empress that the Queen was now wholly occupied with a
jardin à l'anglaise. The rows of frames and flower-beds of Richard's
research garden were doomed.

A visit to the Comte de Caraman, whose garden in Paris was
one of the most successful in the new fashion, provided Marie-
Antoinette with the adviser for whom she was looking. Antoine
Richard's plan for an English garden had been crammed with
every absurdity that ingenuity could contrive, but was utterly
devoid of taste; Caraman was duly appointed 'Directeur des
Jardins de la Reine'.

On the 31st of July the King gave orders that the area was to
be enclosed with a wall and that 'everything that the Queen
should desire was to be carried out with all the care and all the
diligence possible'. Marie-Antoinette happily imagined that there
was nothing else to worry about. She did not know the workings
of the Service des Bâtiments. She had made one of her usual
tactless mistakes in appointing Caraman and Mique to have sole
charge over the gardens at Trianon. The Comte d'Angivillier,
Directeur des Bâtiments, resented their intrusion and was inclined
to make things awkward. Moreover there were the usual difficulties over finance, for Turgot, more anxious to save the royal
exchequer than to gratify the Queen, was at the head of this
department. He and Angivilliers managed to delay matters by
demanding exact details and estimates. Patience, however, was

not one of Marie-Antoinette's virtues. 'You know your mistress,' wrote Fontanien to Mique; 'she likes to have her pleasures promptly.' In the end she had her own way, and the expense of the garden became alarming. 'At first the public took a favourable view of the King's giving Trianon to the Queen,' wrote Mercy in September 1776; 'they are now beginning to be uneasy and alarmed at the expenses which Her Majesty incurs there.'

For the alterations were involving nothing less than a complete transformation. 'I thought I must be mad or dreaming,' wrote Croÿ, visiting Trianon for the first time since the reign of Louis XV; 'never have two acres of land so completely changed their form, nor cost so much money.' The ground to the northeast, where the big hot-houses had formerly stood, had been cast into a miniature range of hills, and a lake had been dug, fed by a cascade which gushed from the mouth of a mysterious grotto. Next to the grotto, and dominating the gardens from its raised plateau, stood the Belvédère, remarkable for the exquisite ornament of the carvings without and the delicacy of the painted arabesques within.

The four pediments frame carved scenes of hunting and gardening, while the bas-reliefs over the window represent the four seasons. The frieze is interesting, being made of lead, closely fitted to the entablature and painted to look like stone. The painting of the arabesques inside was done by Le Riche, and the ceiling—cupids tumbling about in a blue sky—was by Lagrenée.

The Belvédère commanded a prospect over all the garden. Immediately in front of the Château could be seen the blue and gold canopy of the Chinese pavilion known as the Jeu de Bagues. This diversion consisted of a revolving platform, manipulated by men in the basement, on which were several seats, some in the form of peacocks, others in the form of kneeling Chinamen. Seated in these, the ladies were whirled round and tried to tent-peg rings which issued from the perimeter of the canopy. The exotic, pagoda-like form of the pavilion, with its gilt dragons and painted figures, must have introduced a somewhat bizarre note into the general harmony of the gardens. Perhaps it was what Arthur Young had in mind when he wrote: 'There is more of Sir William Chambers here than of Mr. Brown—more effort than nature—and more expense than taste.' Sir William Chambers was the author of a 'Dissertation on Chinese Gardening', while Lancelot Brown was responsible for most of the new landscape gardening in England.

East of the lake, through green meadows and loosely planted groves, wandered a river, now forming a little backwater towards the Château, now dividing its stream to leave an island planted with lilac and laburnum, from which rose the twelve stately columns of Mique's temple, carrying their stone cupola over Bouchardon's statue of Love, from which the temple takes its name. A rich variety of trees, many of alpine species recently acclimatized, formed the background of this artificial Paradise. 'The glory of *La Petite Trianon* [*sic*]', admitted Arthur Young, 'is the exotic trees and shrubs. The world has been successfully rifled to decorate it. Here are curious and beautiful ones to please the eye of ignorance, and to exercise the memory of science. Of the buildings, the Temple of Love is truly elegant.'

Another beauty of the gardens was their perfect silence; only the trickle of water and the song of nightingales was to be heard; 'one could fancy oneself three hundred miles from Court,' wrote the Prince de Ligne, and the truth of his statement is the measure of Marie-Antoinette's success, for this was the very purpose for which Trianon had always been dedicated.

THE GAME OF MAKE-BELIEVE. THE QUEEN'S THEATRE AND THE HAMEAU

At no time during the history of Versailles was there a lack of interest in the theatre. Louis XIV, who had himself appeared on the stage as *Le Roi Soleil*, the Duchesse de Bourgogne, who had frequently got up theatricals at Marly, and Madame de Pompadour had all multiplied the number of Salles de Spectacles in the royal palaces. By about 1780 the vogue for the *Comédie Intime* was at its height. Everywhere young men and women were taking lessons from professionals and plunging into amateur theatricals. At Versailles a small troupe was formed by the Duchesse de Villequier. It was not long before the Queen sought an invitation to one of their performances, and in due time Mercy had the delicate task of breaking the news to Vienna that the Queen had started an amateur company of her own.

Among the various temptations which led the Queen to take this rather inadvisable step, not the least was the possession of a perfect and charming miniature theatre of her own in the gardens of Trianon. She had started to build it in 1778 from the designs of her architect, Mique.

The building of the theatre followed the pattern of construction of all the features of the Trianon domain. After the first sketches had been made and approved, a scale model was presented to the Queen for her inspection. There had been models of the Belvédère and of the Temple d'Amour, with wooden columns and wax capitals, and no fewer than seven different projects for the grotto were offered in this form. The model of the theatre must have been a delightful toy in itself. All the mouldings were done in wax and gilded; the rest was painted and upholstered in silks and velvets, and even lit by twenty-four tiny lamps. Besides this, many of the decorative motifs were modelled life-size to give an idea of the effect that they would produce.

The auditorium was in the shape of a perfect horseshoe, whose elegant curves were marked by two galleries, the lower of which presented a balustrade, and the upper a solid parapet carved with acanthus scrolls and supported on large consoles. The cove of the ceiling was pierced by a number of oval windows through which the performance could be watched from the uppermost gallery. These apertures were linked by a festoon of flowers and *amorini*, and formed an elaborate frame to the ceiling, on which Lagrenée painted the almost inevitable Apollo attended by Graces and Muses.

The colour scheme, which required to be seen by candlelight, was obtained by the sky-blue silk and velvet upholstery and the bronze-coloured gilding of the ornament. The King and any other guests of honour sat in chairs placed in the parterre. Access to these seats was by means of an octagonal vestibule approached from a porch in the Jardin Français. The other spectators, usually drawn from the Queen's staff at Trianon, reached their seats in the galleries by means of subsidiary entrances placed to east and west of the auditorium.

Guests of honour were almost exclusively chosen from the Royal Family: even the Princesse de Lamballe was not invited, though Mercy was once accorded entry—one suspects that this was to ensure that his report to Vienna would not give a distorted account of this innocent amusement. It was the actors themselves who made up, for the most part, the intimate society of the Queen at Trianon, and Marie-Antoinette's attentions to these favoured few probably did more harm to her reputation than anything else. Nobody else at Court knew the facts about the life led at Trianon, so nobody was in a position to contradict the rumours.

The central figure in this tiny society was the Comtesse Jules de Polignac. Among the innumerable eulogies left of her, that of the Comte de Ségur is perhaps the most inclusive: 'It would be impossible to find anyone,' he wrote, 'who combined in their person a more charming countenance, a more sweet expression, a more delightful voice or more lovable qualities of heart and mind.' She was in no way spoilt by the favours which were heaped on her. Only Mercy, among so great a crowd of admirers, found her 'wanting in sense, judgement and any quality worthy of the confidence of a great Princess'. Her husband was a non-entity. For this woman Marie-Antoinette conceived an extravagant affection; in May 1780, when the Comtesse was expectant, the Queen took the Court to La Muette in order to spend most of her time with her friend, an attention so exaggerated as to cause immediate scandal in Paris. Nor was the friendship, of course, disinterested. The family of Polignac had many branches, but few sources of revenue, and to remedy this deficiency the Queen now devoted her attention. Titles, offices and sinecures were heaped upon the Comtesse's relations, and when there was no other benefice to bestow, large sums of money were given instead, and any debts which their extravagance might incur had only to be mentioned to be paid forthwith out of the royal exchequer. 'This family,' wrote Mercy in December 1779, 'without any deserts as regards the State, and from pure favouritism, has already secured for itself, both by Court appointments and other benefices, something like 500,000 livres of annual revenue.' This was only a beginning; the following year the favourite obtained a further 400,000 for discharging a debt, 800,000 as a dowry for her daughter, dukedoms for her husband and Guiche, and the hereditary office of Grand Falconer for Vaudreuil.

Other members of the côterie were the Duc de Guines, the Comte d'Adhémar and the Count Esterhazy. The Duc de Guines, who, as Ambassador in London, had earned for himself the title 'the Magnificent', owed his favour and his ducal rank entirely to the Queen. He was one of the best examples of a French wit—sharp and to the point, and he was a brilliant *raconteur*. Somewhat short, and of an ever increasing stoutness, he had the vanity to wish to appear otherwise. With every suit he had two pairs of breeches made, and every morning his valet inquired gravely: 'Monsieur le Duc s'assoit-il aujourd'hui?' If the answer was in the negative, the Duke would then mount upon two chairs and lower himself cautiously into the tighter pair of breeches; but if it was one of his sitting days, then he ordered the pair which was less flattering to his figure.

The Comte de Vaudreuil, tall, military and accomplished in all the social graces, with a nobility of expression which made up for a countenance marked with the smallpox, was a regular member of the troupe, but if he was a true friend to those for whom he cared, his pleasant qualities were marred by his ferocious temper; 'the slightest thwarting of his will,' said Besenval, 'put him beside himself.' He was as talented an actor as he was a conversationalist, and a persistent patron of Beaumarchais, in whose play, *The Barber of Seville*, he took the part of Almaviva.

It was generally agreed that the first prize for wit and assiduity must be awarded to the Comte d'Adhémar. He had married one of the Queen's *dames du palais*, Madame de Valbelle, a lady considerably his superior both in age and fortune, but his warmest attentions were reserved for the Polignacs. 'Le Comte d'Adhémar,' wrote Madame de Bombelles, 'me paraît toujours occupé tendrement de la favorite.'

Perhaps the least nocuous of the côterie was the Hungarian Esterhazy, whose comparative want of ambition secured for him that freedom of the Queen's apartment which led to a correspondence between the two which greatly displeased the Empress Maria Theresa, who expressed her surprise that 'a young man of no exalted rank should have means of access to her daughter'.

One thing is almost universally agreed about the intimate society of the Queen, and that is that, where moral character was concerned, none of them came anywhere near the standards of Marie-Antoinette herself. She did not, however, set the tone of her society. When she complained of some of the company she had to put up with when she visited the Polignacs she was almost snubbed by her favourite.

The repertoire performed by this princely company is interesting. The plays present, almost invariably, a picture of everyday life; usually the rôles played by the Queen were of humble characters such as Gotte, the maid in *La Gageure Imprévue*, Agathe, the laundry girl in *Le Sorcier*, or of Colette, the simple village maiden in Rousseau's *Devin de Village*. It was as if they were deliberately trying to get away from the responsibilities of their rank in a game of make-believe. On the rare occasions when the play touched on the subject of Royalty, as for instance in *Le Roi et le Fermier*, it is treated in much the same spirit as in *Figaro*. A King, lost while hunting, enters a farmhouse, and is treated by the farmer, who is unaware of his identity, to a witty satire on the Court.

'Who could have taught you so much?' asks the King.

'In faith, I've got around a bit; I've seen,' replies the farmer, 'I've seen what it is not always in the power of a King to see.'

'What's that?'

'Men.'

Such dialogues, pronounced by Princes before a Monarch, had a certain piquancy. They also shed a certain light on the mentality of the Court, and in particular of the Queen, who had the choosing of the piece.

From these entertainments all but the Royal Family and the retainers of the Queen were rigorously excluded. Needless to say there were many who felt that they were entitled to admittance. All the theatrical arrangements were in the hands of Monsieur Campan, but the Duc de Fronsac, First Gentleman of the Bedchamber, considered that such affairs fell by right within his competence; he felt himself aggrieved and made a continual scene about it, in spite of the Queen's firm letter: 'You cannot be First Gentleman when we are actors; besides I have already let you know my wishes with regard to Trianon; I have no Court there; I live as a private individual.'

The disaffection of the Court was only half of the trouble which arose from the Queen's behaviour. The scandal caused in the mind of the public was more serious; it was unfortunate that the obvious comparison was with the private theatrical companies of the Comtesse de Montesson and Mlle Guimard. These companies devoted themselves to the most licentious form of theatricals. Owing to the closely guarded secrecy of Trianon there was nobody to contradict this impression.

To those to whom the Queen extended her hospitality Trianon must have been a Fairyland. One of the loveliest entertainments was the illumination and fête given to Gustavus III of Sweden in June 1784. Marie-Antoinette, according to Madame Campan, 'was strongly prejudiced against Gustavus III and received him very coldly'. They had, however, much in common; both were enthusiastic landscape gardeners and had exchanged plans and drawings of Trianon and Drottningholm; both were keen on amateur theatricals. Gustavus had acted in and produced plays himself, and had even authorized the appearance of the crown jewels on the stage.

Marie-Antoinette was not to be outdone. There was a performance in the theatre at Trianon of Marmontel's *Dormeur Réveillé*, an exuberant piece taken from the Thousand and One Nights and set to music by Grétry. For this the voluptuous scenery done by Mazières some six years earlier for *L'Aveugle de Palmyre* was again utilized. It represented the Palace of the Sun, of which the chief features were the twisted columns of gold studded with diamonds. Needless to say, the diamonds were not real, but in 1789, when the deputies from the States General came to Trianon many of them asked to see the 'Cabinet des Diamants'. In popular rumour the theatre scene had become, by a process of judicious exaggeration, a room encrusted with precious stones, and they could not without difficulty be persuaded, relates Madame Campan, that no such room existed. This is a classical example of how relatively innocent amusements were detrimental to the popularity of the Queen, almost entirely because of the inaccessibility of her life at Trianon.

For the performance of the *Dormeur Réveillé*, the Royal Family had copies of the play specially bound in red morocco tooled in silver with the Queen's armorial bearings, while another copy, bound in green and gold with the royal arms of Sweden, was offered to their illustrious guest.

Besides the theatre, Gustavus was treated to an illumination of the gardens. The buildings were lit by the glow of an encircling fire, hidden from the eye by means of a ditch. Thousands of little pots, some fitted with transparencies, concealed behind green boards, cast a pool of light round every clump of trees and 'brought out the different colours in the most charming and agreeable manner'. A series of paintings by the Chevalier de Lespinasse preserve in some sort the appearance of the gardens by this floodlighting. Above the waters of the lake the Belvédère shone with a lustre that might have been its own, the great light given off by the faggots picking out some of the trees with a pale luminosity, and casting others into a dark, unnatural relief, whitening the surface of the rocks and accentuating the cavernous recesses of the grotto. It brought an unreality to the scene, as if buildings, trees and water were floating in the air.

On the other side, the Temple de l'Amour was aglow, shining 'with a great brightness which made it the most brilliant point in the whole garden'. It is recorded that on this occasion 6,400 faggots were employed in the illumination of the temple alone.

The King of Sweden came to Versailles under the name of the Comte de Haga. It was a sign of the times that Royalty travelled incognito, thereby freeing themselves from some of the inconveniences of their rank without forgoing any of the pleasures of privilege. Although she did not travel under an assumed name, Marie-Antoinette conformed to this attitude. It was possible for a visitor from the provinces to see the Queen cross the Salle des Cent Suisses at Versailles in a white *déshabillé*, her hair in disorder, trailing a cape over one arm and offering the other to the Comte de Vaudreuil. It was a virtual abdication. 'Maintenant je ne suis plus la Reine,' she exclaimed when visiting the Duchesse de Polignac, 'je suis moi!' Her time was almost divided between the apartment of the Polignacs and Trianon. As if to emphasize the desertion of Versailles, the Polignacs did their entertaining in a specially constructed wooden salon appended to the extremity of the Aile du Midi, overlooking the Orangerie.

The Queen's attempt to live 'as an ordinary individual' was certain to embitter all parties: the Court, who expected that noble birth and high position should be sufficient claim to the attentions of the sovereign; and the people, who, while they loudly protested against any undue extravagance, none the less looked to see the dignified tradition of their Monarchy worthily upheld. The portrait of Marie-Antoinette in a simple muslin dress and straw hat, exhibited by Madame Vigée Le Brun in the Salon of 1783, was badly received. A Queen dressed 'like a chambermaid' was as sharply criticized as the elaborate and ridiculous headgear of the previous decade. Nevertheless the simpler garment suited her better. A gentleman from Lorraine, François Cognel, obliged to take sudden refuge in one of the buildings while visiting the gardens at Trianon on account of the unexpected arrival of the

Queen, was so overcome by her presence that he made an involuntary genuflexion as she passed the window: 'In these modest clothes,' he wrote, 'she looked perhaps even more majestic than in the full dress in which we had seen her at Versailles.' The white muslin dress was that prescribed for Trianon, and was worn by all ladies of the little côterie. The men wore scarlet frocked coats.

In the year 1783 the English garden was extended by the laying out, after designs by Mique, of the Hameau—a little toy village which was becoming the vogue for great Princes to possess.

It is perhaps significant that the central building of this picturesque ensemble was called the Tour de Marlborough. The year 1783 saw the opening of peace negotiations with England; the Duke and Duchess of Manchester had come on an embassy to Versailles, and the Duchess had made an immediate impression upon the Court, her dignified demeanour more than compensating for her want of looks. To mark the new friendship with England there was a sudden wave of enthusiasm for the old arch-enemy Marlborough, and anything that was to be considered *à la mode* had to be *à la Marlborough*. The old refrain *Malbrouk s'en va-t-en guerre* was on every lip, and was apparently introduced to Versailles by the Dauphin's appropriately named wet nurse, Madame Poitrine. The tune was to be heard again, for it found its way into Beaumarchais' play, the *Marriage of Figaro*.

The tower thus named originally stood clear of the trees on a rocky promontory into the lake, like a little Ionic lighthouse. The upper balcony was approached by a sweeping spiral staircase lined with pots of wallflowers and geraniums, forming, as Hézecques described it, a sort of 'aerial parterre'. From the elevation thus gained one could see the Palace of Versailles over the treetops, and also enjoy a magnificent view of the Hameau.

Round the borders of the lake were disposed a number of small houses, such as might have formed a tiny rural village, or the background of a picture by Greuze. A farm with a monumental gateway, several thatched cottages, each with a little garden enclosed by a hedge and grown with vegetables and fruit trees, and a mill worked by a rivulet fed from the lake, formed the whole, but the trees were so arranged as to permit here and there a view of the cottages and Church of St. Antoine, giving, as it were, a background of reality to this artificial scene. Cattle grazed upon the meadows, peasants worked in the gardens, and village maidens brought their washing to the mill, to which also the cottagers brought their corn to grind. The whole spectacle was an idealized *tableau vivant* of country life.

In the later years of Louis XVI's reign there was a marked change in the attitude of the French towards country life. This also was borrowed from England. 'La simplicité des coutumes anglaises,' wrote Ségur, 'nous charmait.' Until recently, to be ordered to live on one's estates was virtually exile, but with the falling off of Court life, occasioned by the Queen's predilection for privacy, some of the nobles had come to take an interest in their lands and their tenantry. Of these the Duc de Liancourt is an example who is well known through his friendship with Arthur Young. 'The present fashion in France for passing some time in the country,' he noted, 'is new. . . . Everybody that have country seats are at them, and those who have none visit others who have; this remarkable revolution in French manners is certainly one of the best customs they have taken from England; and its introduction was effected the easier, being assisted by the magic of Rousseau's writings.' The Duke's interest in the agricultural and commercial affairs of his estate appealed to Arthur Young, who also approved the easy relations between the tenants and their lord, 'though modest . . . yet without any obsequiousness offensive to English ideas'. For such was beginning to be the ideal in France.

The Queen was not an exception to this new fashion for country-house life, but with her it had to be a game of make-believe. When she entered the Salon at Trianon the ladies did not rise from the piano or the embroidery frames, and gentlemen did not interrupt their billiards or their tric-trac; the formality of the Court gave place to the simple freedom of the country house. 'The pleasure of wandering about all the buildings of the Hameau, of watching the cows milked and of fishing in the lake,' wrote Madame Campan, 'enchanted the Queen.' There has been a popular misconception that the Hameau was the scene of an elaborate game in which Louis played the rôle of miller, Marie-Antoinette of miller's wife, *Monsieur* of the village schoolmaster and even, in the extremest form, Rohan that of the curé. The idea that Rohan ever entered the precincts of Trianon (except once under false pretences) may be dismissed. He was not even on speaking terms with the Queen. Nor is there any contemporary evidence of the Royal Family playing the part of peasants. What they seem to have been playing at was being 'country squire and wife' after the English fashion.

One of the houses of the Hameau was set apart for the use of the Queen. It was really two buildings joined by a wooden gallery, of which the larger was known as the Maison de la Reine and the smaller as the Maison du Billard. The exterior was painted to represent the dilapidation which was no doubt the general rule for houses of the peasantry, the cracked plaster crumbling away to reveal the brickwork, and the beams riddled with worm holes; vines climbed the walls and hung down over the windows, and wistaria twisted its snaky branches in and out of the wooden balconies. The galleries were lined with flower-pots of blue and white porcelain bearing the Queen's monogram. But all this picturesque and rural beauty was merely external; the inside had all the elegance and sophistication of the rooms at the Château. The very names of the rooms have a boring similarity to those of the royal apartments at Versailles— Cabinet de Jeu, Cabinet Chinois, Salle des Nobles, Cabinet du Billard, Bibliothèque de la Reine. The main apartment, the Salon, was hung with tapestry and adorned with a correct Corinthian entablature and finely chiselled mantelpiece. The country cottage was the merest veneer to another elegant garden pavilion.

There was one building in the Hameau, however, which in all

probability provided the Queen with an occupation more in keeping with her legendary rôle of miller's wife, and that was the dairy. It was the last of the buildings to be put up, and was sumptuously equipped. Marble walls and a marble floor, across which a little conduit enabled a stream of water to flow, kept the dairy cool in summer; between the windows were ornamental niches, one of them containing a marble urn surmounted by a swan and two *amorini*. There were fifteen marble tables, with special porcelain utensils for the making of butter, cream and cheese. It was noted in *La Vie Parisienne sous Louis XVI* that at Chantilly 'the Princesses amused themselves by doing the cooking, dressed in the *déshabillé* of villagers; they also liked to make butter, as did the Queen at Trianon'. This seems to be the best evidence for Marie-Antoinette's actual participation in the life of the Hameau. Otherwise the dairy performed its usual function. There was a superb herd of Swiss cows on the farm, and every morning the cans of fresh milk were carried up to the Château for the consumption of its inmates.

But the enjoyment of these rustic pleasures was short-lived. In 1784 the Queen acquired St. Cloud. It was thought to have a healthier air for her delicate son. Considerable enlargements and alterations were put in hand and Mique consulted on the question of another *Jardin Anglais*. In 1785 the Queen was mainly occupied with these works. On the 9th of August she was back at Trianon. She had decided, somewhat unwisely, to reopen the theatre with a performance of the *Barber of Seville*, and was rehearsing the part of Rosine. It was the last performance she was to give there. Madame Campan had been approached by the jeweller Boehmer to obtain for him an interview with the Queen. He was summoned to Trianon, and as he told his tale, in the little boudoir behind the Queen's bedroom, the whole monstrous fabric known as the affair of the diamond necklace began to come clear in the mind of the Queen. It was a blow from which her reputation never recovered. After the interview Madame Campan found her 'in an alarming condition'. On the 15th of August the Cardinal de Rohan was arrested at Versailles, as he passed from the Cabinet du Conseil into the Galerie. The Queen returned to Trianon and the curtain went up on the *Barber of Seville*. In the audience was Beaumarchais himself, the man whom Maria Theresa had imprisoned for an early calumny on Marie-Antoinette, and whose writings openly attacked the basis of a privileged class. He owed his invitation to the solicitations of Vaudreuil.

In the last few years that remained to her, Marie-Anoinette made a few attempts to redress the damage done by the extravagance of her favourites. Polignac was obliged to resign the *Direction des Postes et Chevaux*—worth fifteen thousand livres annually; Vaudreuil his position as Grand Falconer; the Duc de Coigny was deprived of his place of Premier Écuyer and took it badly. He had an interview with the King, in the course of which both lost their tempers. That was the trouble with the Queen's friends; gifts which they had received from pure favouritism they came to regard as their personal property. 'It is terrible,' wrote Besenval, 'to live in a country where one cannot be sure of possessing one day what one had the day before. That sort of thing only happens in Turkey.' The Queen's attempts at retrenchment only led to the alienation of her society. They were not friends, but they were company; now she was left alone to face the coming storm. It was accompanied by the death of the Dauphin at Meudon on the 4th of June 1789. He died in the morning, racked with suffering but 'with a courage and a resignation beyond his age'. The feelings of the Queen during this ordeal are better imagined than described. She had gone to Marly to hide her misery, but in October she was back at Trianon.

One place in the gardens corresponded to her mood. There was a wood up behind the Belvédère where a heap of moss-grown boulders overhung a little ravine down which a cascade brought its tumbling waters to swell the stream. Here, after many projects had been tried and abandoned, was contrived the grotto. 'This grotto,' wrote the Comte d'Hézecques, 'was so dark that the eyes, dazzled before, needed a certain time to be able to discern objects clearly.' It was carpeted with moss, and cooled by a little stream which flowed through it. A bed, also of moss, invited repose. The grotto was designed for solitude, for either by a chance effect or by the deliberate contrivance of the architect a crevice, which opened above the top of the bed, overlooked the whole meadow, and 'enabled one to detect from afar anybody who might have wished to approach this mysterious retreat'.

It was here, on the 5th of October, that the messenger found the Queen and brought her the news that the mob was marching on the Palace of Versailles. For years she had played at make-believe in this lovely garden, vainly pretending to be an ordinary individual. Now the game was up. There were carriages in readiness which could have taken her to safety, but she refused them proudly. 'Puisqu'il y a du danger,' she said, 'ma place est auprès du Roi.' Now that it was too late she rose magnificently to the occasion, calling upon those deep reserves of heroism and endurance that lie so often beneath unlikely surfaces, and when next day, upon the balcony of the King's bedroom at Versailles, she faced the mob, she showed herself, as never before, the Queen. But the times had changed irrevocably, and she was to be Queen of the Conciergerie and of the Temple. Versailles was not the background of her reign; its story closes with the Queen's departure. As the family bundled into the great berline that was to take them from Versailles forever, Louis turned to the Marquis de la Tour du Pin. 'Vous restez le maître ici,' was all he said, 'tâchez de me sauver mon pauvre Versailles.'

V

Epilogue

THE RESURRECTION OF VERSAILLES

ALTHOUGH NO SINGLE building could have symbolized the *ancien régime* more completely than Versailles, the Palace suffered astonishingly little during the Revolution, popular hatred contenting itself with the demolition of the Bastille. On the whole the Revolution was seldom a destroyer of buildings. Palaces and great country houses, being deprived of their reason for existing, were certainly exposed to the threat of destruction, but when it came, it came usually from the hands of contractors seeking to profit from the materials rather than from *enragés* seeking to obliterate the visible monuments of tyranny.

Versailles survived the Revolution almost intact. The dispersal of all the furniture was indeed an irreparable loss, which largely accounts for the dullness of the interior today, but otherwise the effacing of a quantity of fleurs-de-lis and other insignia of Royalty must be set against the preservation of the fabric as a whole. With the departure of the King, the immediate danger was removed, and, taking advantage of the unlooked-for absence of the Court, the *Service des Bâtiments* started upon a general work of cleaning and restoration. A report made in 1791 by five commissioners shows the whole place empty and unfurnished; the Grande Galerie was full of scaffolding, and the ceiling under repair; stoves had been installed in all the rooms to preserve them from the damp; the Petits Appartements de la Reine had been repainted, and her bathroom 'remise à neuf', but all the charming furniture and appointments of the room, the little details that create the impression of life in a building and relate it to the character of the occupant, had all disappeared; even the books had gone from their shelves, and only a few sheets of music lay strewn upon the Library floor.

With the fall of the Monarchy, the situation again looked ugly. A tumbril full of aristocrats, among whom was du Barry's friend the Duc de Brissac, was set upon by the mob just by the Orangerie gates, and the inmates massacred, but still no violence was done to the Palace buildings. The preservation of Versailles at this time of crisis was largely due to the fact that the citizens of the town felt that their own interests were somehow or other bound up with those of the Palace, which had for so long been the focal point of their existence. On the 21st of September 1792 they successfully petitioned against the removal of all the remaining art treasures to the new 'Museum of Paris', and in due course it was decided to turn the Château into a picture gallery devoted to the French school; formerly the haunt of tyrants, Versailles was to become 'the resort of patriotism and the arts'.

Only Marly, less adaptable to civic purposes, succumbed to the times, and that not until the days of the Empire. A last glimpse may be obtained from the memoirs of Madame Vigée Le Brun; it had made a deep impression on the Court painter, recalling to her the days of the Grand Monarque, and in 1812, returning from her exile, she hastened to renew her acquaintance with the charming spot; 'j'ai couru revoir mon noble et riant Marly' . . . the Palace, the pavilions, the trees, the cascades, the fountains, all were gone; only a single stone remained which seemed to mark the centre of the Salon.

Napoleon could have saved Marly—the mayor specially petitioned him to do so—as he saved the last vestiges of Chantilly. He himself used the Grand Trianon, installing himself in the rooms formerly occupied by Maintenon and Pompadour, but for Versailles he contented himself with grandiose projects for replacing the nymphs throughout the gardens with 'panoramas of masonry'. Quite what he meant by this is not clear, but it sounds as if it is just as well they remained projects.

At the Restoration the Court did not return to Versailles. It had been the creation of *la Monarchie Absolue*; *la Monarchie Constitutionelle* could never aspire to it. Lamartine paints a moving picture of Louis XVIII revisiting the scenes of his gay and gilded youth and 'measuring with a wistful eye the distance which separated his old age from his cradle'. Supported on the arms of his servants, he would mount the stairs which led to his old apartments at the end of the Aile des Princes, in which he had caused such articles of the original furniture as were still in the *garde-meuble* to be replaced 'to give him a momentary illusion of the old days'. Leaving his servants at the door, he would sit there, in his crimson velvet chair, alone with his memories. Then he would order his carriage and drive to Trianon and tune his ears once more to catch the faint and fading echoes of the past. 'Il se retraçait les spectacles, les concerts, les illuminations, les amours de ces délicieux jardins, dont les arbres avaient versé leurs premières ombres sur le pas de cette jeune cour.' The memory of Marie-Antoinette still lingered in the silent alleys and deserted rooms. 'Il trouvait dans cette chaumière royale toute l'âme d'une princesse qui aspirait à l'obscurité pour cacher le bonheur, jusqu'au lit de simple mousseline de la Reine de France.'

He even toyed with the idea of setting up the Court once more in its old haunts, and built the Pavillon Dufour to match the architecture of the Aile Gabriel. That he should have considered returning to Versailles at all testifies to the small extent of the damage done by the Revolution.

In so far as Versailles has suffered, it has suffered mostly at the hands of a King, and from the ill-effects of nineteenth-century taste. For Louis-Philippe turned the palace of the Bourbons into a museum dedicated 'to all the Glories of France', and to make room for his galleries hundreds of the most beautiful eighteenth-century interiors were swept away or disfigured. One of the more pointless mutilations was the levelling out of the Cour de Marbre with the Cour Royale, from which it had been previously elevated by five steps, an alteration which ruins the proportions of Le Vau's façades without serving any very obvious purpose. But regrettable though his taste may have been, the 'Bourgeois King' deserves the indulgence of posterity; he devoted some twenty-four millions of his Civil List to his museum, and thereby saved Versailles from becoming a barracks, a destiny which, for a noble edifice, can only be regarded as a fate worse than death.

The nineteenth century did more to ruin Versailles than the Revolution. Prodigal in its care for relics of the Middle Ages, it was usually blind to the artistic genius of the two preceding centuries. The rooms in the new museum were established regardless of the excellence of the décor which they replaced; where the original carvings were retained they were often pitifully mutilated or coated with a thick and inelegant layer of grey distemper. Old paintings were subjected to a sort of 'bed of Procrustes', being extended or reduced in size to fit the new places assigned them without any consideration for their proportions. New paintings, ordered by the square yard, filled the wall-spaces with indifferent compositions and doubtful likenesses; the public, it was supposed, would be better pleased with a fictitious Clovis than with a genuine du Barry, but in this Louis-Philippe and his advisers were mistaken; the public showed conspicuously little interest in either.

But the destruction was not always complete. Much of the beauty of Versailles had not been irreparably lost; under the dirty whitewash, misnamed 'gris Trianon', lurked the chaste colours of Etienne Martin and the finely chiselled carvings of Verberckt; up in the attics, awaiting classification, were stacked the canvasses of Largillière, Boucher and Nattier; in the gardens, hardly visited except when the fountains were playing, the statues remained as Le Nôtre had placed them, and down by the canal, under the roof of an old workshop, lay rotting the great carcase of Marie-Antoinette's yacht.

During this uneventful period, there was a strange afterglow of the great days when Versailles had been the inspiration of half the palaces of Europe. In 1878 King Ludwig II of Bavaria set about the building of an exact copy of Versailles on the island of Herrenchiemsee. He succeeded in reproducing the whole of the central block on the garden side, with some of its attendant statuary and waterworks, containing its Œil de Bœuf, Salon de Paix, Salon de Guerre and Grande Galerie almost exactly copied to scale. In other parts of the Palace, notably in the King's bedroom, the architect (or his royal patron) appears to have been unable to restrain himself, and has given way to a wild rococo extravaganza in no way suggestive of the majesty of its prototype. Here, and in the Wagnerian castle of Neuschwanstein, Ludwig lived his rather pathetic make-believe existence, roaming alone among the vast halls and galleries wrapped in a black cloak. But enthusiasm for Louis XIV and his monumental architecture at this time was peculiar to this eccentric monarch. The Palace of Versailles remained, like the Sleeping Beauty, neglected and unloved.

In 1887 a young man, unsuccessful in his application for a post in the Cabinet des Estampes, somewhat reluctantly accepted one in this forlorn museum, and an apartment in the Ministers' Wing was prepared for the reception of the family of Pierre de Nolhac. To this apparently unpromising appointment Nolhac brought a scholarly mind with a taste for exactness and an inquisitive disposition. They were not qualifications likely to be acceptable to the head of the department. 'Don't you go too fast, young man,' his chief warned him, when the new attaché suggested a rearrangement of the exhibits, 'our business is to look after them, and what makes it all the easier is that they look after themselves.' A further protestation elicited the further rebuke: 'Write books about Versailles if that amuses you, but leave in peace this museum which no longer interests anybody.'

He did write books on Versailles—the first really reliable ones since the days of Blondel—but his interests were not merely antiquarian. Raised by an early promotion to the rank of Conservateur, Pierre de Nolhac profited by the indifference of the public and ministry alike to start on his own great work of restoration which continues today. It is as complementary to this task that his writings should be considered. Before anyone could undertake an intelligent restoration, the exact topography of the place had to be reconstituted. The break with the *ancien régime* had been complete. Even in the days of Louis XVI only comparatively few persons had really known their way about the Palace. 'One might compare the Château de Versailles to a vast labyrinth,' wrote the Comte d'Hézecques, 'one needed a long familiarity to find one's way about.' The naming of the rooms had always been complicated; now it was forgotten. Only by the sorting of the innumerable plans and documents in the National Archives could questions of the original decorations be solved. To this work Pierre de Nolhac now applied himself, a task undertaken, in his own words, 'par goût de la précision'.

Parallel with the research among the archives ran the rediscovery of Versailles itself. One day, finding a door which did not answer to his master key, Nolhac inquired its purpose. It was a closet, he was informed, where the staff kept their cleaning materials. He had the door opened, and penetrated into a small, obscure chamber whose walls, but dimly visible, revealed a strange and wonderful decoration. Scenes of bathing and aquatic sports framed in oval bulrush borders were carved in the centre of each panel, while swans and dolphins, scissors and shaving utensils formed the unusual adornment of the window recesses. The store cupboard of the charwomen was nothing less than the bathroom of Louis XV, the last of his extensive redecorations of the Palace; four shades of gilding—glossy, matt, green and bronze—had been used by Dutems and Brancour to vary the effects of this exotic décor.

Some of the errors of Louis-Philippe were not without their humorous side. One day, conducting the Duc d'Aumale round the Petits Appartements, Nolhac was asked why the prie-dieu had been removed from one of the smaller rooms. 'That was where the King made his confession with Madame de Maintenon,' explained the Prince. The little closet did indeed bear the name of Louis XIV's celebrated confessor,* but Nolhac knew better than his royal visitor the private function of a 'Cabinet de la Chaise'.

The smallest details of the rooms, checked by careful reference to plans and documents, called forth the memories of a past which had been forgotten with them. On the spiral staircase descending from the Queen's apartment to that of the royal children could be seen the rings that had held the cord which served as a banister. Below them Nolhac noticed another set of rings smaller in size, doubtless for a second cord adjusted for the convenience of the little Dauphin. And thus, piece by piece, the private life of the Royal Family could be put together again in its correct setting, and the details of that setting ascertained from the papers in the archives.

By far the most important 'rediscovery' was Nolhac's systematic and scholarly work on the drawings and documents in the National Archives, by means of which the accurate restoration of Versailles has been made possible. Under the steady pressure of Nolhac's influence a new movement began—the resurrection of Versailles as far as possible in its old original decoration.

The principles of such a restoration were laid down by Vittel: 'As regards ancient monuments, it is better to preserve than to repair, to repair than to restore, to restore than to construct; in no cases should one add or subtract.' His last point is of doubtful value. The subtraction of later additions and the replacement of features which have been removed is often desirable.

This can be illustrated from the works at Versailles. By far the greatest disfigurement which the Palace suffered was the disappearance of the urns and trophies from the balustrade on the garden front. The replacement of accurate copies on the central block and the north wing has restored an essential feature of the whole without which Versailles would present a deplorable skyline towards the gardens. It only remains to apply the same principle to the Grand Trianon, which should also

* Père Lachaise

have its uninteresting silhouette peopled with the lead figures and stone vases which Mansart and Robert de Cotte designed for it.

At Trianon, however, the converse principle, the subtraction of later additions, has been applied with the happiest effect. Louis-Philippe made the Grand Trianon his residence, and was so insensible of its beauties that he masked almost the whole façade behind exterior shutters, and abolished the characteristic feature of the building by filling in the Colonnade with windows. It is thanks to Pierre de Nolhac that this has once more opened its vista from the entrance right through into the gardens, as Louis XIV and Robert de Cotte planned it.

The new signs of life in the curator's department was answered by a quickening of the public interest. To a narrow republicanism which condemned all the works of the *ancien régime* as coming from 'the sweat of the people' succeeded a broader nationalism capable of appreciating the important patronage to the arts given by Louis XIV, and the resulting prestige which is still enjoyed by France. Thus a lecture by Nolhac was warmly received by a socialist audience. 'Ils sentaient bien,' he says, 'que ma sincérité n'était au service d'aucune idée politique.'

The interest of the public was reflected by contemporary artists, and once again Versailles found its place in their subject-matter and provided their inspiration. Henri de Regnier, attracted by the atmosphere of abandoned magnificence, Anna de Noailles, more directly appreciative of the gardens of humanism, and other poets began to sing the praises of the renascent palace. Painters, who had hardly been attracted to this spot since the days of Bonington, began once more to set up their easels in the apartments of the Palace and in the alleys of the garden. First among them was Maurice Lobre, 'portraitiste attitré du vieux Versailles'.

Public interest once aroused, and the great work of restoration started, the former apathy of the government gave way to a fine enthusiasm which was not without danger to the cause which it purposed to support, for the age was still unable to appreciate the finesse of eighteenth-century art. Louis-Philippe had covered the panelling with a grey distemper; the architects of the museum, usually at loggerheads with the curator, would have gilded the whole place. The Bibliothèque du Dauphin, one of the finest examples of the Louis XV style in the Palace, should have been given back the soft colours of its *vernis Martin*, still discernible beneath the whitewash, but the architect, victim of 'a veritable mania for gilding', plastered the cornice with gold leaf, and then claimed the right to treat the remaining wall-surfaces to match. Nolhac objected, and there the matter rested. It is only at the present moment that the Dauphin's library is receiving the attention which it deserves.

The work undertaken by Pierre de Nolhac was only a tentative beginning, for, like most men who have concerned themselves with the building of Versailles, he was hampered by lack of money. The public, however, was beginning to awaken to its responsibility towards the monuments of its great inheritance, and private donations sometimes made their way into the repair fund.

One day a lady entered the Conservateur's office; she was well known to Paris by the contrast afforded by her simple mode of living and her great wealth, almost all of which she devoted to charity. She was a great admirer of Marie-Antoinette, and was particularly hurt by the state of dilapidation into which the Petit Trianon and the Hameau had fallen. She had come armed with two hundred thousand francs, and a promise of more if her conditions were accepted. They were that she was to remain anonymous, and that Pierre de Nolhac was to have full discretion in the administration of her bequest. She had no confidence, she told him, in the administrations of the Republic. Her vote of no confidence caused the Republic to reject her offer, and it remained to the generosity of an American millionaire, less romantic but more tactful in his approach, to render service to Versailles.

After the First World War the condition of many public buildings was serious, either owing to the enforced neglect of the previous four years, or from direct enemy action. Of these two categories the most striking examples were the Palaces of Versailles and Fontainebleau and the Cathedral of Rheims. Of one million dollars offered by Rockefeller for the repair of these three buildings, seven hundred thousand were to be devoted to Versailles, administered by a Franco-American committee working 'in accordance and in collaboration with the works actually undertaken or projected by the State'.

For the most part the Rockefeller Trust was used for securing the actual fabric of the Palace from decay, the roofing and exposed woodwork receiving first attention, but in one respect, and this was at Rockefeller's personal instigation, the money was outlayed on the restoration of a work of art, the Queen's theatre at Trianon. It is thanks to the American's generosity that this charming construction of Mique's can now be seen in its original freshness of blue and gold, and the atmosphere of some of the most intimate anecdotes of the unhappy Queen can be recaptured. A visit should not be made without an inspection also of the tiny rooms over the vestibule where the architect lived and worked, until he and his son paid on the scaffold for the part which they played in ministering to the Queen's extravagance.

The Rockefeller donation is a great landmark in the history of Versailles, for it marks the reinstatement of the Palace in that worldwide position which it originally held. It testifies to what Gabriel Hanotaux called the 'internationalism of beauty', a recognition by the world that all great works of art are the world's irreplaceable heritage, and an acceptance by the whole of civilization of responsibility for their preservation.

It is on this level that restoration is being carried out today, and visitors from every continent who come to see the apartments, attend the lectures, or enjoy the illuminations on summer evenings are contributing to the continued work of resurrection which aims to present to the world as truthfully as is now possible this priceless witness to the life of a bygone age. The rediscovery of the recipe for *vernis Martin* made possible the restoration of du Barry's apartment in all its original brilliance.

It may come as a surprise to some who think of the eighteenth century as an age of quiet and restrained good taste. This impression is perhaps caused by the fact that much of what has survived has faded. But many of the designs in the National Archives, notably those for Madame Sophie's apartment, show that bright and contrasting colours had their vogue in the middle of the eighteenth century.

The most important of the reconstructions has been that of the Opéra. Of all the great reception rooms of the Château this had received the worst disfigurement. Its delicate colour-scheme had disappeared beneath a thick coat of ugly red mahogany; the floors had been levelled and the Royal box enlarged; du Rameau's painted ceiling had been rolled up and stacked with the scenery and replaced by an enormous skylight. In 1871 the stage was equipped with seats and rostrum for the Senate. The atmosphere of a Court theatre had been entirely destroyed. In addition to the obliteration of the décor, the fabric had been allowed to deteriorate. In 1941 the Opéra was in danger of ruin.

The last defect was the first remedied, and once the fabric was secured, the complete rehabilitation of the Salle de Spectacle was put in hand. It was accomplished with the usual mixture of lucky finds and scrupulous attention to detail. Two pieces of the original furniture had been hidden, one by the Prompter, at the time of the sale in the Revolution. These were discovered and provided the colour and the patterning for the velvet upholstery. A remnant of material, still nailed to the back of one of the balustrades, preserved for posterity the colour 'bleu céleste' of the silken hangings. The careful removal of the red paint revealed the marbling of the colonnade and the delicate floral paintings of the Royal box. The detailed specifications of the original contractors were found in the archives and adhered to meticulously. The result is a restoration at once beautiful and historically accurate. We can agree with the original verdict of the Duc de Croÿ: 'c'est la plus belle Salle de l'Europe.'

If the essential interest of architecture is, as was suggested at the beginning of this book, the fact that it is closely bound up with the personalities of the people associated with each building, which thus becomes the proper background for the historical imagination, then intelligent restoration on these lines is by no means to be deplored. It is a vulgar error to value a building merely for its venerable antiquity. Today the Tudor house is still more widely popular than the Palladian, but its charm may be due largely to the mellowing effect of four hundred years upon the original (and often garish) appearance. In the architecture of humanism this mellowing of time has no place. The regularity with which the painting and gilding at Versailles was renewed suggests that they were not intended to lose their original brilliance. That they should be repainted and regilded today is wholly in accordance with seventeenth- and eighteenth-century tradition. Versailles has had its autumn, it should have its spring, rising again with freshness of colour and fullness of form, as from year to year the beauties of the garden are renewed.

For if there is any time of the year at Versailles to rival autumn for beauty, it is the early spring, when the winds of April drive the great white masses of cumulus across the radiant blue of the sky, and the countryside gleams fresh and flourishing in the bright air. The oaks, the chestnuts, the poplars and willows of the park present to the eye their infinite and exquisite blendings of greens and yellows and browns, and the lime shoots are coral red. To either side of the canal the grass verges are golden with buttercups, and the swallows skim low across the face of the waters. To left and right the woods are pierced with long avenues and glades, green and deserted. Walking down their unkempt rides behind the gardens of Trianon, the visitor comes unexpectedly on old forgotten fountains whose leaden cupids still bear the traces of their former gilding. These are the times when the past seems nearest, for comparatively few eyes have gazed upon these figures since their gilding was last renewed, when the fountains played in the heat of the day, and the woods resounded to the fanfare of horns and the baying of hounds, and in the evening when the sun had dipped behind the trees and the fountains died down in their basins, there came the glow of illuminations and the flash of fireworks and a noble noise of music from the canal. The fireworks and the music may be heard again today when the Palace is illuminated, and they help to remind one that the last chapter in the history of Versailles has not been written.

Bibliography

GENERAL

Argenville, D. d'. 'Voyage Pittoresque des environs de Paris, ou Descriptions des maisons royales'. 1762

Blondel, J.-F. 'L'Architecture Française'. Vol. IV. 1907

Cosnac, Comte de. 'Mémoires du Marquis de Sourches sur le règne de Louis XIV'. 1882

Félibien, A. 'Description sommaire du Château de Versailles'. 1674

Guiffrey, J. 'Inventaire Général du mobilier de la couronne sous Louis XIV'. 1882

Josephson, R. 'Relation de la visite de Nicodème Tessin'. In *Revue de l'Histoire de Versailles*. 1926

Laborde, Comte de. 'Versailles ancien et moderne'. 1839

La Force, P. de. 'Nouvelle Description des Châteaux et Parcs de Versailles et Marly'. 1713

Perrault, C. 'Mémoires de ma vie'. 1902

Saint-Simon, Duc de. 'Mémoires'. 1873–86

Sourches, Marquis de. *See* Cosnac above.

Tessin, N. 'Relation de sa visite à Marly, Versailles, Clagny, Rucil et Saint-Cloud en 1687'. 1927

Verlet, P. 'Le Mobilier royal français'. 1945

AUTUMN AT VERSAILLES

Campan, Mme. 'Mémoires sur la vie privée de Marie-Antoinette'. 1823

Hézecques, Comte de France d'. 'Souvenirs d'un page de la Cour de France'. 1895

La Tour du Pin, Marquise de. 'Journal d'une femme de cinquante ans, 1778–1815'. 1914

Nolhac, P. de. 'La Reine Marie-Antoinette'. 1917

Saint-Priest, Comte de. 'Mémoires. Règnes de Louis XV et Louis XVI'. 1929

Tourzel, Duchesse de. 'Mémoires de Madame la Duchesse de Tourzel'. 1883

Weber, J. 'Mémoires concernant Marie-Antoinette'. 1806

LA CHASSE ROYALE

Battifol, L. 'L'Origine du Château de Versailles'. In *Revue de Paris*. 1909

——'Le Château de Versailles et son architecte Philibert Le Roy'. In *Gazette des Beaux Arts*. 1913

Beauchamp, Comte de. 'Louis XIII d'après sa correspondance avec le Cardinal de Richelieu'. 1902

Du Bus, C. 'Le plus ancien plan de Versailles'. In *Gazette des Beaux Arts*. 1926

Marie, A. 'Naissance de Versailles'. 1968

Nolhac, P. de. 'La Création de Versailles'. 1925

Palewski, J. 'La Chasse Royale autour de Versailles'. 1936

Perrin, O. (Ed.). 'L'Encyclopédie de la Vénerie Française'. 1969

THE FIRST ENLARGEMENTS

Félibien, A. 'Description de la Grotte de Versailles'. 1669

La Laurencie, L. de. 'Lully'. 1911

Locatelli, S. 'Voyage de France. Relation de Sébastien Locatelli'. 1905

Marie, M. 'Le premier Château de Versailles construit par Le Vau en 1664–1665'. In *Bulletin de la Société de l'Histoire de l'Art Français*. 1952

Mauricheau-Beaupré, C. 'Un document inédit sur les premiers travaux de Louis XIV à Versailles: La basse cour de 1662'. In *Revue de l'Histoire de Versailles*. 1933

Scudéry, Mlle de. 'La Promenade de Versailles'. 1669

THE FETES

Félibien, A. 'Relation de la Feste de Versailles du 18 juillet 1668 et des Divertissements donnés par le Roy en 1674'. 1679

Marie, A. 'Les Fêtes des Plaisirs de l'Ile Enchantée, 1664'. In *Bulletin de la Société de l'Histoire de l'Art Français*. 1944

Montpensier, Mlle de. 'Mémoires de Mlle de Montpensier'. In C. Petitot, *Collection des mémoires relatives à l'Histoire de la France.* 1824

Prunières, H. 'Grand Divertissement Royal de Versailles'. In *Revue Musicale.* 1931

Racinet, C. 'Les Plaisirs de l'Ile Enchantée, la Fête de Versailles du 18 juillet, 1668, et les Divertissements donnés par le Roi en 1674'. 1859

THE CHATEAU NEUF
Clément, P. 'Lettres, Instructions et Mémoires de Colbert'. 1868

Kimball, F. 'Genesis of the Château Neuf at Versailles: 1668–1671'. In *Gazette des Beaux Arts.* 1949

Micheili & Visconti. In *Venetian Ambassadors' Despatches*. Bibliothèque Nationale, Fonds Italien. 1872

THE FIRST OFFSHOOTS. *The Trianon de Porcelaine.*
Danis, R. 'La Première Maison Royale de Trianon'. 1927

Marie, A. 'Trianon de Porcelaine et Grand Trianon'. In *Bulletin de l'Histoire de l'Art Français'*. 1945–46

Nolhac, P. de. 'Trianon'. 1927

Clagny

Bonnassieu, P. 'Le Château de Clagny et Mme de Montespan d'après les documents originaux'. 1881

Harlay, C. 'Le Château de Clagny à Versailles'. s.d.

Nolhac, P. de. 'Le Château de Clagny'. In *Revue de l'Histoire de Versailles.* 1900

THE COMPLETION OF VERSAILLES
Bourget, P. 'Jules Hardouin Mansart'. 1960

Kimball, F. & A. Marie. 'Unknown Versailles. The Appartement du Roi'. In *Gazette des Beaux Arts.* 1946

Margry, P. 'Un fils de Colbert'. 1873
Nolhac, P. de. 'Versailles Résidence de Louis XIV'. 1925

THE GRAND APPARTEMENT
Bourdelot, P. M. 'Relation des Assemblées faites à Versailles dans le Grand Appartement du Roy pendant le carnaval de l'An 1683'. 1683
Weigert, R.-A. 'Le meuble brodé de la Salle du Trône de Louis XIV à Versailles'. In *Revue de l'Histoire de Versailles*. 1930

FURTHER OFFSHOOTS. *Marly*
Josephson, R. 'Le plan primitif de Marly'. In *Revue de l'Histoire de Versailles*. 1928
Magne, E. 'Le Château de Marly d'après les documents inédits'. 1934
—— 'Louis XIV et les "Marlys" '. *In Revue de Paris*. 1934
Marie, J. & A. 'Marly'. 1947
Mauricheau-Beaupré, C. 'Le Château de Marly'. 1927

Trianon de Marbre
Deshairs, L. 'Le Grand Trianon'. 1908
Hallays, A. 'Le Grand Trianon'. 1924
Josephson, R. 'Le Grand Trianon sous Louis XIV'. In *Revue de l'Histoire de Versailles*. 1927
Nolhac, P. de. 'Trianon'. 1927

THE PROBLEM OF WATER
Barbet, L.-A. 'Les Grandes Eaux de Versailles'. 1907
Evrard, F. 'Les Eaux de Versailles'. In *Annales de Géographie*. 1933
Le Roi, J.-A. 'Ancienne Machine de Marly'. 1860
—— 'Travaux Hydrauliques à Versailles sous Louis XIV'. 1865
Nolhac, P. de. 'Versailles Résidence de Louis XIV'. 1925

THE REDECORATIONS OF 1701
Haussonville, Comte d'. 'La Duchesse de Bourgogne'. 1898

Marie, J. & A. 'Marly'. 1947
Nolhac, P. de. 'Versailles Résidence de Louis XIV'. 1925

MADAME DE MAINTENON & THE CHAPEL
Champigneulle, B. 'La Chapelle Royale de Versailles'. 1947
Deshairs, L. 'Documents inédits sur la Chapelle du Château de Versailles'. In *Revue de l'Histoire de Versailles*. 1906
Haussonville, Comte d' and G. Hanotaux. 'Souvenirs de Mme de Maintenon'. 1902
Kimball, F. 'The Chapels of the Château de Versailles'. In *Gazette des Beaux Arts*. 1944
Nolhac, P. de. 'La Chapelle Royale de Versailles'. 1912

VERSAILLES IN THE EIGHTEENTH CENTURY
Colombier, P. du. 'L'Art français dans les Cours rhénanes'. 1956
Nolhac, P. de. 'Versailles au XVIIIe Siècle'. 1926
Nonnotte, D. 'Vie de François Le Moyne'. In *Réunion des Sociétés des Beaux Arts*. 1902
Réau, L. 'Histoire de l'expansion de l'art français'. 1924
Voltaire. 'Siècle de Louis XIV'. 1751

THE PETITS CABINETS
Argenson, Marquis d'. 'Journal du Marquis d'Argenson'.
Cheverny, Comte de. 'Mémoires du Comte Dufort de Cheverny'. 1886
Croÿ, Duc de. *See* Grouchy.
Dunlop, I. 'The Petits Appartments de Louis XV at Versailles'. In *Connoisseur Year Book*. 1955
Fels, Comte de. 'Ange-Jacques Gabriel'. 1912
Grouchy, Vicomte de. 'Journal inédit du Duc de Croÿ'. 1906
Luynes, Duc de. 'Mémoires du Duc de Luynes sur la Cour de Louis XV'. 1865
Nolhac, P. de. 'Versailles au XVIIIe Siècle'. 1926
—— 'Versailles Inconnu. Les Petits Cabinets du Roi'. 1922
Racinais, H. 'La Vie inconnue des Petits Cabinets de Versailles'. 1951

MADAME DE POMPADOUR

Campardon, E. 'Madame de Pompadour et la Cour de Louis XV'. 1867

Chamchin, B. 'Le Château de Choisy'. 1910

Devismes, P. 'Le premier Ascenseur du Château de Versailles'. In *Revue de l'Histoire de Versailles*. 1924

Jarry, P. 'La Cuve de Marbre de l'Appartement des Bains'. In *Revue de l'Histoire de Versailles et de Seine-et-Oise*. 1934

Marigny, Marquis de. 'Correspondance du Marquis de Marigny'. 1904

Nolhac, P. de. 'Louis XV et Mme de Pompadour'. 1904

THE PETIT TRIANON AND MADAME DU BARRY

Desjardins, G. 'Le Petit Trianon'. 1885

Nolhac, P. de. 'Trianon'. 1927

Saint-André, C. 'Madame du Barry d'après les documents authentiques'. 1909

THE QUEEN. MARIE-LECZINSKA

Argenson, Comte d'. 'Correspondance publiée par le Marquis d'Argenson. Lettres de Marie-Leczinska et du cercle de la Reine'. 1922

Hénault, C. 'Mémoires'. 1911

St-Yves, 'Observations sur les Arts'. 1748

Jallut, M. 'Marie-Leczinska et la peinture'. In *Gazette des Beaux Arts*. 1969

Nolhac, P. de. 'Louis XV et Marie-Leczinska'. 1928

Langlois, R.-M. 'L'Opéra de Versailles'. 1958

Japy, A. and others. 'Opéra de Versailles'. 1957

LOUIS XVI AND MARIE-ANTOINETTE

Arneth, A. d'. 'Correspondance inédite du Comte de Mercy-Argenteau avec l'Empereur Joseph II et le Prince de Kaunitz'. 1889

Besenval, Baron de. 'Mémoires du Baron de Besenval'. 1821

Mercier, S. 'Les Mémoires de M. de Séguret'. 1782. In *Tableau de Paris*. 1897

Mercy, Comte de. *See* Arneth, above

Levis, Duc de. 'Souvenirs et Portraits'. 1813

Ségur, Comte de. 'Mémoires, ou Souvenirs et Anecdotes'. 1824

Séguret. *See* Mercier, above

Jallut, M. 'Château de Versailles. Cabinets Intérieurs et Petits Appartements de Marie-Antoinette'. In *Gazette des Beaux Arts*. 1964

THE QUEEN'S GARDEN

Granger, A. 'La replantation des Parcs de Versailles et des Trianons en 1775'. 1932

Laplace, G. 'Le Hameau de Marie-Antoinette'. 1913

Ligne, Prince de. 'Coup d'Œil sur Belœil'. 1786

Nolhac, P. de. 'Le Mobilier de Marie-Antoinette'. In *Gazette des Beaux Arts*. 1896

Young, A. 'Travels during the Years 1787, 1788 & 1789'. 1792

THE GAME OF MAKE-BELIEVE
THE QUEEN'S THEATRE AND THE HAMEAU

Laplace, G. 'Le Hameau de Marie-Antoinette'. 1913

Nolhac, P. de. 'Le Trianon de Marie-Antoinette'. 1924

Rey, L. 'Le Petit Trianon et le Hameau de Marie-Antoinette'. 1936

THE RESURRECTION OF VERSAILLES

Davillier, Baron. 'La vente du Mobilier du Château de Versailles pendant la Terreur'. 1877

Francastel, P. 'Le Château de Versailles sous Louis-Philippe'. In *Revue de Paris*. 1930

Fromageot, P. 'Le Château de Versailles en 1795 d'après le journal de Hughes Lagarde'. In *Revue de l'Histoire de Versailles*. 1903

Hallays, A. 'La donation de M. Rockefeller II à Versailles'.
In *Journal des Débats*. 1926

Kreisel, H. 'The Castles of Ludwig II of Bavaria'. 1954

Marcel, H. 'Louis-Philippe et le Château de Versailles'. In *Revue
de l'Histoire de Versailles*. 1909

Marie, A. 'Le Château de Versailles sous Napoléon I'. In *Bulletin
de l'Institut Napoléon*. 1953

Nolhac, P. de. 'Versailles pendant la Révolution'.

—— 'La Résurrection de Versailles. Souvenirs d'un
Conservateur 1887–1920'. 1937

Vigée Le Brun, Mme. 'Souvenirs'. 1835

Index